T0369564

Analytic Philosophy and Human Life

Analytic Philosophy and Human Life

THOMAS NAGEL

OXFORD
UNIVERSITY PRESS

Oxford University Press is a department of the University of Oxford. It furthers
the University's objective of excellence in research, scholarship, and education
by publishing worldwide. Oxford is a registered trade mark of Oxford University
Press in the UK and certain other countries.

Published in the United States of America by Oxford University Press
198 Madison Avenue, New York, NY 10016, United States of America.

© Oxford University Press 2023

CIP data is on file at the Library of Congress

ISBN 978-0-19-768167-1

DOI: 10.1093/oso/9780197681671.001.0001

Printed and bound by CPI Group (UK) Ltd, Croydon, CR0 4YY

*To the memory of my parents
and of my brother Andrew*

Contents

MORAL PSYCHOLOGY

REALITY

TRIBUTES

Preface

Most of the essays collected here are reviews, but they provided the occasion to reflect broadly on developments and controversies in philosophy and related subjects in recent years. Ethics and moral psychology figure prominently, but the pieces on Theresienstadt and Plantinga on science and religion deal with topics I specially care about. I have also included tributes to some of the people who have been particularly important to me—most of them eulogies occasioned by their deaths, but not all.

—T.N.

New York, August 2022

Acknowledgments

Earlier versions of these essays appeared in the following places:

1. *Economia Politica* 26, no. 1 (2009)
2. *The New York Review of Books*, February 10, 2011
3. *The New York Review of Books*, January 9, 2014
4. *Times Literary Supplement*, June 4, 2010
5. *London Review of Books*, October 6, 2011
6. *The New York Review of Books*, September 28, 2017
7. *The New York Review of Books*, March 25, 2010
8. *Times Literary Supplement*, November 20, 2015
9. *The New York Review of Books*, March 21, 2019
10. *London Review of Books*, April 3, 2014
11. *London Review of Books*, February 10, 2022
12. *The New York Review of Books*, November 21, 2013
13. *The Boston Globe*, Jan. 26, 2003
14. *The New York Review of Books*, October 9, 2014
15. *The New Republic*, February 16, 2012
16. *The New Republic*, November 11, 2013
17. *The New York Review of Books*, December 6, 2012
18. *The New York Review of Books*, April 5, 2018
19. *The New York Times* (Opinionator), August 18, 2013
20. *The New York Review of Books*, September 27, 2012
21. *Times Literary Supplement*, August 12, 2011
22. *The New York Review of Books*, September 29, 2016
23. *The New York Review of Books*, March 9, 2017

1

ANALYTIC PHILOSOPHY AND HUMAN LIFE

Philosophy in the second half of the twentieth century, the period
during which I entered the field, saw complex activity and growth
in a number of areas. What is most conspicuous in the analytic tradition in which I was formed is the focus on language, both as a
subject of great philosophical importance in itself, and as a path
into the philosophical understanding of other topics, from metaphysics to ethics. I myself have never worked in the philosophy of
language, but the background of an education in this type of philosophy has had an effect on the way I think and write.

I was exposed to analytic philosophy in its three leading
branches, through the accident of the three institutions at which
I studied. I was an undergraduate at Cornell University, at a time
when the philosophy department there was dominated by the
influence of Ludwig Wittgenstein, through the presence of his
student and follower Norman Malcolm. We studied with great intensity Wittgenstein's later writings, published and unpublished,
and assimilated the method of discovering the root of many philosophical problems in misunderstandings of the way language
functioned. I then went to Oxford as a graduate student, at a time
when J. L. Austin, Paul Grice, and others were pursuing a close attention to the precise details of how ordinary, natural language was
used, insisting on the subtleties it contained, in contrast with the
oversimplification of general theories expressed in artificial and

This is the *Sintesi Panoramica* that I presented on the occasion of the award of the Balzan
Prize for Moral Philosophy in 2008.

Analytic Philosophy and Human Life. Thomas Nagel, Oxford University Press.
© Oxford University Press 2023. DOI: 10.1093/oso/9780197681671.003.0001

often obscure philosophical vocabulary. After two years at Oxford I went to Harvard to complete my graduate studies, and there encountered the more systematic, logically based approach to language represented by W. V. Quine, which descended from the work of logical empiricists such as Rudolf Carnap and Bertrand Russell.

I am not really a follower of any of these traditions, but they provided the intellectual environment in which I have worked, very different from the environment of continental philosophy of the same date, with its strong elements of Marxism, existentialism, and phenomenology. Temperamentally, in a subterranean way, I have been drawn to aspects of these continental movements—to the egalitarian utopianism of Marx, the sense of the absurd of the existentialists, and the inescapability of the subjective point of view of phenomenology. But I have pursued these interests in an analytic framework.

The attention to language brought with it standards of conceptual clarity and an insistence on careful testing of philosophical hypotheses by argument and counterargument. But against this background, there are three broad developments of analytic philosophy that mark its relatively recent history, and that have been important to me in a more substantive way. One is the close connection between philosophy and science. Another is the great revival of moral, political, and legal philosophy. And the third is the return to at least partial respectability of *Lebensphilosophie*— philosophical reflection on basic questions of life and death.

The close connection of analytic philosophy with the natural sciences and mathematics is characteristic of the last of the three branches of the tradition I mentioned—the logical empiricist branch. Indeed it also gave rise to mathematical logic, which is now a branch of mathematics more or less independent of philosophy. There is a tendency in this dominant strain of analytic philosophy to aspire to a role for philosophy as the most abstract and general form of the scientific understanding of the world. The good side of this tendency is that it requires those interested in philosophy to know something about the natural sciences; as a result, the scientific and mathematical literacy of analytic philosophers is relatively high—usually much greater than their historical or artistic literacy. But the bad side is that analytic philosophers are often susceptible to scientism—i.e., the view that the natural sciences, mathematics, and logic both define the questions that it makes sense to ask and provide the only methods of true understanding, whatever the subject matter. This I believe is an obstacle to full understanding of ourselves, in particular, and it limits the capacity to explore seriously questions of value of all kinds.

My work in the philosophy of mind grows out of this background. I believe that philosophy in this case enables us to see why the mind cannot be adequately understood by means of the types of theory that have been so successful in explaining the physical world since the scientific revolution—simply because those theories were developed to account for a very different type of phenomenon. The problem of the relation between subjective experience and objective reality has been a central issue of philosophy from its beginnings, but in our time it has been affected by the growing authority of the physical sciences, extended into an understanding of living beings through evolutionary theory and molecular biology. The idea that mind can somehow be explained as part of the physical world, through a combination of behavioristic functional analysis and neurophysiological identification, has seemed to many theorists to be the next step on the forward march of physical science to provide a theory of everything.

While I believe the pursuit of a more and more objective conception of reality, less and less attached to the particular forms of human sensory experience, is a great manifestation of the capacity of human reason and its aim of transcendence, I believe that this pursuit of objective reality inevitably leaves something very important behind. That was the point of an early article of mine, "What Is It Like to Be a Bat?"—whose title really contains its entire argument. The subjective character of human experience—or the experience of any particular type of creature with an individual perspective on the world, cannot be understood only in terms of behavior or the physical functioning of the central nervous system, even though these three elements are inextricably connected.

The real problem is to try to understand this connection in a way that does not eliminate the irreducibly subjective aspect of mental reality, and also to ask what conception of the natural order might do justice to the fact that the most objective description of the physical world cannot be a complete description of what there is. This is a problem for the future, and I do not think much progress can be expected on it during the lifetime of anyone here today The search for a physicalistic understanding of the mental is due to a natural human weakness: the desire for closure—to reach a solution using the tools available before one departs from the scene—and a refusal to recognize that we are at an early stage in the progress of human understanding. Progress on the mind-body problem will take many intellectual generations.

Moving to the subject of ethics, I was very fortunate to be involved in a reawakening of the field that has transformed philosophy. When I began my studies, the dominance of linguistic analysis meant that analytic philosophers were for the most part interested only in metaethics—the analysis of moral language and the logic of moral concepts—rather than in first-order moral questions. It was widely thought that there was no way to think rationally about substantive questions of right and wrong, good and bad, justice and injustice. However, one of my teachers at Cornell was John Rawls. He was then in his early thirties and had published only two articles, but he was engaged in a project of substantive moral theory—the defense of definite principles of justice for a modern liberal democracy—that would by its example do more than any other work of the twentieth century to bring moral thought back into the center of philosophy. The focus of his work on institutional questions, including social, economic, and legal issues, made philosophers think again in systematic ways about the political problems of their time.

Beginning in the 1950s there was a gradual development of philosophical interest in substantive moral theory and substantive questions of policy. Elizabeth Anscombe wrote about the morality of warfare and the distinction between combatants and noncombatants—a crucial issue in the cold war nuclear age of Mutually Assured Destruction. H. L. A. Hart wrote about the enforcement of morals, and debated with Patrick Devlin the legitimacy of laws against homosexuality, pornography, and prostitution. But it was not only intellectual changes that caused the awakening of moral and political philosophy. In the 1960s the civil rights movement, the Vietnam War, and conflicts about abortion and homosexuality became large elements in public debate in the United States, and a number of moral, political, and legal philosophers began to write and teach about these questions, partly in response to the interests of our students, and partly because some degree of engagement seemed mandatory in a politically disturbing time.

My first teaching position was at Berkeley, just at the time when the student movement exploded there. Subsequently I moved to Princeton, where I was involved in the creation and editing of a journal called *Philosophy & Public Affairs*, whose title is emblematic of these developments, and which played a significant role in connecting philosophy with issues of contemporary public concern. Such issues are among the things I have written about since that time: war, taxes, privacy, affirmative action, global inequality, sexual freedom, religion and the state, and so forth. At New York University my joint appointment in the philosophy department and the law school reflected those interests.

In ethical theory, as in metaphysics and epistemology, I have been concerned with the relation between the point of view of the individual and the transcendent, objective point of view—represented in this domain by moral impartiality. This was already a theme in my first book, *The Possibility of Altruism*, derived from my doctoral dissertation, but it has reappeared in many guises in subsequent writings. The tension between the very fruitful transcendent impulse of human reason and the subjective perspective that it leaves behind and that must coexist with it is a source of philosophical problems in metaphysics, epistemology, ethics, political theory, and the understanding of human action. I have discussed the parallels most fully in *The View from Nowhere*, but the topic is also treated in *Mortal Questions*, *Equality and Partiality*, and *The Last Word*. In ethics and political theory the contrast of standpoints underlies traditional questions about the relation between individual self-interest and the collective good, and what form and degree of impartiality is the appropriate basis of ethics and political justice. I have written about that issue with reference to Hobbesian, utilitarian, and Kantian theories of the foundations of morality, and have been especially concerned with how the drive to reduce social and economic inequality can be reconciled with the natural partiality we all feel toward ourselves and those we particularly care about.

The positive moral outlook I have tried to develop depends on the crucial human capacity to see oneself from outside, as merely one person among others. If we wish to affirm our own value from this objective point of view, and the importance of our life, happiness, and flourishing, then we must in consistency accord equal objective value to the lives of all other persons, since from the objective standpoint everyone else is as much an "I" as I am. The only alternative is to abandon all value when one moves to the objective standpoint, and this I believe is impossible. We cannot regard our own lives as objectively valueless, so that others have no reasons except subjective ones to care whether we live or die. This point was embodied in the claim that morality includes "agent-neutral" reasons, such as the reason that any person has to relieve person A's pain—and not just "agent-relative" reasons, such as the special reason A has to relieve A's pain, or to care for A's children.

However, even though the objective standpoint provides a powerful source of moral reasons, it cannot replace the subjective standpoint completely, but must be integrated with it. However much we recognize the equal value of all persons, our own life is always the life of a particular individual, with particular aims, projects, needs, and personal attachments. The question of whether to subordinate this point of view to the claims of moral impartiality, or rather how and to what extent to do so, seems to me to be the central issue of moral theory. The utilitarian tradition has defended the requirement of a fairly radical subordination of agent-relative reasons to agent-neutral ones—though it admits agent-neutral justifications for allowing people to pursue individualistic aims, as with the special responsibilities among members of a family, which can be justified in utilitarian terms by their contribution to the general welfare. I have been more drawn to the Kantian tradition, which gives to impartiality a regulative role over our motives, while leaving the independent rational authority of the subjective point of view over our lives in place within the framework of a harmonizing system of universal standards. This is the intent of the categorical imperative, and more vividly of Kant's conception of the kingdom of ends.

In political theory these issues extend to the evaluation of legal, economic, and social institutions. On what terms can we live with our fellow citizens, that take fully into account both the equal value of all of us from an objective point of view and the special concerns each of us naturally has about our own life and attachments? The relation of collective public power to individual freedom and various kinds of equality must, I believe, be evaluated in these terms, and I think they make it possible to defend a form of egalitarian liberalism in which there is a moral division of labor between the state and the individual. In other words, public institutions should have a greater role in recognizing the equal importance of everyone than personal morality, which should leave people substantially free to follow their own path in life against this background, so long as they do not harm others.

The third topic that has always interested me is matters of life and death: the absurdity or meaning of life, the right attitude toward death, the relation of human life to the larger cosmos. These are questions that have a natural place in philosophy, but that are very hard to think about with the clarity that the analytic tradition prizes. However, in recent years these issues have ceased to be regarded as the exclusive province of the continental tradition, and I have written about them from time to time. I have never been dislodged from the conviction that death is the end of our existence, and that it is a very bad thing, even though it happens to everybody. More recently, I have become interested in the relation between science and religion, and in secular expressions of the religious tempera- ment. It remains unclear whether it is legitimate to seek a satisfying account of the cosmos and our place in it, one which will make us feel at home in the universe. Like the other questions of philosophy, we can expect this one to be around for a long time. I believe that progress in philosophy consists not in answering questions defini- tively, but in deepening our understanding of the problems that in- evitably arise in the attempt to find our place in the world, once we become afflicted with the pervasive self-consciousness that makes us human.

LIFE AND DEATH

2

TONY JUDT: LIFE AND MEMORY

The title of *The Memory Chalet* refers to its method of composition. Locked inside a body made inert by amyotrophic lateral sclerosis, and faced with his shrinking future and approaching death, Tony Judt decided to revisit his past. Physically unable to write, but with a mind as sharp and active as ever, he plotted the twenty-five short essays that compose this book in his head, while he was alone at night, using a mnemonic device taken from accounts of the early modern "memory palace," whereby elements of a narrative are associated with points in a visually remembered space; but instead of a palace, he used a small Swiss chalet that he had once stayed in on vacation as a boy, and that he could picture vividly and in detail. He was then able to dictate these feuilletons the next day from the resulting structure. All but four of them were originally published as separate pieces, but their impact is much enhanced as a single book, a book which is at once memoir, self-portrait, and credo.

Judt says that ALS is in both senses an incommunicable disease, yet his articulacy in describing the condition almost makes you think you can understand what it is like to be helpless in this way:

> Having no use of my arms, I cannot scratch an itch, adjust my spectacles, remove food particles from my teeth, or anything else that—as a moment's reflection will confirm—we all do dozens of times a day.
>
> It is not as though you lose the desire to stretch, to bend, to stand or lie or run or even exercise. But when the urge comes

This was a review of Tony Judt, *The Memory Chalet* (Penguin, 2010).

Analytic Philosophy and Human Life. Thomas Nagel, Oxford University Press.
© Oxford University Press 2023. DOI: 10.1093/oso/9780197681671.003.0002

over you there is nothing—nothing—that you can do except seek some tiny substitute or else find a way to suppress the thought and the accompanying muscle memory.

Ask yourself how often you move in the night. I don't mean change location altogether . . . merely how often you shift a hand, a foot; how frequently you scratch assorted body parts before dropping off; how unselfconsciously you alter position very slightly to find the most comfortable one. Imagine for a moment that you had been obliged instead to lie absolutely motionless on your back . . . . . .for seven unbroken hours and constrained to come up with ways to render this Calvary tolerable not just for one night but for the rest of your life.

But he believes that the deeper experience of isolation and imprisonment cannot be conveyed; he feels as out of reach of the imagination of others as Kafka's Gregor Samsa.

The articulate recreation of the active life that he has lost is Judt's answer to his imprisonment and impending death, and it gives him a more personal posthumous existence than do his historical and critical writings, important as they are. These eloquent personal recollections are infused with historical consciousness, but they also explain and reflect the strong opinions and attitudes that marked Tony Judt as a distinctive presence among us, unforgettable to those who knew or read him. Wary of group identity, he was an Englishman but exceptionally cosmopolitan, a Jew who became an outspoken critic of Zionism, and an egalitarian social democrat who was also an elitist and a defender of meritocracy.

Judt was born in London in 1948, to secular Jewish parents with roots in Eastern Europe, and he experienced both the austerity of postwar Britain and the extraordinary social mobility and social transformation that followed it. He remained throughout his life a grateful beneficiary of the welfare state and of its educational largesse. He also loved public transport, and is lyrical in the description of the trains, buses, and ferries of his youth, which have declined sadly since:

> I would park my bike in the luggage wagon at Norbiton Station on the Waterloo line, ride the suburban electric train out into rural Hampshire, descend at some little country halt on the slopes of the Downs, cycle leisurely eastward until I reached the westerly edge of the old London to Brighton Railway, then hop the local into Victoria as far as Clapham Junction. There I had the luxuriant choice of some nineteen platforms—this was, after all, the largest rail junction in the world—and would entertain myself with the choices from which to select my train back home. The whole exercise would last a long summer day.

Judt expresses affection for the material world in which he grew up, but words, ideas, and human institutions are the real substance of his life. He was one of those clever lower middle class boys who benefited from the opening up of British education after World War II. He went to a selective independent "direct grant" school that was funded by the local municipal authority and open without fee to those who did well on the eleven-plus exams. Judt says he hated school and remembers with respect only one of the masters, a ferocious teacher of German who instilled high standards through fear of his scorn. But he must have learned other things there, because he did so well on the entrance exams for King's College, Cambridge, that he was admitted without having to take the school-leaving exams (A levels); in consequence, he quit school halfway through his final year.

King's when he went there in 1966 was "the very incarnation of meritocratic postwar Britain," an ancient establishment with beautiful buildings and a distinguished tradition, now filled with students from selective state schools who had done well on exams, and who were invited to take on the inherited self-confidence that permeated the institution. Within a few years the formality, the gowns, the gate hours had been done away with, but while Judt was there he had the sense of membership in an elite, not of descent but of merit:

> Promoted on merit into a class and culture that were on their way out, we experienced Oxbridge just before the fall—for which I confess that my own generation, since risen to power and office, is largely responsible.

One of Judt's fundamentals is an unapologetic belief in the importance of recognizing the distinction between excellence and mediocrity, and making it count. He is pitiless about the intellectual and cultural egalitarianism and anti-elitism that have made such progress in English education since his day:

> For forty years, British education has been subjected to a catastrophic sequence of "reforms" aimed at curbing its elitist inheritance and institutionalizing "equality." . . . [T]he worst damage has been at the secondary level. Intent upon destroying the selective state schools that afforded my generation a first-rate education at public expense, politicians have foisted upon the state sector a system of enforced downward uniformity. . . . Today, when the British government mandates that 50 percent of high school graduates should attend university, the gap separating the quality of education received by the privately schooled minority from that of everyone else is greater than at any time since the 1940s.

Although he is politically on the left, and a believer in reducing social and economic inequality, he has no sympathy for the notionally equalizing forces of multiculturalism and political correctness. Becoming an American academic, he found much to deplore:

> Undergraduates today can select from a swathe of identity studies: "gender studies," "women's studies," "Asian-Pacific-American studies," and dozens of others. The shortcoming of all

these para-academic programs is not that they concentrate on a given ethnic or geographical minority; it is that they encourage members of that minority to study *themselves*—thereby simultaneously negating the goals of a liberal education and reinforcing the sectarian and ghetto mentalities they purport to undermine.

He is likewise dismissive of the taboos on sexual expression and sexual relations that have closed in since the sexual liberation of his youth:

> Since the 1970s, Americans assiduously avoid anything that might smack of harassment, even at the risk of forgoing promising friendships and the joys of flirtation. Like men of an earlier decade—though for very different reasons—they are preternaturally wary of missteps. I find this depressing. The Puritans had a sound theological basis for restricting their desires and those of others. But today's conformists have no such story to tell.

Because of these views some of his academic colleagues regarded Judt as a "reactionary dinosaur." That doesn't bother him, but at one point he suggests that there may be some incoherence in being politically on the left yet a defender of the elitism of universities:

> In my generation we thought of ourselves as both radical and members of an elite. If this sounds incoherent, it is the incoherence of a certain liberal descent that we intuitively imbibed over the course of our college years. It is the incoherence of the patrician Keynes establishing the Royal Ballet and the Arts Council for the greater good of everyone, but ensuring that they were run by the cognoscenti. It is the incoherence of meritocracy: giving everyone a chance and then privileging the talented. It was the incoherence of my King's and I was fortunate to have experienced it.

I suppose this is irony; but it is worth spelling out that there is no incoherence in wanting to reduce economic stratification while preserving educational selection based on ability. That is just the common sense of the old left, which recognizes that not all kinds of inequality are the same, and that it will not help the poor to level the educational system. Judt was the kind of old-fashioned, academically conservative leftist who could make distinctions—now an endangered species.

He was also old-fashioned in his commitment to social democracy, his distrust of market capitalism and the privatization of essential public services, and his belief that a decent society should prevent the large inequalities of wealth that market economies tend to generate. He even goes so far as to liken the broad current acceptance of market orthodoxy to the earlier abasement of European intellectuals before the historical inevitability of communism. That, I think, is rhetorical overkill; while ideological dogmatism is plentiful, there is much more honest uncertainty and debate, both empirical and moral, about how governments can best harness the evident innovative and productive power of capitalism in the service of the common good.

The most complex feelings expressed in this memoir are about the Jews, Jewishness, and Israel. There was no religious observance in Judt's immediate family, and they always had a Christmas tree. He was one of only about ten Jews in his school, out of more than a thousand pupils. But he must have inherited a very strong sense of Jewish identity, because from the age of fifteen he was deeply engaged with left-wing Zionism, as an official of one of its youth movements, and he spent three summers working on Israeli kibbutzim, plus six months just before starting at Cambridge. He was a true believer:

I idealized Jewish distinction, and intuitively grasped and reproduced the Zionist emphasis upon separation and ethnic difference....

The essence of Labour Zionism, still faithful in those years to its founding dogmas, lay in the promise of Jewish work: the idea that young Jews from the diaspora would be rescued from their effete, assimilated lives and transported to remote collective settlements in rural Palestine—there to create (and, as the ideology had it, recreate) a living Jewish peasantry, neither exploited nor exploiting.

In the end, he says, he became disaffected for two reasons. The first was the appalled reaction of his fellow kibbutzniks to his intention to take up a place at Cambridge instead of settling permanently in Israel. The second was what he saw during auxiliary participation in the Israeli armed forces, on the Golan Heights just after the Six-Day War. He was shocked by the attitude of young Israelis toward the recently defeated Arabs. "The insouciance with which they anticipated their future occupation and domination of Arab lands terrified me even then." The experience inoculated him against many forms of seductive commitment:

> I knew what it meant to be a "believer"—but I also knew what sort of price one pays for such intensity of identification and unquestioning allegiance. Before even turning twenty I had become, been, and ceased to be a Zionist, a Marxist, and a communitarian settler. . . , Unlike most of my Cambridge contemporaries, I was thus immune to the enthusiasms and seductions of the New Left, much less its radical spin-offs: Maoism, gauchisme, tiersmondisme, etc. For the same reasons I was decidedly uninspired by student-centered dogmas of anticapitalist transformation, much less the siren calls of femino-Marxism or sexual politics in general. I was—and remain—suspicious of identity politics in all forms, Jewish above all.

But Jewishness is an indelible identity, and Judt struggles over what it means to him. He says he is not a "lapsed" Jew, but he is certainly a lapsed Zionist: His most provocative publication was an essay in *The New York Review of Books* advocating the end of the Israeli Law

of Return and hoping for the eventual formation of a binational
Jewish-Arab state in greater Palestine—a deliberately utopian fantasy that takes his rejection of identity politics to its limit.

Yet Judt emphatically thinks of himself as a Jew, so he must ask,
"what can it mean—following the decline of faith, the abatement of
persecution, and the fragmentation of community—to insist upon
one's Jewishness?" His uncomfortable answer involves memory,
and all the awkwardness of secular Jewish identity appears in his
remarks about the Holocaust:

> In this sense, American Jews are instinctively correct to indulge
> their Holocaust obsession: it provides reference, liturgy, example,
> and moral instruction—as well as historical proximity. And yet
> they are making a terrible mistake: they have confused a means
> of remembering with a reason to do so. Are we really Jews for
> no better reason than that Hitler sought to exterminate our
> grandparents?

I am afraid that I am one of those secular Jews who regards that and
the larger history of anti-Semitism as a sufficient reason, without
which the other alleged nonreligious reasons would not carry much
weight. Judt appeals to an intellectual tradition:

> Judaism for me is a sensibility of collective self-questioning and
> uncomfortable truth-telling: the *dafka*-like [contrarian] quality
> of awkwardness and dissent for which we were once known. It is
> not enough to stand at a tangent to other peoples' conventions;
> we should also be the most unforgiving critics of our own. I feel a
> debt of responsibility to this past. It is why I am Jewish.

Yet I doubt that this would be enough without the horrible need
to identify with the victims of Hitler, to which Judt is not immune.
The chapter in which his reflections on Judaism occur is entitled
"Toni," and at the end he tells us that Toni Avegael was a female

cousin of his father who was gassed at Auschwitz, and after whom he is named.

It is natural to react to persecution not only by defense but by a heightened pride in the traditions and characteristics of the persecuted group. In spite of his universalist convictions, this mechanism is at work in Judt's feelings, even though he condemns the "uncompromising Israelophilia" and "lachrymose self-regard" that is often associated with commemoration of the Holocaust in the United States.

But his dominant identification is with the values of Western liberalism in its social democratic form. He is rueful about the failure of Western radicals of his generation to recognize that the real revolution in 1968 was taking place in Prague and Warsaw, though it would culminate only twenty years later. He taught himself Czech and became a historian not just of modern France, as he had begun, but of the whole of Europe. He loved New York because so much of the world converges here. I was a friend of Tony Judt, and we spoke during his final illness about death, and the importance to someone's life of the things he does that reach beyond it and what remains of him after he is gone. The magnificent and defiant gesture of writing this book in these circumstances is the fitting legacy of an extraordinary man who wanted us to know who he was.

3

AFTER WE'VE GONE

1.

We are all going to die, and the world will go on without us. In his highly original book *Death and the Afterlife* Samuel Scheffler explores the powerful but often unnoticeable ways in which these obvious facts affect the values that govern our lives and the motives that shape them.

The afterlife referred to in the title is not the personal afterlife, the continued existence of the individual in some form after death. Scheffler does not believe in a personal afterlife, and some of the book is taken up with the question of how we should feel about our own mortality if death is the end of our existence. But his main topic is what he calls the collective afterlife, the survival and continued renewal of humanity after our personal death—not only the survival of people who already exist, but the future lives of people born long after our deaths. Scheffler argues that the collective afterlife is enormously important to us—in some respects more important than our individual survival—though its importance escapes our attention because we take it so much for granted.

The book derives from Scheffler's two Tanner Lectures on Human Values, together with a third lecture about death delivered at a conference on the work of Bernard Williams. In keeping with the usual format of the Tanner Lectures, these are followed by a set of comments and a response by Scheffler.

To reveal the place of the afterlife (henceforth I'll generally omit the qualifier "collective") in the structure of our concerns, motives,

This was a review of *Death and the Afterlife*, by Samuel Scheffler, with commentaries by Susan Wolf, Harry G. Frankfurt, Seana Valentine Shiffrin, and Niko Kolodny (Oxford University Press, 2013).

Analytic Philosophy and Human Life. Thomas Nagel, Oxford University Press.
© Oxford University Press 2023. DOI: 10.1093/oso/9780197681671.003.0003

and values, Scheffler employs the classic philosophical method of counterfactual thought-experiments: to understand the significance of something, imagine its absence and see what else changes. He offers two imaginary situations, the doomsday scenario and the infertility scenario.

In the doomsday scenario, you are to imagine that, although you will live a normal lifespan and die of natural causes, the earth will be completely destroyed thirty days after your death in a collision with a giant asteroid. In the infertility scenario (taken from P. D. James's novel *The Children of Men* (1992), later made into a film by Alfonso Cuarón), the human race has become infertile, so that after everyone now alive has died of natural causes, there will be no more human beings. These are both terrible possibilities, but the interesting question is, exactly how are they terrible? What values are at work in our reaction when we contemplate the extinction of humanity?

Part of our response, of course, concerns the fate of people now living. In the doomsday scenario, those who survive your own natural death would have their lives cut short in a mass catastrophe. In the infertility scenario, those who are now young would see the population of the world gradually dwindle until there were only small numbers of lonely old people unable to maintain a civilized existence. But this is not the aspect of our response that interests Scheffler. He believes that if we think about the cases carefully, we will notice that the prospective absence of future persons would itself have major negative consequences for the living. And this reveals that the afterlife, the survival of humanity far into the future, has great importance for our lives in the present. As he summarizes his conclusion:

> In certain concrete functional and motivational respects, the fact that we and everyone we love will cease to exist matters less to us than would the nonexistence of future people whom we do not know and who, indeed, have no determinate identities. Or to put it more positively, the coming into existence of people we do not

know and love matters more to us than our own survival and the survival of the people we do know and love.

Scheffler's ground for this paradoxical claim is that the disappearance of the afterlife would undermine our sense of the value of most of what we do in the present, in a way that our own personal extinction does not. The value of our actual expiration-dated lives and activities depends on their being situated in a history of human life that stretches far beyond us into the future.

2.

Some examples of the dependence of present value on the existence of future persons are obvious: It would make no sense to pursue a long-term project like the search for a cure for cancer, or the reversal of global warming, or the development of an effective system of international law, if humanity were going to be extinguished shortly. But Scheffler believes that the prospect of extinction would probably undermine the motivation for many other types of activity as well: procreation, of course (in the doomsday scenario); but also artistic, musical, and literary creation, humanistic scholarship, historical and scientific research—even though these seem to be temporally self-contained. Their place in traditions that extend greatly beyond our own lives and contributions, Scheffler believes, is a condition of the value we assign to them, and of our motivation for pursuing them.

In part, what he says here is foreshadowed by his discussion of the relation between value, time, and history in an earlier essay, "The Normativity of Tradition." There he wrote:

Traditions are human practices whose organizing purpose is to preserve what is valued beyond the lifespan of any single individual or generation. They are collaborative, multigenerational enterprises devised by human beings precisely to satisfy the deep human impulse to preserve what is valued. In subscribing to a tradition . . . , one seeks to ensure the survival over time of what one values. And in seeking to ensure the survival over time of what one values, one diminishes the perceived significance of one's own death.[1]

But this exploration of the comprehensive impact of the future on the present through the afterlife greatly expands the topic and gives us something entirely new to think about. It isn't just that we want what we value to survive our deaths. Rather, even the present value of much that makes up our lives depends on its continuation and development long after we are gone.

Scheffler grants that some things would be exempt from this decline into pointlessness, such as friendship, personal comfort and pleasure, the avoidance of pain, and perhaps some activities that are pointless already, like games, which he says create "self-contained bubbles of significance." But a life whose value is limited to the quality of immediate personal experience is an impoverished life. We care about much more than our own experiences. This, says Scheffler, is one important way in which we are not individualists: we are dependent, for much of what we value in our own lives, on the survival of humanity into the future. Scheffler goes further. He finds "not implausible" the idea, taken from the P. D. James novel,

that the imminent disappearance of human life would exert a generally depressive effect on people's motivations and on their confidence in the value of their activities—that it would reduce their capacity for enthusiasm and for wholehearted and joyful ac-. tivity across a very wide front. . . . We cannot simply take it for

---

[1] Samuel Scheffler, *Equality and Tradition: Questions of Value in Moral and Political Theory* (New York: Oxford University Press, 2010), p. 305.

granted that the activity of, say reading *The Catcher in the Rye*, or trying to understand quantum mechanics, or even eating an excellent meal would have the same significance for people, or offer them the same rewards, in a world that was known to be deprived of a human future.

In spite of its tentativeness, this broader speculation invites skepticism. Indeed, the prospective end of humanity might heighten rather than diminish the value of many experiences. Think what it would be like to listen to *Don Giovanni* knowing that it was one of the last times anyone would ever hear it—that it would soon vanish forever because there were no longer any humans. One might feel the same about many aspects of human life—a desperate wish to give them an intense final realization before the lights went out for good.

On the other hand, Scheffler seems right that motivation for the kind of work that contributes to our culture, our knowledge, our economy and society would be hard to sustain under these scenarios, and that this would drain a good deal of meaning from our lives, and might well result in a general social breakdown. Yet this is most plausible with regard to creative activities of a kind that most people don't engage in. Would it be natural for an electrician, a waitress, or a bus driver to think of what they are doing as essentially part of the collective history of humanity, stretching far into the future—so that it would lose meaning if there were no future?

Except for the link to their direct descendants, I suspect that for most people, horizontal connections with their contemporaries are far more significant in underwriting the value of their lives and activities than vertical links to the distant future. But while the exact scope of the effect may be hard to determine, it is clear that Scheffler has succeeded in posing a genuinely new philosophical question of great interest and importance. Value evidently has a long-term historical dimension.

3.

The third of Scheffler's essays, "Fear, Death, and Confidence," though also quite original, deals with more familiar questions. Much of the discussion responds to Bernard Williams's famous essay, "The Makropoulos Case: Reflections on the Tedium of Immortality,"[2] but it refers to an extensive literature going back to Epicurus and Lucretius, and takes up topics such as whether death is an evil if there is no personal afterlife, why we find our future nonexistence alarming but are not disturbed by our past nonexistence, and whether it would be a good thing to live forever. Williams argued that while death is usually a bad thing for the person who dies, endless life would not be a good thing. He also suggested that we have reason to fear death. Scheffler defends his own versions of these three claims, whose compatibility is not obvious.

Williams held that an endless life would eventually collapse into infinite boredom. Scheffler has a different objection; he believes that mortality is a condition of the meaning of our lives. "The basic point," he says, "is simple. Our lives are so pervasively shaped by the understanding of them as temporally limited that to suspend that understanding would call into question the conditions under which we value our lives and long for their extension." Scarcity, in particular scarcity of time, is, he believes, a condition of the value we place on most of the things we want and do. So although (except in cases of terminal agony) death whenever it occurs is an evil because it deprives us of more of the life we value, we wouldn't be able to value life in the way we do if death never occurred. Scheffler is eloquent about how bizarre noncelestial immortality would be:

> We are somehow imagining creatures who are meant to be like us but who are not embodied in the way we are, who pass through no

---

[2] In Bernard Williams, *Problems of the Self* (Cambridge: Cambridge University Press, 1973).

stages of life, who know nothing of the characteristic challenges, triumphs, or disasters associated with any of those stages, who need not work to survive, who do not undergo danger or overcome it, who do not age or face death or the risk of it, who do not experience the reactions of grief and loss that the death of a loved one inspires, and who never have to make what they can of the limited time and opportunities that they have been given. More generally, we are trying to imagine creatures who have little in their existence that matches our experience of tragic or even difficult choices, and nothing at all that matches our experience of decisions made against the background of the limits imposed by the ultimate scare resource, time. But *every* human decision is made against that background, and so in imagining immortality we are imagining an existence in which there are, effectively, no human decisions.

All this is true. Eternal lives would not be just like mortal lives, only endless: they would have no shape. But does that imply they would be devoid of meaning altogether? Humans are amazingly adaptable, and have developed many forms of life and value in their history so far, in response to changing material circumstances. I am not persuaded that the essential role of mortality in shaping the meaning we find in our actual lives implies that earthly immortality would not be a good thing. If medical science ever finds a way to turn off the aging process, I suspect we would manage.

Still, Scheffler could be right, and if he is right, that would have interesting consequences for the structure of our values. He holds that much of the value in our lives depends on the fact that they will end in death, but death is almost always a bad thing for us because it brings to an end so much of what we value. This may look like a contradiction, but it is not. It just means that good is inseparable from evil in human life.

Scheffler is also very good on the fear of death. He quotes Philip Larkin: "This is a special way of being afraid / No trick dispels . . ." and he insists, convincingly, that the debates about whether death is a misfortune for the one who dies, and if so why, are beside the point when it comes to the assessment of this fear. It cannot be explained as a manifestation of regret that one will not see one's grandchildren grow up, or will never visit Angkor Wat, or by any deprivation of specific future experiences or activities that one will miss. The fear of death is sui generis and does not, in Scheffler's view, require any such justification:

> Although I have had the experience before of losing things that mattered to me or of having good things end, it is *I* who have had those experiences. . . . But I take death to mean that the very *I* that has had those experiences is what is now going to end. The egocentric subject—which is what has provided the fixed background for all my previous endings—is itself to end. My only resources for reacting to this prospect seem to involve turning back on myself a set of attitudes—such as sadness, grief, rage, anxiety—that are tailored to circumstances in which the self endures and undergoes a loss. But those attitudes become unmoored when directed toward their very subject. And this induces, or can induce, *panic*. It can seem completely incomprehensible and terrifying, even impossible.

Scheffler therefore endorses a strange combination of attitudes. He believes it is reasonable to fear death, and to regard its occurrence as an evil in most cases; yet personal immortality would be undesirable. By contrast, the collective afterlife is very important:

> Although our fear of death may be reasonable, our confidence in our values depends far more on our confidence in the survival of other people after our deaths than it does on our confidence

in our own survival. Indeed, our own eternal survival would itself undermine such confidence. To put it a bit too simply: what is necessary to sustain our confidence in our values is that we should die and that others should live.

He makes the interesting further point that belief in a personal afterlife, of the kind associated with some religions, "may reconcile people too readily to the disappearance of life on earth, and make it seem less urgent to prevent this from happening." (This surmise may be supported by the fact that some believers in a personal afterlife not only expect earthly life to end in the Apocalypse, perhaps in the near future, but welcome the prospect.) Scheffler contends that for those of us who do not believe in a personal afterlife, recognizing the importance of the collective afterlife should motivate us to do more to avert global catastrophe:

> We are not unreasonable for fearing death, even though it does not threaten our confidence. But we may be unreasonable if we fail sufficiently to fear, and so do not try to overcome, the ever more serious threats to humanity's survival, upon which our confidence does depend.

The motivation is not an altruistic concern for future persons, but a concern for the meaning of our own lives. We want the future to be in some respects our future—a place in which we could be at home, even though we will never get there.

4.

Two of the four commentators, Susan Wolf and Harry Frankfurt, are unconvinced by Scheffler's suggestion that the prospect of human extinction would result in a general erosion of our confidence that anything matters. Frankfurt insists that many things are

important to us for their own sakes—not only pleasure and friendship, but music, artistic creation, the pursuit of scientific and historical understanding—and would not lose their value if there were
no afterlife. Yet Scheffler is clearly right that the value of some of
these things is not contained in the individual's experience. Wolf is
more sympathetic to the view that we conceive of our activities

> as entering or as being parts of one or another ongoing stream—
> of the history and community of art or of science; of an ethnic
> or religious culture; of legal, political, industrial, technological
> developments, and so on.

But she thinks that if humanity had no future, our commitment to
the care and comfort of others would be undiminished and perhaps
enhanced, and would give our lives meaning.

Wolf also takes up an interesting question posed by Scheffler: We
all know that humanity will not last forever—if only because the
evolution of the sun will make the earth uninhabitable eons from
now—yet that doesn't affect us in the way that the doomsday or
infertility scenario would. Most of us, Scheffler points out, are not
susceptible to the despair of Woody Allen's character Alvy Singer,
in *Annie Hall*, who at the age of nine sees no point in doing his
homework because the universe is expanding and will break up
billions of years from now. Wolf suggests that if we reject Alvy's reaction, consistency may require that we also reject the reaction of
pointlessness to the doomsday or infertility scenarios. But Scheffler
responds that the cases are not comparable, because our judgments
of value are simply baffled by time scales like that of the death of
the sun or the breakup of the universe; we can't take them in, so we
can't take our lack of response as a reliable guide to the relevance of
human extinction to the meaning of our lives.

Seana Shiffrin is generally sympathetic to Scheffler's position,
but suggests, in a Kantian spirit, that perhaps the future existence
of other rational beings who would continue the practice of valuing

would be enough to sustain us—that the survival of humanity is not essential. Scheffler replies:

> Although I don't have firm views about this, my feeling is that we are more attached to the specifically human than Shiffrin is inclined to suppose. That may partly be because I think history counts for more than she does, and partly because I think biology counts for more.

Niko Kolodny concentrates on the third essay, and doubts that it makes sense to fear one's own impending nonexistence per se. I find Scheffler's sympathetic interpretation of this special form of panic persuasive, but these disagreements are not easy to settle, and Scheffler himself is reluctant to claim that only one set of responses is objectively correct. Whether there could even be such a thing as the right way to feel about our own deaths is itself a difficult question. Perhaps there are irreconcilable differences between the reactions and attitudes of different persons to the end of life.

That does not diminish the value of the inquiry. With its careful arguments, counterarguments, and comparative evaluation of alternative hypotheses, this book is a superb example of the application of analytic philosophy to a subject that is of fundamental concern to everyone, not only to academic philosophers. Scheffler has opened up a new range of questions about life and death.

4

CAN WE SURVIVE?

If your existence depends on the life of a particular human being, you will vanish when that creature dies: the center of consciousness that is now reading this sentence will be annihilated, and the universe will close over you. In his ambitious and quixotic book, *Surviving Death*, Mark Johnston shows a deep understanding of the natural fear of death and rejects a number of traditional religious and philosophical accounts of how we might survive it. He then offers his own explanation of how, even if one assumes a naturalistic world view, surviving our own biological death may be theoretically possible. But since the hope of survival he offers, apart from its philosophical implausibility, is one which neither the author nor his readers have a significant chance of achieving, the book offers little comfort. Still, it is stimulating, written with skill and charm, and packed with illuminating philosophical reflection on the questions of what we are, and what it is for us to persist over time—on the relations among selves, persons, human beings, bodies, and souls.

What is it that you care about, if you don't want to die? Not the survival of a particular organism, as such. The survival of that human animal concerns you because it is a condition of *your* continued existence; if you could survive its death, then even though you might miss the old jalopy, the worst would be averted. But can we give sense, and perhaps even credence, to this possibility? Most of us can easily imagine waking up on the day of judgment, or being

This was a review of Mark Johnston, *Surviving Death* (Princeton University Press, 2010).

Analytic Philosophy and Human Life. Thomas Nagel, Oxford University Press.
© Oxford University Press 2023. DOI: 10.1093/oso/9780197681671.003.0004

reincarnated as someone else, but perhaps that is just a trick of the imagination, a projection of the self that corresponds to no real possibility.

Johnston is moved in this inquiry not only by the pure wish to survive, but by another wish that seems to require survival for its fulfilment: the wish that goodness should be rewarded. Those who are good are not good for the sake of reward, but if great sacrifice in the name of the good is not rewarded, Johnston believes, the importance and even the rationality of goodness are threatened. He concludes, like Kant, that faith in the importance of goodness requires hope of reward in an afterlife. I have no sympathy for this view, because I believe that the reasons to be good are self-sufficient, even if they require sacrifice. But Johnston's conviction leads him to seek a demonstration that death is better for the good than for the bad, and that will be the key to his analysis of survival.

First, however, he has to dispose of the considerable array of alternative theories. These fall into three types: immortality of the soul, resurrection of the body, and psychological continuity. Johnston rejects each of them as a way we might survive death, for different reasons, and his arguments constitute an excellent tour of the territory of theological and philosophical theories of personal identity. He says that there is no evidence against the naturalistic view that nothing but a properly functioning brain is necessary for conscious mental life; in particular, psychical research has turned up no credible evidence for a detachable soul. He argues on subtle metaphysical grounds that even a body just like yours, reassembled by God at the day of judgment out of the same atoms that constituted your body shortly before your death, would not be the same body. And he maintains that, though we care about the continuation of our memories and personalities, such psychological continuity alone is not enough to guarantee that a future psychological replica will be you.

Though the issues are far from settled, Johnston makes a good case for the view that none of these three forms of survival is available. His weakest argument is that even if you had an immaterial soul, that would not justify your special concern for its future, since everyone else would also have such a soul—to which the reply is that your soul's future experiences are the only ones that would be *yours*. Suppose, however, that we concur with Johnston in setting aside these three types of account; what is the alternative?

To decide whether surviving death is possible, we need to know what would make a future experience mine. One of Johnston's important and plausible claims is that we cannot discover this by *a priori* reflection on what to say about various possible cases, because our concept of personal identity does not work that way. Instead, it operates by "offloading" the conditions of identity onto the real nature of certain actual persisting things—human animals, in our own case—which we reidentify only by their manifest properties. As he puts it: "The idea of offloading can be expressed by means of a motto, 'I don't know what the (non-trivial) sufficient conditions for identity over time are, but I do know a persisting object when I see one.'" This phenomenon of offloading is familiar from the case of "natural kinds" like water or gold, whose real essences can't be discovered by *a priori* reflection on our concepts, but require empirical investigation.

We can offload the criteria for identity over time by referring to what metaphysicians call a *substance,* that is, "something whose present manifestation determines what it would be to have that very same thing again." Living things are the clearest examples of substances, in virtue of their active disposition to maintain themselves over time. To determine personal identity—identity of the self—we offload onto persisting human beings, a class of living things that we regard as possessing embodied minds. And now that we have learned about the dependence of mental life more specifically on the operation of the brain, we add that if a brain could be kept alive without its body, it would continue to embody the same mind. This seems to imply that the true conditions of personal identity are determined by how mental life is generated in the brain, and it seems to rule out decisively any possibility that we might survive biological death. I think that is the correct conclusion. Johnston, however, believes he can escape it.

To do so, however, he must dismantle the ordinary idea of the persisting self, an idea he evokes vividly as follows: "The most immediate way in which I am given to myself is as the one at the center of this arena of presence and action." This is the subjective sense of "I," and it is this subjective I for whose interests he has an immediate, absorbing concern, and whose death he finds terrifying. "My sheer desire to survive may *feed* a desire that Johnston survive, but it is not itself a desire that Johnston survive. It is the desire that there will continue to be someone with the property of being me."

The crux of Johnston's argument is that there is no such property—or none that could justify the special future-directed self-concern to which it is supposed to give guidance. The way the world is, independent of our attitudes, does not determine what it would be for this same arena of presence and action to exist at a later time. Johnston denies, (unconvincingly, I believe) that this subjective sameness can be secured by offloading onto the persistence conditions of the particular human being who occupies this arena of presence and action at the present moment. Instead, he claims that the self is a merely intentional object, whose identity is not an objective matter, but depends on what the subject *takes* it to be. Like the dagger that Macbeth hallucinates, its reidentification at different times is wholly determined by how the subject sees it. Johnston's relativism about personal identity is a radical inversion of the traditional dependence of your future-directed concerns on your belief about who will be you. He contends that personal identity is response-dependent: it is the disposition of your future-directed concerns that determines who will be you, instead of the other way around.

To introduce this idea, Johnston imagines three tribes of human animals, whom he calls Hibernators, Teletransporters, and

Humans. The Hibernators fall into a deep sleep during the winter months, and they do not regard the person who will wake up in the spring in their body, with their memories and personality, as being numerically the same person as they are; they do not believe they survive dreamless sleep. The Teletransporters, on the other hand, are accustomed to superfast travel of the kind familiar from science fiction. They step into a machine that takes a complete reading of the microconstitution of their body, destroys the body, and sends the information at the speed of light to a target machine at the destination, where a body physically and mentally indistinguishable from the original is produced from local materials. The Teletransporters believe they survive these trips and unproblematically regard the person who will step out of the target machine as themselves. Finally, the Humans believe that they survive dreamless sleep and don't believe they would survive teleportation: they wouldn't get into one of those machines for a million dollars. In each case, the conviction is immediate and shows itself in unreflective patterns of special future-directed concern.

Johnston says that the Hibernators, the Teletransporters, and the Humans are all right, each on their own terms. There is no objective fact that could make one belief right and the others wrong. Identity is response-dependent, and it is the disposition to deeply and consistently identify with some future person—to care about what happens to him in the first-person way—that constitutes the identity-determining disposition.

And here is the punch line: You can survive the biological death of the human being who is now at the center of your arena of presence and action, if you develop a disposition of future-directed concern for all of the human beings who will exist after he is gone— if, in other words, you become someone who literally loves your posterity as yourself. But once the independent reality of the self is recognized as an illusion, this becomes the rational attitude to take: "If there is no persisting self worth caring about, the premium or excess that special self-concern expects and rejoices in cannot represent a reasonable demand or expectation. . . . One's own interests are not worth considering *because* they are one's own but simply because they are interests, and interests, wherever they arise and are legitimate, are equally worthy of consideration."

Therefore *agape*, the universal love that is the Christian ideal of goodness, brings with it its own reward, for those who can attain it. Persons are Protean: a single person may be constituted by one human being, or by a series of human beings, or even by a huge crowd of human beings, "the onward rush of humanity," depending on which interests he is immediately disposed to incorporate into his practical outlook. Johnston's theory vindicates the importance of goodness by making absolute goodness the condition of continued life.

This form of survival through extreme selflessness would require a transformation that is out of the reach of almost everyone, and in any case not subject to the will. Johnston adds, though, that even if we cannot attain this perfect goodness, it is important to transcend natural selfishness and nepotism in a more familiar way, by recognizing that everyone's interests have the same importance as our own. Even if we cannot be truly good, we can become "good enough," not to survive death but to "face death down, to see through it to a pleasing future in which individual personalities flourish. . . . For the utterly selfish, however, the obliteration of their individual personalities is the obliteration of everything of real importance to them." But this is a familiar point, and does not cancel the absoluteness of one's own death.

To accept Johnston's theory—that identity is relative, that persons are Protean, and that we could survive death by coming to identify with future human beings—would require at least as large a dose of wishful thinking as belief in the immortality of the soul or the resurrection of the body. It seems far more likely that the world, in particular the facts about how the brain sustains the mind, determines what we are, even though those facts are still largely unknown. Johnston's skepticism about a purely mental substance as the carrier of personal identity is reasonable, but the familiar, and alas perishable human animal is harder to dislodge from its decisive control over our fate.

5

ASSISTANCE IN DYING

It would be best not to have to die at all, but failing that, many of us would like to have some control over the time and manner of our deaths, should we find ourselves in a condition so hopeless that there is no point in going on. At this date, in most of the world, including Britain and most of North America, the legally permissible forms of such control do not include voluntary euthanasia or assisted suicide. A physician may not, in most jurisdictions, administer or prescribe for self-administration a lethal drug for the purpose of ending life, even at the explicit request of a fully competent patient. Yet a physician is legally permitted (sometimes legally required) to take other steps that hasten death, if requested to do so by the patient or a proxy: he may end or withhold treatment (chemotherapy, antibiotics, surgery); withdraw or fail to initiate life support (respirators, feeding tubes); give high doses of opiates to relieve pain or induce coma, where these may also shorten life.

In his lucid and powerful book, *Assisted Death*, the Canadian philosopher L. W. Sumner argues that this distinction is indefensible. His target is what he calls the Conventional View, namely that there is "an ethical 'bright line' between assisted death, on the one hand, and all other end-of-life measures which may hasten death, on the other." By assisted death Sumner means either providing (assisted suicide) or administering (euthanasia) a lethal medication in order to cause the patient's death as a means of relieving his suffering. Sumner argues that the differences between assisted death

This was a review of L. W. Sumner, *Assisted Death: A Study in Ethics and Law* (Oxford University Press, 2011).

and the legally permitted measures, such as turning off a respirator, are for the most part morally irrelevant. He favors a regime like that which now exists in the Benelux countries, where both assisted suicide and euthanasia are allowed, under carefully specified conditions.[1]

Sumner holds that end-of-life treatment, like all medical treatment, should be governed by two values: respect for the patient's autonomy and concern for the patient's well-being. Usually they coincide, but where autonomy is not possible, as with an infant, well-being must govern. And if autonomy and well-being conflict, in the decision of a competent patient, Sumner believes autonomy should take priority.

With respect to the value of well-being, the most important and obvious point to be made is that one is justified in hastening death only in cases where death is better or at least no worse for the patient than continued life. Death may either be good, when it ends intolerable suffering, or neither good nor bad, when it ends a state of irreversible unconsciousness. Normally death is a great evil for the person who dies, which explains the stringency of prohibitions against killing; but death is not always an evil, by comparison with the alternative. Sumner accepts the "deprivation account" according to which death is bad because it deprives us of the goods that would be brought by continued life. If continued life would bring nothing but misery, in the form of intractable pain, nausea, delirium, and helplessness, then a death that relieves us of that misery is not bad but good. That is what leads competent patients in sufficiently dire conditions to refuse further treatment, request removal of respirators and feeding tubes, or ask for terminal sedation. Evidently the same end could often be achieved more quickly and effectively by a lethal injection, so the value of the patient's

---

[1] Since Sumner's book was published, euthanasia has become legal in Colombia, Canada, New Zealand, and parts of Australia.

well-being does not draw a "bright line" between assisted death and other measures.

If we turn to the value of autonomy, we do find a difference. The currently recognized right of a patient to refuse treatment is very powerful, because it can be exercised for any reason that is consistent with the patient's mental competence, and not just to end unbearable suffering. For example, adult Jehovah's Witnesses are permitted to refuse blood transfusions on religious grounds, even if it will result in their deaths. This is the consequence of a general right to bodily integrity: no one, including a physician, may intrude on that integrity by surgery, injection of drugs, or other physical transgression contrary to the wishes of the patient. Without the patient's explicit consent it would normally be a form of impermissible assault. (Exceptions for the treatment of an unconscious patient in an emergency are usually construed in terms of presumed consent: we believe the patient would agree if he were conscious and understood the situation.)

The right of bodily integrity introduces an asymmetry between withdrawing treatment and assisted death: a physician must end treatment if the patient demands it, even if the death that results is not in the patient's interest; but no one, including Sumner, proposes that patients should have a right to request assisted death unless their medical condition makes life not worth continuing. The strong "negative" obligations on others—obligations to refrain from interference—that are entailed by individual rights do not entail corresponding "positive" obligations. There is a general negative obligation not to provide life-saving treatment against my wishes; but there is no general positive obligation to help me end my life just because I wish it. (Sumner gives the startling information that "In the Netherlands approximately two-thirds of requests for euthanasia or assisted suicide are refused by physicians," presumably because they are thought to be inadequately grounded.) Still, this asymmetry with respect to obligation does not imply that there is a corresponding asymmetry between the *permissibility* of withholding treatment and the permissibility of assisted death, in the more usual case where both autonomy and well-being are served by either measure. Sumner's position is that when the two values coincide, either method of hastening death is permissible.

However, he needs to defend this position against the objection that there are two further differences between assisted death and the other methods that distinguish them morally. This is a crucial part of his argument, because it is those differences that are at the heart of the Conventional View. Euthanasia and assisted suicide have two features at least one of which is absent from each of the other measures. First, the lethal medication causes death directly, rather than merely removing an obstacle to its occurrence from other causes. Second, the death of the patient is the intended aim of administering the medication, not merely an effect that is foreseen.

By contrast, when treatment is withheld or life support is terminated, death is caused by the disease or by one of its consequences, like the inability to breathe or eat. And when death is caused by extremely high doses of opiates, the intended aim is to relieve pain, and death is merely a foreseeable side-effect. The claim that needs to be answered is that assisted death involves direct, intentional killing, and that this is wrong even if supported by values of autonomy and well-being that would justify allowing a terminal cancer patient to die of a treatable infection or shortening his life as a side-effect of pain relief. This is clearly the assumption behind the Conventional View. This is the alleged moral "bright line."

The distinctions between doing and allowing, and between intending and foreseeing, are the subject of extensive and continuing discussion in moral philosophy, and there is disagreement about their significance. Sumner summarizes the discussion, but his main point is that, whatever may be the moral importance of those distinctions in other contexts, they cannot mean the same in end-of-life choices, for a stunningly simple reason.

As applied to choices that lead to someone's death, those distinctions have been developed to deal with cases that have the following three features: (1) death is a bad thing for the person who dies; (2) that person does not agree to it; (3) the choice is motivated by the aim of benefiting, or avoiding harm to, a different person. In those painful circumstances where someone or other will suffer harm no matter what we do, it is essential for a usable morality to determine which alternatives must be excluded, and which remain permissible. There is controversy over the correct standards to govern such cases, which include self-defense, collateral damage in warfare, and triage in medical care or rescue operations. But such standards have no bearing on end-of-life decisions, because *all three* of these crucial features are absent in typical cases of assisted death. When a competent patient requests euthanasia to end his suffering, (1) death is a good thing for him, (2) he agrees to it voluntarily, (3) its purpose is to benefit him and no one else. Even in the euthanasia of a noncompetent patient for whom there is no hope, such as an infant, the first and third conditions hold.

The whole point of identifying certain "indirect" ways of causing death as morally permissible is to distinguish them from what is strictly forbidden, namely the intentional killing of an innocent person in order to benefit another. (Killing one person to harvest his organs and save five others is wrong; rescuing five persons and leaving a sixth to die, when one cannot rescue all six, is not wrong.) But euthanasia is not killing one person to benefit another; it is benefiting a single person by ending his life. The fact that the killing is intentional and causally direct is, to be sure, a feature that it shares with culpable murder, but it lacks the other features that make that morally significant. There is no moral reason, therefore, to contrast intentional euthanasia with the more indirect measures that are permitted by the Conventional View. The intentional/foreseen distinction has moral relevance only in cases of interpersonal tradeoffs where death is an evil. Neither of these features is present in euthanasia and assisted suicide.

The same applies to the treatment of noncompetent patients who cannot exercise autonomy, such as infants born with a congenital defect that will end their lives after a year of suffering. The Conventional View permits hastening their death by not treating an infection, or not surgically correcting a bowel obstruction, for example. Sumner points out that these "failures to treat" aim at the death of the infant just as much as active euthanasia; but the main point is that for both types of measure that fact is morally irrelevant, since the infant is not being harmed for the benefit of someone else: he is not being harmed at all, but spared a worse fate. (Sumner emphasizes that all measures to hasten an infant's death, "active" or "passive," are completely unjustified in cases of congenital disability that would allow the patient to lead a life worth living, such as Down's syndrome.) The Conventional View depends on the confused transfer to this case of standards that apply to cases of a completely different kind.

The final major topic addressed by Sumner is that of respect for the autonomy of patients who are not now competent but who once were. Examples are cases of advanced dementia, and unconsciousness or semi-consciousness produced by stroke or brain damage. Advance directives in the form of a living will are designed for such cases, but they are not always available. Sometimes relatives offer evidence from things said in the past for what the patient "would have wanted." Where an explicit or inferred past wish of the now incompetent patient clearly coincides with the patient's present interest (relief of irreversible suffering), or does not conflict with it (terminating irreversible coma), there is no objection to any of the methods of hastening death. However, the priority Sumner gives to autonomy over well-being creates problems, which he recognizes, for cases where an advance directive requests euthanasia or nontreatment under more ambiguous conditions.

Suppose, for example, that you sign a directive asking to be euthanized, or allowed to die of a treatable infection like pneumonia, if you should reach a condition of advanced dementia in which you don't remember anything and can't recognize anyone. It is possible to be in such a condition without intolerable suffering, and even to enjoy eating peanut butter and jelly sandwiches. Does autonomy really give your past self the authority to kill off this later self, even though its life retains the simple experiential value available to an infant? One response, proposed by Ronald Dworkin, is that we must distinguish between the experiential and the critical value of a life. Your directive expresses the view that in such circumstances, despite its primitive experiential value, your existence would not be worth continuing—it would be, in the critical sense, bad for you to go on living in such a condition. So there is not really a conflict between autonomy and well-being in such a case.

Sumner is torn. He says it is hard to imagine administering a lethal injection to such a person. Yet he also says, "As a general thesis, it is hard to see how one might argue that current pleasures and enjoyments, under conditions of diminished or non-existent autonomy, always take precedence over previous, fully autonomous, expressions of one's deepest and most enduring values." I am doubtful of this grant of authority to the competent former self, whose values have not in fact endured, since they mean nothing to the demented present self. On balance there may be no right answer to the question whether it is good or bad for that person to go on living in that condition. But Sumner's general point still applies here: the same standard should be required to justify withholding life-sustaining treatment on the basis of such an advance directive as would be required to justify euthanasia: either both are permissible, or neither is.

Sumner's detailed description of the legal landscape and its history is highly instructive. We are at the beginning of a great cultural shift in end-of-life treatment, made necessary by medical advances that can slow down the progress of fatal diseases, while offering the patient continued life that is sometimes of doubtful value. Decisions to withhold further treatment and provide only palliative care are becoming common, and the provision of palliative care and adequate pain relief is now taken seriously by the medical profession. For most terminal patients those options are sufficient.

Even where euthanasia and assisted suicide are available, in the Netherlands, they accounted for 1.7 per cent of all deaths in 2005, whereas withdrawing treatment or terminal sedation accounted for nearly one out of four deaths in that year. Sumner argues that there should be much more regulation of the latter methods of shortening life, since they are so much more common, and stand equally in need of justification.

Sumner poses the question whether the wider availability of assisted death would reduce the incentive to provide adequate palliative end-of-life care, since there would be a much cheaper and quicker alternative. He replies that this has not happened so far in the jurisdictions where assisted death has been legalized. Though the two types of measures have the same aim, to eliminate suffering, physicians apparently feel a strong motive to ensure that assisted death is chosen only as a last resort, when palliative measures fail. This optimistic view may hold for wealthy societies; I am not confident that it would hold up if assisted death became legal in societies with much more limited resources.

Sumner's book provides a superb example of the relevance of philosophy to public policy. The reason is that public policy governing treatment at the end of life is to a great extent shaped by philosophical confusions. It may not be too much to hope that a book such as this will help to rectify the situation.

6

THERESIENSTADT

1.

Theresienstadt, the concentration camp about forty miles north of Prague, held a unique place in the Nazis' campaign of extermination. While its main purpose was to gather Jews from Czechoslovakia, Austria, and Germany for deportation to the death camps in Poland, it was presented to the outside world as a self-governing Jewish settlement, to support the fiction that the removal of Jews from German society was being carried out in a humane fashion. The camp had an internal Jewish administration which, under the absolute control of the SS, played an important part in carrying out both of these tasks. As the Czech writer and historian H. G. Adler says, this made Theresienstadt "into the most gruesome ghost dance in the history of Hitler's persecution of the Jews."

To begin with the numbers: Between November 1941 and April 1945, approximately 141,000 people were sent to Theresienstadt. During this period about 33,500 died there, mostly of disease and malnutrition.[1] Eighty-eight thousand were deported from Theresienstadt to the East, of whom 3,500 survived; the others were murdered in Auschwitz or other camps. A further 2,400 were

---

This was a review of H. G. Adler, *Theresienstadt 1941–1945: The Face of a Coerced Community* (Cambridge University Press, 2017).

[1] Among them my grandfather Ludwig Nagel, a violinist who had been concertmaster of the Düsseldorf symphony. After *Kristallnacht* in 1938 he returned to his native Czechoslovakia, and was trapped when the Nazis occupied Prague in 1939. His sister Ottilie Nagel also died in Theresienstadt, and his brother and sister-in-law Teofil and Irma Nagel were sent from there to the gas chambers at Treblinka.

Analytic Philosophy and Human Life. Thomas Nagel, Oxford University Press.
© Oxford University Press 2023. DOI: 10.1093/oso/9780197681671.003.0006

released to neutral countries or escaped; and there were 17,500 survivors in the camp when the SS relinquished control to the Red Cross, shortly before Germany's surrender. In the final weeks of the war thousands of inmates were transferred to Theresienstadt from other concentration camps, but of the total number who had been sent there originally, slightly fewer than one in six survived the war.

One of those survivors was Adler (1910–1988), a writer and scholar from Prague whose first language, like that of many Czech Jews, was German, and who after the war had a productive career as a poet and novelist in that language, though he lived in England. He and his family were deported to Theresienstadt in February 1942. His wife, Gertrud, a physician and chemist, served as a doctor and headed the medical laboratory in the camp, but he himself held only menial or clerical positions in the camp's workforce. In October 1944, they were sent to Auschwitz in one of the last transports from Theresienstadt. Gertrud could have lived but would not leave her mother, and died with her in the gas chamber.[2] Adler, selected for forced labor, survived Auschwitz and several other camps until the end of the war, after which he returned to Prague. He had lost eighteen close relatives in the Holocaust.

When Adler entered Theresienstadt, he did not expect to survive, but resolved that if he did, he would write about it in detail. He left notes and materials behind when he was sent to Auschwitz and recovered them later. He accumulated more material after his release, before emigrating to England in anticipation of the Communist takeover of Czechoslovakia in 1947. The major study that emerged from this research, *Theresienstadt 1941–1945*, was originally published in German in 1955, with an expanded second edition appearing in 1960. It was reprinted in 2005 with an afterword by his son, Jeremy Adler, who was born after the war, and has

[2] The Nazis have left us a vast legacy of what is unbearable to imagine. Another example reported by Adler: in July 1944, six hundred women from Theresienstadt went voluntarily to the gas chamber with their children, even though they could have been included in labor kommandos without the children.

now finally been translated into English. Running to more than eight hundred carefully annotated pages, including numerous original documents and records, it is a monumental work of information, analysis, and moral reflection, painful to read and historically indispensable.[3]

The book is divided into three sections—History, Sociology, and Psychology—of which the second, with twelve chapters on every aspect of the camp, from nutrition to culture, is by far the longest. Half of the book consists of primary sources—official documents, administrative communications, tables of statistics, organizational and legal protocols, and quotations from the testimony of others who had been in the camp—rather than Adler's own words. The avalanche of data embeds the reader in the reality of a pathological situation, and serves Adler's intention to treat the subject as if he were a cultural anthropologist immersed in an alien community. But when it comes to his own observations and commentary, this is not value-free social science. What Adler writes is pervaded with moral judgment, and the attempt to draw a moral lesson from the human response to these unspeakable circumstances is a chief aim of the work.

2.

In the autumn of 1941 deportations to Poland began from Germany, Austria, and the occupied "Protectorate" of Bohemia and Moravia (corresponding to the present-day Czech Republic minus the Sudetenland, which had been annexed by Germany under the

---

[3] Adler also published a trilogy of novels based on his experiences, but they are modernist works written in a stream-of-consciousness style, totally different from the dense factuality of *Theresienstadt*. They have been translated into English by Peter Filkins: *Panorama*, *The Journey*, and *The Wall*, all published by Random House. Filkins has also written a biography, *H. G. Adler: A Life in Many Worlds* (Oxford University Press, 2019).

Munich agreement of 1938). Though the extermination camps were being built and began operation in December 1941, the Nazis managed to keep them secret for some time. Nevertheless, the unknown fate of those deported to the East made "transport" the most terrifying word for every Jew. To the official Jewish organization in Prague, the *Jüdische Kultusgemeinde* (JKG), the establishment of a nearby camp seemed like a safer alternative. Adler writes:

> The men of the JKG told themselves that anything was better than deportation to Poland, and, like the "Reich Association" in Berlin [the Jewish organization there], they hoped at least to delay the deportations. The course of events would disappoint these hopes.
>
> From the beginning, there were only two possibilities: (1) They might have decided in March 1939 [when the Nazis dismantled Czechoslovakia and marched into Prague], even at the cost of their lives, to dissolve all Jewish communities and institutions and destroy all records and documents. (2) They would have to follow policies aimed at delaying the worst and cleverly negotiating and easing the situation. This second path was followed to the bitter end, with ever more terrible entanglements, and it led to failure.

The first course was advocated by some Jewish officials, but the second won out. In spite of the complete failure of the second strategy to achieve what the JKG leaders hoped, Adler refrains from condemning them for this choice; his blame is focused elsewhere.

Theresienstadt was a walled garrison town created under the Habsburg Empire. Its barracks made it easy to pack in large numbers of prisoners when it was emptied out and converted to a ghetto. The maximum population of the camp, in September, 1942, was over 58,000. (It is now an ordinary civilian town called Terezin, with a population of about three thousand.) The crowding and the sanitary conditions were atrocious. Men and women were housed separately, except for members of the Jewish Council of Elders, the internal administration of the camp, who were allowed to live with their families.

The camp was controlled by a small number of SS—about twenty—and guarded by 120 Czech gendarmes. Most prisoners had almost no contact with the SS, and the SS rarely killed a prisoner inside the camp. Only the head of the Jewish Council of Elders and his deputy were allowed to speak to the camp commandant, to make daily reports and receive orders. (The Council of Elders came initially from the Prague JKG, but after transports arrived from Germany and Austria in June 1942, they were joined by Jewish officials from Berlin and Vienna.[4]) Orders from the SS were delivered orally, never in writing, but they were carried out by the Jewish administration through a blizzard of written instructions, forms, records, and memoranda so elaborate that the problem of insufficient supplies of paper was a frequent complaint.

Amid all this coercive machinery, the rich culture of the Central European Jews continued to express itself. Musical instruments had been brought by some prisoners, and performances were possible; composers continued to compose, artists to draw, and writers to write. There were frequent lectures by specialists in many fields; Adler himself arranged a commemoration of Kafka to celebrate his sixtieth birthday. But an elaborate bureaucracy controlled the material and practical conditions of life in the camp; and it created the possibility of dreadful corruption, which in this setting was equivalent to murder.

---

[4] One of them, Rabbi Benjamin Murmelstein of Vienna, was the subject of a film by Claude Lanzmann, *The Last of the Unjust*. He was the last chief elder of Theresienstadt and survived the war. Adler's attitude to him is complex: he describes Murmelstein as "smart, clear, superior, cynical, sly, and far superior to his colleagues in intelligence, and especially in cunning." But Adler is repelled by his icy, autocratic character and the absence of any sign of compassion.

3.

The main obsession of prisoners, apart from not being on the next transport, was food. The diet was barely sufficient to sustain life, and there was persistent theft from the miserable common food supply by those who controlled its preparation and distribution, for themselves and their allies—with the result that others, especially the helpless old, were left to starve. A few members of the administration strove to prevent these abuses, with only occasional success. It is one of Adler's many examples of the general failure of humanity and decency in a desperate situation:

> Even if they held out physically, people fell almost irretrievably into a struggle of all against all, in which only people with a deeply anchored morality could keep from sacrificing their souls.

A different kind of moral failure appeared in the way the administration exercised its power to determine who would be deported to the East, when transports were ordered by the SS:

> The story of a transport or a series of transports within a short period went according to the following pattern. Eichmann gave orders to the SS "office" in Theresienstadt on the number of transports and persons, the date, general guidelines, and "special instructions." The camp leader, sometimes together with other SS officers, gave more specific orders to the Jewish Elder, who was told what age groups, countries of origin, and other categories of people to choose or to protect. . . . The SS went no further in choosing the victims but left this entirely, or largely, to the Jews.

The choice was made by a "Transport Department," which was part of the central administration. Until the final transports in the autumn of 1944, when two thirds of the inmates were shipped to Auschwitz in the course of a month, the members of the Council of

Elders and their families were exempt from deportation, and others tried desperately to secure positions in the camp's workforce or bureaucracy that made them indispensable.

Even without knowing about the gas chambers, everyone feared what awaited them in the East. Then, early in 1943, the leaders of the internal administration learned the truth through some escapees from Auschwitz, but kept it a secret—even Rabbi Leo Baeck, the honorary chairman of the Council of Elders, whom Adler singles out as a person of exceptional humanity and rectitude.

This decision to hide the truth strikes me as comprehensible but appalling—though none of us can know what we would have done in the circumstances. Adler, who must have learned about it after the war, seems unable to come to a judgment about the Elders' decision; he reserves his condemnation for individuals who, knowing the truth, not only tried to spare their friends but used the transports to get rid of people who were giving them trouble. For example, after Vladimir Weiss, a member of the "Detective Department," sent the Jewish Elder Paul Eppstein a detailed complaint of flagrant corruption in the allocation of food, he and his family disappeared on the next transport.

Adler also indicates that even someone like himself, who deliberately avoided any position of authority, nevertheless belonged to the "community of guilt" that the camp created. This feeling is obviously genuine, and it seems to refer to any form of participation in a structure whose ultimate aim was murder.

4.

It is hard to guess what the Nazis would have said about the disappearance of the Jews from Europe if they had won the war. The policy of extermination was concealed from the time of its formulation at the Wannsee Conference in January 1942, and Theresienstadt was described at the time by Adolf Eichmann as an element in the process that would allow them to "save face towards the outside world." The deception included forcing some of those who arrived at Auschwitz to write reassuring postcards to relatives left behind, which were sent at intervals after they were gassed. Secrecy about the outcome was of course useful in making the deportations go smoothly; but there seems also to have been a sense that this project, unlike the campaign of military conquest or the preliminary policies of racist exclusion, depended on values that even the Nazis were unwilling to proclaim publicly.

Theresienstadt served as camouflage in more than one way. It was described as a retirement colony for deportees from German territory too old to be sent for labor in the East. It received a certain number of "notables"—prominent Jews known to the outside world, whose fate might arouse interest beyond their friends and relatives. On two occasions, in 1944 and before it was liberated in 1945, the camp (described as a "Jewish Settlement Area") underwent a program of "beautification" in order to be shown to a few foreigners, including representatives of the Red Cross. And it was the subject of a propaganda film.

The first beautification of Theresienstadt, during which 7,500 people were sent to Auschwitz to reduce the population density, included not only polishing the streets and the outsides of buildings, planting 1,200 rose bushes, building a "children's pavilion" with sandbox, wading pool, and carousel, and doubling the food ration. It also involved staging concerts, cabaret and theatrical performances, a soccer match, and even a trial for theft before a Jewish court. Everything that would be seen was carefully planned and rehearsed.

The first international visitors, in June 1944, were two representatives of the Danish government and a Swiss representative of the International Red Cross. (There were 400 Danish Jews in the camp who had not managed to escape the Nazis when the Danes, warned of an imminent roundup, accomplished their remarkable feat of evacuating more than 7,000 Jews from Denmark to neutral

Sweden.) The Jewish Elder Eppstein was presented as mayor of the town, dressed in a morning coat and derby, though he had a black eye from a blow delivered by the camp commandant a few days earlier. His carefully scripted speech to the visitors under the eyes of the SS, and their guided tour of the camp, left them with no way of gathering independent evidence.

One would think that this might have induced wholesale skepticism on the part of the visitors. In fact, the Danes produced cautious reports that received almost no attention. The report of the Red Cross representative, on the other hand, took everything he had seen and heard at face value but was suppressed by his superiors in Geneva as evidently much too favorable. So in a sense the masquerade had worked, but it yielded no propaganda. That September, a film was made depicting life in the camp under the same idyllic aspect. (It was produced by three prisoners with show-business backgrounds, including the well-known actor and film-maker Kurt Gerron, who was deported to Auschwitz and gassed after the film's completion.)

Intended for foreign consumption, the film was never distributed, though excerpts were included in a German newsreel, contrasting the easy life of these Jews (most of them dead by then) with the hardships being endured by German soldiers. It is doubtful that Theresienstadt had much of a sanitizing effect on Germany's image in the outside world. By the time of the second Red Cross visit, in April 1945, Eppstein had been shot by the SS, the war was almost over, and the visitors were not fooled, in spite of a renewed beautification effort.

As the inevitability of Germany's defeat became clear, the Nazi leadership split over what should be done with the Jews who still survived in Theresienstadt and other camps. Heinrich Himmler, of all people, presented himself as a moderate, and hoped to use some live Jews as a bargaining chip in negotiations; in February 1945, 1,200 Jews from Theresienstadt were transferred to Switzerland with Himmler's authorization. Others, following Hitler, pursued extermination to the end. Eichmann was one of these: he wanted all the remaining Jews in Theresienstadt to be killed before the Russians arrived, but his plans were not carried out.

5.

Adler's book is not autobiographical, but it is highly personal. What obsesses him is the moral and psychological interpretation of human conduct in extreme circumstances. He believes there is something of universal value to be learned from what he has observed. In a letter to a friend written just after his return to Prague in 1945, and quoted in the afterword, he makes the following extraordinary statement: "I have experienced some terrible things, but since I experienced them, it is not something I regret, and I would not do without them." This is Nietzsche's "love of fate" with a vengeance.

Given what Adler went through, it is not surprising that his view of human beings and human institutions is profoundly pessimistic—though he may have been predisposed in this direction. He writes in his conclusion:

Paradigmatically, and in rare concentration, the developments, experiences, and crimes at the camp in Theresienstadt contained the sum of all suffering and evil that could and actually do otherwise, with a wider dispersion and less visibly, operate in other communities. The unique aspect of the camp we have considered is that everything skewed, dangerous, foolish, and mean that proliferates in humans and human institutions, often in secret and ornamented with aesthetic conventions, emerged in Theresienstadt so uncannily and in such unmerciful nakedness that no one . . . was spared insight into the prevailing situation.

The one positive conclusion he drew from his dark experiences is that there is nonetheless a ground of morality that is in principle always available. Adler calls this personal quality "humaneness" (*Menschlichkeit*, also translatable as "humanity")—an inner resource that enables individuals of sufficient strength to act morally in any circumstance, however horrible.

That is the standard by which he judges the camp officials and their entanglement with the Nazis.

> The Jewish leadership had an enormously difficult task. Not even the greatest integrity could have prevented the sum of its decisions, in an absolute sense, from being bad. No freedom but self-destruction would have remained to the leadership had it offered the kind of resistance that would have countered absolute evil with absolute good. But an infinite amount of good could have been done within the existing boundaries. The SS's special plans to preserve this camp might have been better used to the advantage of thousands of people. Here, apart from its purely tragic responsibility, begins the leadership's much more terrible guilt. . . . A much more determined battle was possible against dirt, corruption, theft, and the worst kind of protectionism. . . . Almost nothing that could have improved these circumstances was done.

Adler blames them not for serving as instruments of the Nazis, which was the result of a tragic choice to cooperate in the vain hope of slowing the deportations, but for the failure of humanity in the way most of them conducted themselves in office.

6.

That is why, in spite of his own severity, Adler objected strongly when Hannah Arendt cited his book in support of her indictment of Jewish officials for collaboration. When Arendt's *Eichmann in Jerusalem* appeared in German translation, Adler published a scathing response, "What Does Hannah Arendt Know about Eichmann and the 'Final Solution'?"[5] In maintaining that Jewish officials could have impeded the exterminations by acting differently, Adler charges, Arendt completely failed to understand their trapped situation. He also captures her imperceptiveness about Eichmann. In his appearance at the trial, no traces of his demonic character remained, because it had come into effect only with the enormous power conferred on him by the Nazi regime:

> [It is] the Eichmann who acted in the Third Reich . . . , not the scatter-brained defendant 15 or 16 years later, who demands the attention of posterity. . . . Alone, most of the evil have little power, they need their Hitler, with whose downfall and without an equally strong replacement they are rendered impotent and also lose their demonic character, burnt out, disintegrated, shadows of themselves and finally as survivors, pitiful and banal.

Adler is not of the view that the Holocaust was a unique and incomprehensible cataclysm in the history of humanity, as it is sometimes seen. He believes it resulted from general characteristics of both individuals and political institutions that are still in place.

> Theresienstadt is still possible. It can be imposed on a massive scale, and, in the future, the Jews—who in mankind's overall history of suffering so often have had to serve as harbingers and as those most especially at others' mercy—might not be the only victims. Theresienstadt stands not as an experiment but as the

---

[5] "Was Weiß Hannah Arendt von Eichmann und der 'Endlösung'?," *Allgemeine Wochenzeitung der Juden*, November 20, 1964. Before this their relations had been cordial. He cited several of her writings, including *The Origins of Totalitarianism*, and she tried without success to interest American publishers in his book.

writing on the wall, and it is more alluring than our disgust at the horror is yet willing to admit.

The history of ideologically driven massacres and persecutions in the intervening years would not have surprised him. Organized power repeatedly creates the opportunity for evil on a large scale, which heroic individual humaneness is too weak and rare to resist.

In his informative and illuminating afterword Jeremy Adler says that his father's political outlook was anarchistic. He seems to have believed that morality depends on the inner resources of individuals, and cannot be found in institutions. But no inner source of human decency can solve these problems by itself. Even if H. G. Adler is right that individual morality can operate under the most monstrous of coercive institutions, that does not mean that it is our only, or even our chief, moral resource. Other coercive institutions, such as due process of law, can themselves embody morality—and in a way that relieves the pressure on individual morality, whose fragility he so unsparingly observes.

Adler's encounter with the outer limits of human wickedness and debasement led him to a fully justified fear of human nature, and his perception of the danger of collective power led him to a distrust of the state that even residence in the relatively benign society of postwar Britain did not dislodge. Yet liberal democratic institutions, with their guarantee of individual rights, are the best protection so far devised against both the struggle of all against all and the bottomless capacity for collectively empowered evil in human nature. If the fragile humaneness that is also part of our nature can bring people together in attachment to such institutions, that, rather than reliance on individual morality, is probably our best hope.

ETHICS

7

PETER SINGER AND YOU

1.

We all want to know how to live. That includes not only knowing how to get what we want, but knowing what to want, and what we should and shouldn't do. Peter Singer is prepared to tell us, and because his advice would require most of us to change our lives, and because it is offered with such force and clarity, he is an important figure in moral philosophy. He has also had a larger practical impact on the world than any other philosopher of our time. His 1975 book, *Animal Liberation*, led to effective movements to reduce the suffering of animals in factory farming, scientific experiments, and the testing of commercial products such as cosmetics, and it has persuaded many people to become vegetarians to one degree or another.

Singer's claims about what well-off people in affluent societies should do to help those living in absolute poverty elsewhere in the world have had less effect so far, but he hopes to remedy that with his latest book, *The Life You Can Save*. "The ultimate purpose of this book," he says, "is to reduce extreme poverty, not to make you feel guilty." But making the reader feel guilty is one of his specialties, and a key to his effectiveness as a writer. Whether he is describing cruel and pointless experiments on heroin addiction in monkeys or the devastating effects of easily reparable obstetric fistulas on

This was a review of Peter Singer, *The Life You Can Save: Acting Now to End World Poverty* (Random House, 2009) and Jeffrey A. Schaler, ed., *Peter Singer Under Fire: The Moral Iconoclast Faces His Critics* (Open Court, 2009).

impoverished third-world women who have given birth in their teens, he acts on our emotions, and the impact is heightened by his calm, cerebral style.

The exchanges with critics in *Peter Singer under Fire* cover the full range of his views, but I will start with what he says about affluence and poverty. *The Life You Can Save* repeats and develops an argument he originally offered in 1972, in an article that has probably been read by more students of moral philosophy than any other text, ancient or modern.[1] He begins with an example: You are walking past a shallow pond, and you notice that a small child has fallen into the water and is about to drown. Should you wade in and rescue the child, even though it will ruin your shoes and get your clothes muddy?

Most people agree that anyone who didn't rescue the child would be a moral monster. Even if the case is more demanding—the child has to be taken to a hospital, and that will make you miss a flight for which you have a nonrefundable ticket—it would still plainly be wrong not to save the child's life. The next question is, what is the principle that explains why failing to rescue the child would be wrong? Singer argues that any plausible explanation of what is wrong in this case has vast implications. He offers the following simple principle: "If it is in your power to prevent something bad from happening, without sacrificing anything nearly as important, it is wrong not to do so."

The Life You Can Save is mainly occupied with drawing the implications of this principle for people who have more money than they need to lead a decent life, in a world like ours where a billion people suffer from malnutrition and millions die from easily preventable diseases. He needs only two other premises: (1) Suffering and death from lack of food, shelter, and medical care are bad. (2) By donating to aid agencies, you can prevent suffering and death from lack of food, shelter, and medical care, without

---

[1] "Famine, Affluence, and Morality," *Philosophy & Public Affairs* vol. I, 229–243.

sacrificing anything nearly as important. It is typical of Singer to spell out the first of these two premises, just to make sure that the reader is not a complete moral idiot. But most of the book offers detailed empirical support for the second premise, describing and evaluating what aid agencies do, how effective it is, and how much it costs.

The facts are complicated, and there is controversy over the most useful forms of aid. Singer is fully aware of the problems posed by corruption in recipient countries, the importance of self-sustaining development rather than handouts, the difficulty of ensuring that medical care and preventive measures are actually delivered to those who need them. He acknowledges that sometimes conditions may be so bad that there is nothing we can do.

But he makes a strong case that private aid has done a lot of good, and could do a lot more if it had more resources. He quotes estimates that programs to provide safe drinking water cost $250 per life saved; programs for mosquito nets against malaria cost $820 per life saved; surgery to cure cataract blindness, obstetric fistulas, and deformities like cleft palate costs from $50 to $1,500. And the per capita annual development aid that would enable people in extreme poverty to reach self-sustaining subsistence is estimated to be less than $200.

If you accept these estimates, what should you do? How much of your income and wealth could you contribute to the prevention of death, deformity, and chronic hunger "without sacrificing anything nearly as important?" According to *The New York Review of Books*, the median household income of its subscribers is $123,600 a year.[2] If that is your pretax income, my guess is that Singer's principle applied literally would require you to give away more than half of it. You could survive perfectly well on what was left, though you'd have to move to cheaper housing, give up travel, restaurants, wine,

---

[2] The figure is from 2010, when this essay appeared in *The New York Review*.

opera, taxis, and cable television, and perhaps buy your clothes at Walmart.

But you and I know that you are not going to do this, and so does Singer. In fact, Singer says he himself doesn't give away as much as he thinks he should; (a *New Yorker* profile ten years ago reported that he gave away 20% of his income). And that poses the question whether any of us believes Singer's principle, plausible though it sounds. Does Singer himself really believe it? Or rather, in the sense in which he believes it, does it mean something different from what it appears at first to mean—something less radically demanding? The answer to these questions depends on the relation between morality and human motivation, a difficult topic in moral philosophy, for which Singer's claims are crucially important. Singer's principle seems to explain why we must rescue the drowning child. On the other hand, it seems to require us to do much more, in order to save hundreds of distant children. Most of us accept the first demand and balk at the second. Does that show that there is probably something wrong with the principle, even if we cannot easily say what it is?

2.

There are three possible responses to this problem. The first is to say that the principle is correct, that it tells us we have a decisive reason to give away most of our income, and that our resistance, however natural, is due to motives of self-interest which do not provide reasons that outweigh the impartial demands of morality. The second is to say that the principle is incorrect, and to look for an alternative principle that explains why it is wrong not to save the drowning child but not wrong to keep most of our income. The third is to say that the principle is correct, but that it tells us only what morality requires us to do, not what we have decisive reason to do. What we have most reason to do, all things considered, depends on how much we care about not doing what is morally wrong; and since most of us care about many other things as well, we have significant reasons not to act in accordance with Singer's principle.

You might think that Singer's answer would be the first. That is what made his 1972 article so electrifying. But in later writings he explains, though with some ambivalence, that his answer is the third. This means that his position is more philosophically complex and less threatening than it at first appears. But before examining this aspect of his view, let me say something about the second type of response, which Singer clearly rejects. Responses of the second type are based on a different conception of morality from Singer's, one according to which moral principles attempt to say how we should act in relation to other people, all things considered, by identifying and taking into account a complex set of reasons bearing on our choices.

Someone who thinks of morality in this second way still faces a serious challenge from Singer's argument, because Singer makes you feel that even for a person of modest means, the very strong reason to accept a sacrifice in the case of the drowning child does not disappear when we focus instead on an anonymous distant child. And efforts to explain away the latter reason often seem like lame excuses for a patent inconsistency. The question is whether there can be moral principles that include impartiality but are not dominated by it—principles that acknowledge both that everyone's life is of equal value and that everyone has his own life to live.

One example of such resistance to Singer's argument is the proposal of the moral and legal philosopher Liam Murphy that our responsibility to aid those in desperate need is a collective responsibility, and that each of us is required only to do our fair share. What makes Singer's principle so demanding is that most affluent people contribute nothing to alleviate extreme poverty,[3] so that anyone

---

[3] What they contribute through taxes is trivial. The U.S. foreign aid budget is 18 cents per 100 dollars of national income, and only one fifth of that amount goes to countries classified by the OECD as "Least developed."

who acknowledges a reason to do so is faced with the apparent de-mand to fill the gap and empty his pockets. If all well-off people gave a modest amount, the problem would be solved, and that, Murphy argues, is what each of us should contribute, whether or not others do their share. Morality should not make us hostages to the bad behavior of others.[4]

This seems to distinguish the drowning child case from the case of generalized aid, but Singer points out that it doesn't seem to work if one is faced with a dozen drowning children, and a dozen bystanders. If all the others do nothing, it isn't acceptable for you to rescue just one child and let the others drown. You have to help as many as you can. If the "fair share" limitation is to survive, it prob-ably has to be coupled with a more stringent requirement of im-mediate rescue. But Singer would reply that it is morally irrelevant whether someone who needs help is right in front of you or halfway around the world.

3.

Singer rejects all moral theories that, as a matter of principle, limit the subordination of our personal interests to the requirements of strict impartiality. He holds that you would be morally justi-fied in keeping most of your income only if, improbably, doing so would promote the general welfare better than giving it away.[5] He is an adherent of utilitarianism, the moral theory developed by Jeremy Bentham, John Stuart Mill, and Henry Sidgwick, and fa-vored by Singer's teacher R. M. Hare. According to utilitarianism

---

[4] See Liam Murphy, *Moral Demands in Nonideal Theory* (Oxford University Press, 2000).

[5] One example Singer cites with approval is Warren Buffett, whose brilliance in reinvesting almost all of his income has left him with much more to give away at the end of his life.

the rightness or wrongness of actions or omissions depends on their contribution to the overall balance of happiness minus unhappiness for all those sentient creatures affected, with the benefit or harm to any creature counting the same as comparable benefit or harm to any other. Your own happiness and that of the people you love do not count any differently than the happiness of strangers.

In Bentham's version of utilitarianism the sole measures of happiness and unhappiness are pleasure and pain. In Singer's version what counts is the satisfaction of preferences, including but not limited to the preference for pleasure and against pain. For example, human beings typically have a strong preference to go on living, and are prepared to accept considerable pain and other sacrifices, if necessary, to avoid their own death. Utilitarianism simply counts the preferences of all persons, and other creatures, impartially in determining what any individual should do.

However, as Singer emphasizes, this does not mean that we should continually calculate the effects of each of our actions as we go through life. First, as a practical matter, the ends of utilitarianism are better achieved if we follow rough general rules of conduct, avoiding harm and being kind, considerate and reliable in our dealings with others. Second, some of the greatest sources of happiness in human life are attachments and commitments that involve giving priority to the interests of particular people, for example one's children. The general happiness is best served if people's close personal relations are not governed by concern for the general happiness. Still, Singer says, "this doesn't mean that parents are justified in providing luxuries for their children ahead of the basic needs of others."

Third, there is special value from a utilitarian standpoint in accepting and inculcating certain strict rules such as the rule against murder, which blocks the use of utilitarian calculation as a way of deciding whether to kill an innocent person deliberately. The reason is that the general bad effects of not having such a rule, supported by a widespread revulsion against murder, would be much worse than the loss of the occasional happiness-enhancing murder that the rule might prevent. Something similar is true of the rule that torture is always wrong. Here is what Singer says:

> Given the well-documented tendency of police and guards to abuse prisoners, and the low probability that torture will yield useful information, that rule seems likely to have the best consequences. Yet, I would argue, if I find myself in the highly im-probable scenario where only torturing a terrorist will enable me to stop a nuclear bomb from going off in the middle of New York City, I ought to torture the terrorist. What the individual ought to do, and what the best moral rule directs one to do, are not neces-sarily identical.

This is the utilitarian strategy for explaining the apparent force of all strict rules of ordinary morality, such as the wrongness of lying, promise-breaking, and theft. None of those rules is morally basic, but their automatic acceptance is useful. This is another feature of utilitarianism that is widely contested, by those who believe an ad-equate moral theory cannot be just a matter of adding up costs and benefits but needs to explain how torture, murder, and betrayal are wrong in themselves.

4.

In a different way, Singer applies the idea of a disparity between what individuals really ought to do and what is the best rule for their guidance when formulating his recommendations about aid from the affluent to the destitute. The principle he believes to be morally correct would require the affluent to lower their standard of living drastically, but he recognizes that to insist on this might be counterproductive:

Daunted by what it takes to do the right thing, they may ask themselves why they are bothering to try. To avoid that danger, we should advocate a level of giving that will lead to a positive response.

So he proposes a target that, if everyone met it, would generate more than enough to solve the problem of extreme poverty: "5 percent of annual income for those who are financially comfortable, and rather more for the very rich." He provides helpful tables of progressive rates to allow you to calculate your recommended contribution, and the median *New York Review* household would contribute $6,180. If your income is higher, say $200,000, you would contribute $12,600; if it is $500,000, you would contribute $48,450. If the top 10 percent of American earners alone contributed at these rates, it would raise $471 billion a year to help the world's poorest billion people. But even if many will not contribute, Singer believes promulgating a norm of this kind is likely to be more helpful than battering people with the more stringent demand of his original principle, which would require most readers of *The New York Review* to contribute more than half of their gross income.

He supplements the argument with comments on Larry Ellison's $200 million yacht, and the $45 million the Metropolitan Museum paid recently for a Duccio *Madonna and Child* (using philanthropic contributions):

> In buying this painting, the museum has added to the abundance of masterpieces that those fortunate enough to be able to visit it can see. But if it only costs $50 to perform a cataract operation in a developing country, that means there are 900,000 people who can't see anything at all, let alone a painting, whose sight could have been restored by the amount of money that painting cost. At $450 to repair a fistula, $45 million could have given 100,000 women another chance at a decent life. At $1,000 a life, it could have saved 45,000 lives. . . . How can a painting, no matter how

beautiful and historically significant, compare with that? If the museum were on fire, would anyone think it right to save the Duccio from the flames, rather than a child? And that's just one child.

5.

Peter Singer under Fire is a valuable though uneven volume in which Singer, responding to fifteen critics, explains and defends his views. It begins with an intellectual autobiography that is of great interest. He was born in Australia after World War II to Jewish refugees from Austria. Three of his grandparents died in the Holocaust, and no doubt this background has left its mark on him, in the form of a countervailing hope for the transformative power of morality.

Singer formed his basic views early. As an undergraduate he did not react as expected to the classic argument that utilitarianism must be wrong because it would justify framing one innocent person for a crime if that were the only way to prevent the lynching of five innocent people by a mob intent on revenge. Instead of taking this as a refutation of utilitarianism, he thought it might well be the right thing to do. This exemplifies the moral equivalence between harms you produce and harms you fail to prevent that is such an important element of utilitarianism, and that determines his controversial later views on the irrelevance of the distinction, in medical ethics, between killing and letting die.

His beliefs about our duties toward animals and toward people in desperate need were formed when he was a graduate student at Oxford. He later drew another consequence from his rejection of "speciesism": the denial of the sanctity of human life, according to which all human beings, whatever their particular characteristics, have a value that no other creatures have, and should therefore be kept alive and above all not killed. Singer holds that human beings without a conception of their own future existence, such as newborns, have no interest in not being killed. He defends not only abortion but the killing of irreversibly comatose patients, and even infanticide for severely disabled infants, instead of permitting them to die slowly of afflictions that could be cured but are not, as is now sometimes done.

This last position has provoked outrage, but he insists that severe disabilities impair the quality of life, and that this should have consequences. In response to an essay by the late Harriet McBryde Johnson, an advocate for the disabled who was seriously disabled herself, Singer says:

> We could even rescind the ban on thalidomide—why should pregnant women not take advantage of this drug, so helpful in reducing morning sickness, if the fact that your child is likely to be born without arms or legs has no tendency to reduce his or her quality of life? If this sounds grotesque, that is because the view that implies it is so difficult to take seriously.

On the other hand, he recognizes that as a practical matter, there probably has to be a legal bright line against killing after a certain point, and that although it is morally arbitrary "there is something to be said for taking birth as the cut-off line, at least in terms of the criminal law."

Among the most interesting critical essays in *Peter Singer under Fire*, which prompt the most interesting responses from Singer, are those by Bernard Williams on humanism (his term for the solidarity with our own species that Singer condemns as "speciesism") and Michael Huemer on metaethics, that is, Singer's conception of the meaning of ethical claims and the grounds of their correctness. The last of these topics brings together many of the concerns of the other essays, and poses the most philosophically difficult questions about Singer's position.

Unlike Williams, a famous opponent of utilitarianism, Singer believes that the content of ethics depends on our taking up what Sidgwick called "the point of view of the universe," and thereby transcending not only our individual point of view but the point of view of our society and that of our species. Of course Singer does not believe that the universe has a point of view, but he thinks this is an apt metaphor for the human capacity to take up a standpoint of impartial and equal concern for the welfare of all sentient beings.

Singer's conviction that this is the standpoint from which moral judgments must be made depends on a theory of the meaning of moral language that he takes from R. M. Hare. Hare holds that moral judgments express what he calls "universal prescriptions," which means, roughly, that when I say that someone morally ought to do something, I am not saying merely that I want him to do it, but that I would want everyone in similar circumstances to do the same thing. This includes wanting it to be done in all the hypothetical cases with the same structure, in which I myself occupy each of the roles of those affected by the act.

To decide whether you in your present circumstances are morally required to give away half your income to Oxfam, for example, you have to decide whether you would want this to happen in the full set of structurally similar circumstances in which you were each of the potential donors and each of the potential beneficiaries. Hare claims that the only way to decide whether to endorse this universal prescription is to ask yourself what you would actually want if you were each of the persons affected, and then to weigh up the strengths of their preferences pro and con. This amounts to a criterion of preference utilitarianism. Moral requirements derive from an equal and impartial consideration for the interests of all.

Hare thus attempts to ground utilitarianism in the analysis of moral language and the universal prescriptions he believes such language entails. However, this turns out to be a very weak foundation, since Hare does not believe that there is any rational requirement to engage in moral judgment, to govern one's conduct by moral standards, or to use moral language at all. If someone just didn't care about what he would want everyone to do in parallel circumstances, then morality would have no grip on him. He could say, "Of course if I were starving I would want rich people to contribute to famine relief, but so what? Whether my conduct is 'wrong' in that sense doesn't interest me."

6.

The more radical and demanding a moral claim is, the more pressing is the question what reason we have to live in accordance with it. This is an acute problem for Singer, both because he espouses a radical morality, and because, like Hare, he is drawn to the view, associated with David Hume, that all our reasons for action depend on our desires, and that the desires themselves are neither rational nor irrational:

> So if some people prefer to follow my arguments and give almost all their money to aiding those in great need, there is nothing at all irrational about this. Equally, giving away money to those in great need is not rationally required.

When he is thinking in this vein, Singer searches outside morality for reasons to be moral, and he has argued, for example in his book *Practical Ethics*,[6] that living by principles of radical impartiality will make us individually happy by giving meaning to our lives—something we presumably care about already. But another approach also tempts him, one which he suggests in a later book,

---

[6] Cambridge University Press, 1979; second edition, 1993.

The Expanding Circle—namely that the impartiality that underlies utilitarian morality is itself a requirement of reason:

> That one's own interests are one among many sets of interests, no more important than the similar interests of others, is a conclusion that, in principle, any rational being can come to see.[7]

This idea is found in Sidgwick, and it is opposed to the Humean outlook because it asserts that not only our factual and logical beliefs but also our motives are subject to rational requirements. In other words, it is contrary to reason to prefer eating a meal in a good restaurant to saving a child from death by malnutrition at the same cost. In the end, however, Singer doubts that the appeal to reason can serve as a basis for ethics, since if someone doesn't care about the interests of others, telling him he has an objective reason to care won't get him to act any differently.

I think Singer has taken the wrong path here. Huemer argues forcefully and convincingly that Singer's overall moral position is more consonant with Sidgwick's reason-based outlook than with Hume's desire-based one. Sidgwick's argument requires that reason should be capable of getting us to change our desires at the most basic level, and also to refuse to act on some desires for reasons that do not derive from other, already existing desires. Yet that is precisely what seems to happen when, in response to Singer's arguments, someone becomes a vegetarian or a major donor to Oxfam for reasons of consistency.

The heart of Singer's case is that it is inconsistent to be very concerned about human pain but hardly at all about animal pain, and inconsistent to care about the drowning child in front of you but not about the dying child in a distant country. When people change their conduct to avoid such inconsistency, their motives have been

---

[7] Peter Singer, *The Expanding Circle: Ethics and Sociobiology* (Farrar, Straus and Giroux, 1981), p. 106.

altered by reasoning. Singer also works on our feelings, but in large part he is calling on us to transcend by rational thought the motivational habits of nature and culture toward a truer understanding of how we have reason to live—he is not just describing a moral life that is rationally optional.

Such a reason-based defense of utilitarianism would be opposed not only by antirationalists but also by other rationalists, many of whom think that the impartiality demanded by utilitarianism oversimplifies the complex territory of true reasons for action. Sidgwick, though he defends impartiality as a requirement of reason, despairs of reconciling it with the competing principle of rational self-interest, which seems also intuitively self-evident. That is one of the problems that discourages Singer from accepting reason as the basis of morality. But a reason-based morality may have to take on both these types of reason, and perhaps others, in constructing the principles by which we should live—principles that aspire to the reflective endorsement of everyone, even when their personal interests conflict.

That is the likely outcome if we take as the aim of ethics, as Singer is reluctant to do, the discovery of standards that everyone has reason to meet. The result might be a pluralistic morality that combines impartiality with respect for each individual's inviolability and personal autonomy.[8] It would probably include some version of the relatively modest duties to others in need that Singer recommends as a "realistic" fall-back from what morality truly requires.

Singer's own message is very different. He believes that the moral truth is very demanding. In spite of his expressed ambivalence, I get the sense from his writings that deep down he is convinced that everyone is not just morally required to give equal consideration

---

[8] Significant recent books that develop such alternatives to utilitarianism are Samuel Scheffler's *Human Morality* (Oxford University Press, 1992), T. M. Scanlon's *What We Owe to Each Other* (Harvard University Press, 1998), and David Wiggins's *Ethics: Twelve Lectures on the Philosophy of Morality* (Harvard University Press, 2006).

to the interests of all, but has decisive reasons to do so—and that the recognition of those reasons has the power over time to transform the world. Even those who are not persuaded that he is correct about the content of morality should be grateful to him for posing these questions so vividly.

8

EFFECTIVE ALTRUISM

It has become a moral cliché to deplore the exploding economic in-equality that plagues our planet, both within individual states and across their boundaries. What is to be done about the obscene earn-ings of financial tycoons and the vast gap in standard of living be-tween rich and poor countries? How can we change the economic and political institutions that permit this? William MacAskill, Peter Singer, and others in the effective altruism movement have a different reaction. While others bemoan the political obstacles to institutional reform, they see these huge inequalities as an ideal op-portunity for individual action, because they make it possible for some people to do a great deal of good at very little cost. MacAskill's *Doing Good Better* and Singer's *The Most Good You Can Do* set out the position.

Global capitalism may generate extreme inequalities along with production and growth, but there is no reason to stop there. The winners don't have to spend it all on themselves: they can do vastly more good for others—the poorer the better (Bill Gates and Warren Buffett are spectacular examples). The dual aim of effective altruism is to persuade people who are fortunate to employ their lives and resources in this way, and to determine the best way of doing it—where the need is greatest and what methods will alle-viate the most suffering at the lowest cost.

This was a review of William MacAskill, *Doing Good Better: Effective Altruism and a Radical New Way to Make a Difference* (Random House, 2015) and Peter Singer, *The Most Good You Can Do: How Effective Altruism Is Changing Ideas about Living Ethically* (Yale University Press, 2015).

Analytic Philosophy and Human Life. Thomas Nagel, Oxford University Press.
© Oxford University Press 2023. DOI: 10.1093/oso/9780197681671.003.0008

The argument is not addressed merely to the rich or well-to-do. The first chapter of MacAskill's book provides a sobering account of the overall pattern of inequality in the world. In real purchasing power—not just money—someone living below the U.S. poverty level, earning $11,000 a year, is in the top 15% of the world income distribution. Someone earning $28,000 a year, the median individual income in the U.S., is in the top 5%. Someone earning $52,000 or more is in the top 1%. The bottom 20% of the world's population earns less than $550 a year in U. S. purchasing power, and lives at an almost unimaginable level of want. These data suggest that most people living in the advanced economies are in a position to do substantial good for others at much less cost to themselves. But just what should they do? Effective altruism answers this question by recommending both ends and means.

To begin with ends: there is a difference between the two books, marked by their titles, which reveals an ambivalence in the aims of the movement. Singer defends a radical moral outlook, utilitarianism; that is what his title, *The Most Good You Can Do*, means. Utilitarianism is founded on two principles that have been stated with exemplary clarity by the philosopher Henry Sidgwick: first, that the good of any one individual is of no more importance, from the point of view of the Universe, than the good of any other; and second, that as a rational being, each of us is bound to aim at good generally—so far as it is attainable by our efforts—not at a particular part of it. The rational ideal, then, would be to subordinate one's own point of view completely, for evaluative purposes, to the point of view of the Universe, and to find a way to live that produces more good, impartially measured, than any available alternative. As Singer acknowledges, even those who accept this rational ideal, himself included, almost never live up to it fully; but that, he says, is because they are human, and humans are not fully rational.

The claim that such strict impartiality among persons is rationally required (Sidgwick's second principle) is highly contestable, and I shall return to it. But strict utilitarianism is not essential to explain the choices of many effective altruists, and this is reflected in MacAskill's different title, *Doing Good Better*. His primary goal is not to persuade us to do the most good we possibly can, but to show those who want to benefit others how they can do so most efficiently—whatever their general moral outlook. Perhaps MacAskill too is a utilitarian, and is just keeping it quiet for tactical reasons; but you don't have to be a utilitarian to find his advice useful.

What he takes over from utilitarianism is the method of cost-benefit analysis in comparing strategies of benefit. If the aim is to do good as effectively as possible, a measure of value is needed to compare the effects on people's lives of different acts or policies designed to help them. In the calculations of the effective altruism movement this measure is sometimes provided by the concept of the quality-adjusted life year, or QALY—a concept developed originally to compare the effects of treatments for debilitating medical conditions. A year of life in good health has a value of one QALY. So if you save from death an adult with a life expectancy of thirty years in good health you have produced thirty QALYS. And if you cure someone of a disease that would otherwise reduce the quality of his life by 25% over the next eight years, you have produced two QALYS. (The 25% reduction is established if the victim would be willing to accept a treatment that would free him from the disease for four years, but shorten his life by one year.) This metric, though crude, can be extended to compare the value of other material benefits and disadvantages that affect the quality of life. The point, taken from utilitarianism, is to have a single measure for all value.

One problem for cost-benefit analysis is that we generally do not know for certain what the results of different acts or policies will be, so we must make do with probabilities. The method for doing this is to aim at maximizing "expected value," which means picking the course of action whose different possible outcomes, when their respective values are multiplied by their different probabilities, add up to the greatest total. This will sometimes mean picking an alternative that has a small chance of producing a great good or preventing a great evil over one that is nearly certain to produce a more modest benefit.

To turn to the means recommended: while these authors would like us to change our lives, perhaps radically, they emphasize that altruism should not be identified with self-sacrifice. As they both illustrate with various life stories, benefiting others for their own sake generally produces happiness in the donor, even though that is not its aim. (The lack of interest in self-sacrifice also explains why they don't give especially high marks to the exceptional altruism of donating a kidney to a stranger: it does far less good than giving $5,000 to distribute mosquito nets that prevent malaria.)

If the question is how one can best benefit others, the first obvious choice is between donation and direct action. One striking tactic is called "earning to give"—choosing a career that will maximize one's income (on Wall Street, for example) so that one can give away half of it to appropriate charities. This path has been followed for example by a student of Singer's at Princeton who decided to forgo graduate school in philosophy for finance, and by a doctor described by MacAskill who calculated that by becoming an oncologist in England and giving away half his earnings he could save many more lives than by going to Ethiopia to practice medicine with an NGO. An important part of the calculation, as always for utilitarians, was that the *extra* good he could do by donating was much greater. If he went to Ethiopia, he would save lives, but most of them would have been saved by another doctor who took that job with the NGO if he did not. Whereas by donating he could substantially increase the number of lives saved by allowing the NGO to hire more doctors. For a utilitarian or anyone who evaluates actions like a utilitarian, what matters is not the good you do but the difference you make.

There are four private organizations dedicated to the program of effective altruism. MacAskill is a founder of two of them: Giving

What We Can, which tries to get people to give at least 10% of their income to the most cost-effective charities, and "80,000 Hours" (named for the length of a typical life's work), which coaches young people on how to choose a career that will make the most difference. An earlier book by Singer inspired The Life You Can Save, which urges people to pledge donations on a graduated scale, depending on their income. Finally, and crucially, Give Well (founded by two hedge-fund managers who went in the opposite direction from earning to give) is an organization that conducts rigorous empirical research to identify charities that do the most good per dollar received, and publicizes the results.

Determining which charities should receive donations is at the heart of effective altruism. Singer and MacAskill begin by noting the thoughtlessness with which most people give—motivated by sentimental media appeals, associations with personal experience (funding research on a disease that killed one's child), local connections (the local museum or hospital or community chest), or salient current disasters (earthquakes, tsunamis), without any attempt to find out how much good a donation would do by comparison with other destinations for that amount of money. This is partly a matter of motivation: a great deal of charitable giving is just a form of self-expression or a mark of solidarity rather than an attempt to have an effect. Or if it aims to do good, it does not aim to do so impartially, by the utilitarian metric, but deliberately favors some types of good and some people over others. Still, there are plenty of donors who want to benefit the worst-off people in the world, but who still make no effort to determine on the basis of evidence how to do so most efficiently. Or they rely on irrelevant evidence, such as the percent of the charity's budget that is spent on fund-raising and administration. As MacAskill says, one would never decide to buy a computer based on the size of the manufacturer's executive salaries or its advertising budget. What one wants to know is how much value one is getting for the price, compared with the alternatives, and that is what should determine charitable giving as well.

This kind of empirical calculation, if it accepts utilitarian impartiality, gives stark results. Westerners should give to no beneficiaries in their own countries, only to charities that benefit the poorest people in the world in the cheapest possible way—usually by preventing or treating illnesses that hardly exist in our countries because they are so easy to eliminate. To give one of Singer's and MacAskill's favorite examples, you might think it worthwhile to contribute for the provision of guide dogs for the blind, which certainly improve the quality of life for blind people. But it costs $50,000 to train one such dog which will work for nine years, and for that amount of money it is possible to pay for surgery that will save 500 people in the developing world from blindness caused by trachoma.

Give Well does empirical research to identify the most cost-effective charities, and recommends only a few each year: narrowly targeted charities that alleviate the worst evils at the lowest cost. Evidence for this kind of quantification is easier to obtain for health benefits than for something like economic growth. Nevertheless, one of the charities Give Well rates highly is Give Directly, which simply transfers money from donors to some of the poorest people in Kenya and Uganda—households for which a gift of $1,000 will more than double their income for a year. Give Directly has verified that the recipients invariably use the money for necessities like improved diet, shelter, transport, and education.

Singer and MacAskill are clearly right that people should give much more thought to how to choose the targets of their charitable giving. Showing people on the basis of convincing evidence how they can do the most good is a wholly admirable enterprise. However, what makes the effective altruism movement controversial is its broadly utilitarian outlook, both with respect to how one should live and with respect to the choice of where to direct one's beneficence. Utilitarianism appears both in its strict form, advocated by Singer, and in a weaker form, as expressed in the standards for choosing among beneficiaries. The former presents the rational ideal of turning oneself into a servant of the point of view of the Universe; the latter says only that whatever portion of one's resources one decides to devote to the benefit of others, those resources should be allocated so as to maximize the quantity of impartial utilitarian good that results—the expected value in QALY's.

Even though strict utilitarianism in the sense of radical impartiality among all persons, including oneself, is not essential to the effective altruism project, the ideal of rationality that underlies utilitarianism plays an essential part in shaping the project. Doubts about that ideal will also suggest doubts about whether effective altruism is the only justifiable form of charity. So let me ask first whether perfect rationality would consist in counting the good of every person (or every sentient creature) as of equal importance, and trying to produce as much of that good, impartially measured, as possible.

I think it must be granted that everyone's good is equally important "from the point of view of the Universe," and that rational beings can imaginatively occupy that point of view, as part of their outlook on the world. This form of impersonal detachment plays an important part in reasoning about the world—in the sciences, for example, where it allows us to transcend the perceptual appearances and get closer to objective reality. But should it dominate our reasoning in the practical domain, so that we recognize as objectively valid only the equal importance of everyone? Or is the fact that we each have our own life to live fundamental to human rationality? Does our own perspective—the unequal importance different lives and different goods have when seen not from the point of view of the Universe but from our personal point of view—have independent reason-giving force?

Bernard Williams was one of the most forceful critics of utilitarianism on the ground that it ignores the perspective of the individual. Singer takes issue with Williams's claim that utilitarianism entails a radical alienation from ourselves, our projects, and what gives meaning and substance to our lives. To this, I believe Singer is right to reply that "those who earn to give are, to a greater extent than most people, living in accord with their values—that is, with their core conviction that we ought to live our lives so as to do the most good we can. It is hard to see any alienation or loss of integrity here." If one takes such a leap, it will determine what one's life means. But it is a leap, and Williams is certainly right that it seems to leave behind or downgrade a great deal that there is also reason to value.

The thought that motivates effective altruists—that the needs of the worst-off people in the world overwhelm in importance the goods on which we who are well off spend most of our resources—is a very compelling one. It is easy to understand how it leads them to change their lives. Yet this is nonetheless a choice, and it cannot be rationally mandatory unless the only good reasons are those that appear from the impersonal standpoint. The essence of resistance to utilitarianism is that it is not unreasonable to aim at all kinds of goods even if they are not the greatest goods one can achieve. These suboptimal but reasonable aims include one's own success and enjoyment and that of one's friends and family, the advancement of knowledge for its own sake, the creation or preservation of beauty, the support of institutions from which one has benefited, and so forth. On this view, we are rationally permitted to care about some goods more than others without impartial justification, and to act accordingly.

I believe Williams went too far in claiming that the point of view of practical reason was entirely "from here," and that pure impartiality had no authority in the domain of conduct. But values that are specifically dependent on the perspective of the individual agent seem to be at least an important part of the ground for what we have reason to do, and to recognize those values is not inconsistent with acknowledging that, from the impersonal point of view, all individuals are equally valuable.

If, contra Singer, this is correct, two things follow. First, it is not a failure of rationality if one fails to arrange one's life so as to accomplish the most good one can do. There is more than one rational way to live, and while rationality certainly requires giving some weight to the equal importance of everyone, it allows us to choose many other values in choosing a form of life.

Second, if one is committed to doing something for the good of others, it is rationally permissible to choose the form of that beneficence at least partly on grounds that depend on the personal perspective—not only special concern for family and friends, but personal gratitude and solidarity with causes and institutions with which one has a connection. I agree with Singer and MacAskill that such preferences are often carried to ridiculous lengths, with very wasteful results. The effective altruism movement is doing great service in focusing attention on the greatest needs, which can be met at the smallest cost. But we can acknowledge the importance of this work without admitting that a donation to the local symphony orchestra or Planned Parenthood or one's alma mater is necessarily irrational.

9

KORSGAARD, KANT, AND OUR FELLOW CREATURES

Christine Korsgaard is distinguished within the field of philosophy for her penetrating and analytically dense writings on ethical theory and her critical interpretations of the works of Immanuel Kant. Now, for the first time, she has written a book about a question that anyone can understand. *Fellow Creatures: Our Obligations to the Other Animals* is a blend of moral passion and rigorous theoretical argument. Though it is often difficult—not because of any lack of clarity in the writing but because of the intrinsic complexity of the issues—this book provides the opportunity for a wider audience to see how philosophical reflection can enrich the response to a problem that everyone should be concerned about.

Since the publication of Peter Singer's *Animal Liberation* in 1975, there has been a notable increase in vegetarianism or veganism as a personal choice by individuals, and in the protection of animals from cruel treatment in factory farms and scientific research, both through law and through public pressure on businesses and institutions. Yet most people are not vegetarians: approximately 9.5 billion animals die annually in food production in the United States, and the carnivores who think about it tend to console themselves with the belief that the cruelties of factory farming are being ameliorated, and that if this is done, there is nothing wrong

This was a review of Christine M. Korsgaard, *Fellow Creatures: Our Obligations to the Other Animals* (Oxford University Press, 2018).

Analytic Philosophy and Human Life. Thomas Nagel, Oxford University Press.
© Oxford University Press 2023. DOI: 10.1093/oso/9780197681671.003.0009

with killing animals painlessly for food. Korsgaard firmly rejects this outlook, not just because it ignores the scale of suffering still imposed on farmed animals, but because it depends on a false contrast between the values of human and animal lives, according to which killing a human is wrong in a way that killing an animal is not.

Korsgaard deploys a complex account of morality to deal with this and many other questions. What makes the book especially interesting is the contrast between her approach and Singer's. She writes, and Singer would certainly agree, that "the way human beings now treat the other animals is a moral atrocity of enormous proportions." But beneath this agreement lie profound differences. Singer is a utilitarian and Korsgaard is a Kantian, and the deep division in contemporary ethical theory between these two conceptions of morality marks their different accounts of why we should radically change our treatment of animals. (Equally interesting is Korsgaard's sharp divergence from Kant's own implausible views on the subject. As we shall see, she argues persuasively that Kant's general theory of the foundations of morality supports conclusions for this case completely different from what he supposed.)

Utilitarianism is the view that what makes actions right or wrong is their tendency to promote or diminish the total amount of happiness in the world, by causing pleasure or pain, gratification or suffering. Such experiences are taken to be good or bad absolutely, and not just for the being who undergoes them. The inclusion of nonhuman animals in the scope of moral concern is straightforward: the pleasure or pain of any conscious being is part of the impersonal balance of good and bad experiences that morality tells us to make as positive as possible.

But the existence or survival of such creatures matters only because they are vessels for the occurrence of good experiences. According to utilitarianism, if you kill an animal painlessly and replace it with another whose experiences are just as pleasant as those the first animal would have had if it had not been killed, the total balance of happiness is not affected, and you have done nothing wrong. Even in the case of humans, what makes killing them wrong is not the mere ending of their lives but the distress the prospect of death causes them because of their strong conscious sense of their own future existence, as well as the emotional pain their deaths cause to other humans connected with them.

Korsgaard, in contrast, denies that we can build morality on a foundation of the absolute value of anything, including pleasure and pain. She holds that there is no such thing as absolute or impersonal value in the sense proposed by utilitarianism—something being just good or bad, period. All value, she says, is "tethered." Things are good or bad *for* some person or animal; your pleasure is "good-for" you, my pain is "bad-for" me. Korsgaard says that the only sense in which something could be absolutely good is if it were "good-for" everyone. In the end she will maintain that the lives and happiness of all conscious creatures *are* absolutely good in this sense, but she reaches this conclusion only by a complex ethical argument; it is not an axiom from which morality begins, as in utilitarianism.

Before getting to that argument, however, let us consider how she understands the value of life for humans and for the other animals. Korsgaard believes that "life itself is a good for almost any animal who is in reasonably good shape." Humans, with their capacity for language, historical record-keeping, long-term memory, and planning for the future, have a strong consciousness of their lives as extended in time. But because the other animals are capable of learning and remembering, we know that they also have temporally extended conscious lives, not just successions of momentary experiences; what happens to an animal at one time changes its point of view at later times, so that it acquires "an ongoing character that makes it a more unified self over time." It is a matter of degree, but the lives of most mammals and birds, at least, have this kind of unity, so we can think of them as having good or bad lives, not just good or bad experiences.

The big difference between us and the other animals is that we are self-conscious in a way they are not. Korsgaard marks this as the distinction between instinctive and rational lives. Unlike the other animals, we act not just on the basis of our perceptions, desires, and inclinations. We can step back from the immediate appearances and withhold endorsement from them as grounds for belief or action if we judge that they do not provide adequate justifying reasons—as when we discount a visual impression as an optical illusion or a negative evaluation as the product of jealousy. This type of rational self-assessment has given rise to both science and morality. Animals, by contrast, as far as we know, do not evaluate their own beliefs and motives before acting on them.

So the lives of humans and of other animals are very different. But does that mean that human lives are more important or more valuable than the lives of animals? Korsgaard asks, in keeping with her skepticism about untethered absolute value, "More important or valuable *to whom*?" Your life is more valuable to you than it is to a rabbit, but the rabbit's life is more valuable to the rabbit than it is to you. And if you protest that the rabbit's life is not as important to the rabbit as your life is to you, Korsgaard's response is that even though you have a conception of your life as a whole that the rabbit lacks, this does not show that your life is more valuable:

> For even if the rabbit's life is not as important to her as yours is to you, nevertheless, for her it contains absolutely *everything of value*, all that can ever be good or bad for her, except possibly the lives of her offspring. The end of her life is the end of all value and goodness for her. So there is something imponderable about these comparisons.

Korsgaard denies that the human capacity to appreciate literature, music, and science makes human lives more valuable. She observes that in comparing humans with one another, most of us do not think that one individual is more valuable simply because more good things happen in his or her life, and she holds that we should take the same view when comparing humans with other animals. There are just different individuals, and the life of each of them is of ultimate value to the creature itself.

But if we start from a conception of value according to which what is good or bad is always what is good or bad for particular individuals, and nothing is good or bad in itself, it is not clear where we can find a basis for morality and for our obligations to others. What reason do we have to care about anything but what is good or bad for ourselves, or for a limited group of others who matter to us because of some connection or identification? The history of moral philosophy offers various answers to this question, most of which I will not discuss. Korsgaard endorses the one provided by Kant.

Kant held that we ourselves are the source of the requirements of morality, by virtue of our status as rational beings. As Korsgaard puts it:

> Because of the way in which we are conscious of the motives for our actions, we cannot act without endorsing those motives as adequate to justify what we propose to do. But this is just what it means to value something—to endorse our natural motives for wanting it or caring about it, and to see them as good reasons. So as rational beings, we cannot act without setting some sort of value on the ends of our actions.

Most important, Kant believes that the value we cannot help assigning to our ends is absolute value—value from everyone's point of view. This is a condition of our ability to endorse our actions from an external point of view toward ourselves, which is the essence of rationality. And it has a momentous consequence:

> Your right to confer absolute value on *your* ends and actions is limited by everyone else's (as Kant thinks of it, every other rational being's) right to confer absolute value on *her* ends and actions in

exactly the same way. So in order to count as a genuinely rational choice, the principle on which you act must be acceptable from anyone's (any rational being's) point of view—it must be consistent with the standing of others as ends in themselves.

This gives us Kant's fundamental principle of morality, the categorical imperative, in two of its familiar formulations: act in such a way that you can will your principle as universal law; and treat all rational beings as ends and never merely as means. To treat others as ends in themselves is to regard the achievement of their goals or ends as good in itself, and not just for them. The practical upshot is that each of us has a strong reason to pursue our own ends in a way that does not interfere with the pursuit by others of their ends, and some reason to help them if they need help.

But what does this imply about animals? In Kant's view, we impose the moral law on ourselves: it applies to us because of our rational nature. The other animals, because they are not rational, cannot engage in this kind of self-legislation. Kant concluded that they are not part of the moral community; they have no duties and we have no duties toward them.[1]

It is here that Korsgaard parts company with him. She distinguishes two senses in which someone can be a member of the moral community, an active and a passive sense. To be a member in the active sense is to be one of the community of reciprocal lawgivers who is obligated to obey the moral law. To be a member in the passive sense is to be one of those to whom duties are owed, who must be treated as an end. Kant believed that these two senses coincide, but Korsgaard says this is a mistake. The moral law that

---

[1] Though Kant says we may treat animals purely as means to our ends, he qualifies this by adding that we have a duty *to ourselves* not to treat them cruelly, since cruelty to animals results in a callousness that may affect the treatment of our fellow humans. Korsgaard suggests plausibly that this is "a product of desperation" on Kant's part, "an attempt to explain the everyday intuition that we really *do* have at least some obligation to be kind to animals."

we rational beings give to ourselves can give us duties of concern for other, nonrational beings who are not themselves bound by the moral law—duties to treat them as ends in themselves:

> There is no reason to think that because it is only autonomous rational beings who must make the normative presupposition that we are ends in ourselves, the normative presupposition is only *about* autonomous rational beings. And in fact it seems arbitrary, because of course we also value ourselves as animate beings. This becomes especially clear when we reflect on the fact that many of the things that we take to be good-for us are not good for us in our capacity as autonomous rational beings. Food, sex, comfort, freedom from pain and fear, are all things that are good for us insofar as we are animals.

I find this argument for a revision of Kant's position completely convincing. Korsgaard sums up:

> On a Kantian conception, what is special about human beings is not that we are the universe's darlings, whose fate is absolutely more important than the fates of the other creatures who like us experience their own existence. It is exactly the opposite: What is special about us is the empathy that enables us to grasp that other creatures are important to themselves in just the way we are important to ourselves, and the reason that enables us to draw the conclusion that follows: that every animal must be regarded as an end in herself, whose fate matters, and matters absolutely, if anything matters at all.

Having secured the admission of the other animals to the Kantian moral community as passive members, Korsgaard turns to a further problem: "Nature," she says, "is recalcitrant to moral standards." Not only are the other animals not subject to the moral law; their interests are irreconcilably opposed in a way that makes impossible the kind of moral harmony that we can aspire to as an ideal for the human world. What is good for the lion is necessarily bad for the antelope, and even if we recognize our own duty to treat both of them as ends in themselves, that doesn't provide a moral resolution of the conflict.

Korsgaard concludes her book with discussion of responses to this problem by those who write about animal ethics, some of which outsiders to the field may find bizarre. One proposal is to eliminate predation by arranging the gradual extinction of predator species. Other defenders of the rights of animals believe that we should preserve their habitats and otherwise leave them alone entirely, so that all animals are wild.

Korsgaard rejects both these extremes. She believes we obviously shouldn't kill or exploit animals for food, but we have no obligation to take up the position of a creator by bringing it about that the world is populated by creatures who are better off than the ones who would otherwise be there. She also believes that it's all right to keep animals as pets, provided the society ensures that they are not abused. (Her book is dedicated, by name, to the five cats she has lived with over the past thirty-five years.)

Korsgaard also notes the curious fact that many people are much more concerned with the preservation of species from extinction than they are with the welfare of individual animals, and she thinks this makes no moral sense. Species don't have a point of view, and their survival doesn't have value for them.

> If you accept the idea that everything that is good must be good for someone, for some creature, then you must deny that it makes sense to say that species or ecosystems have intrinsic value. According to the view I have been advocating, it is plain that the health of an ecosystem matters because it matters to the creatures who depend upon it, and the extinction of a species matters when it threatens the biodiversity and so the health of the ecosystem and with it the welfare of its members.

Her claim is that species have no value in themselves. They may have value for individuals, but only individuals have value in themselves. (This leaves aside aesthetic value, which I suspect plays a part in many people's attachment to species as such.)

Korsgaard's position is undeniably powerful, and if it prevailed it would be one of the largest moral transformations in the history of humanity. Let me close by describing two possible grounds of resistance to it. They would also apply to the utilitarian argument for somewhat different but equally radical conclusions about how we should treat animals.

The first ground would be a rejection of the crucial idea of absolute value, either as a moral starting point or as the conclusion of a Kantian moral argument. According to this view, all we have to work with in justifying moral requirements are the interests, motives, or feelings of the individuals to whom they are supposed to apply, rather than some transcendent or impersonal point of view. This does not mean moral principles can't be justified. If, for example, it is in the collective interest of members of a human community to govern their interactions by certain rules that permit peaceful coexistence and cooperation, that would provide a basis for morality that depends only on what is good-for individuals, and not what is good absolutely. And if there is a shared human sentiment of empathy toward the other animals, or some of them, then that would support a requirement of humane treatment as part of morality, though its content would depend on the strength and scope of the sentiment, not on the absolute badness of animal suffering.

Korsgaard acknowledges this type of position in her discussion of reciprocity as a basis for morality. She points out that it has an implication that most people would find unacceptable: namely that if we encountered rational beings so powerful that they had nothing to fear from us, and who didn't feel any sympathy for us, they could kill or enslave or experiment on us without doing anything wrong.

But those who deny that anything has absolute value may be willing to accept that consequence.

The second possible ground of resistance is also mentioned by Korsgaard. One might hold that although humans are not more important or more valuable than other animals, it is morally permissible for us to be partial to our fellow humans and to count their interests more, out of a "sense of solidarity with our own kind." We recognize the moral acceptability of such partiality toward the interests of our own families, for example, and Korsgaard considers the possibility that in situations of life-or-death emergency (rats spreading plague) we would be morally justified in putting the interests of our own species first, to lethal effect. But even if this is granted, it is a far cry from endorsing a degree of partiality for the human species that allows the lives of other animals to be routinely sacrificed to the pleasures of the table. In effect, that seems to be the principle to which most carnivores adhere, though they are probably helped by the assumption that Korsgaard has gone to great lengths to combat: that the loss of life is not really so bad for an animal.

Moral disagreement is a constant feature of the human condition, as we struggle to find the right way to live. Whether we should kill animals for food is one of the deepest disagreements of our time; but we should not be surprised if the issue is rendered moot within the next few decades, when cultured meat (also called clean meat, synthetic meat, or *in vitro* meat) becomes less expensive to produce than meat from slaughtered animals, and equally palatable. When that happens, I suspect that our present practices, being no longer gastronomically necessary, will suddenly become morally unimaginable.

10

REGRET AND ITS LIMITS

In *The View from Here*, an interesting, careful, and occasionally outrageous book, R. Jay Wallace explores the complex interaction and competition between the attitudes of affirmation and regret that are almost inevitable as we look back on our lives and celebrate or deplore the conditions and choices that have made us what we are—that underlie our successes, our failures, and our personal attachments. Wallace's aims are very broad and his conclusions radical, but he begins by examining closely several examples of the phenomenon, real and imaginary, that are already familiar from recent philosophical literature.

First example: the young girl's child. A girl of fourteen decides to have a child, though she is clearly not in a position to care for it adequately, as she would be if she waited till she was an adult. The decision also disrupts her life and limits her opportunities in ways that having a child later would not. But she loves the child, and despite its disadvantages the child itself is glad to have been born. Neither of them can wish the child did not exist, or regret the young girl's decision to give it birth. Yet it seems that it was a decision she should not have made.

Second example: disability. An amputee dedicates himself to becoming a world-class athlete and competes successfully in the Paralympics. Or a person born deaf finds the meaning of his life through immersion in the kinds of communication available

This was a review of R. Jay Wallace, *The View from Here: On Affirmation, Attachment, and the Limits of Regret* (Oxford University Press, 2013).

only to people who lack the ability to hear. The way these people value their lives seems to exclude regretting their disabilities; but does that imply that such disabilities should not be prevented or repaired, if possible?

Third example: Gauguin. In his famous essay "Moral Luck" Bernard Williams imagined an artist, loosely modeled on Gauguin, who abandons his wife and children in France to go to South Seas, where he achieves the fulfillment of his talent and ambition, producing the work that gives meaning to his life as an artist. While his family continues to have a bitter complaint against him for the way he treated them, he cannot look back on his desertion with regret. Even if he acknowledges that it was morally objectionable, Williams says, it is retroactively justified, for him, as a necessary condition of the creative projects that he most values in life. (If on the other hand he had failed in his own eyes as a painter in Tahiti, he would be forced to look back on the abandonment of his family with nothing but regret and self-reproach.)

Wallace's title, "The View from Here," is a phrase Williams used to capture the contingent and perspectival determinants of our values and commitments. Although Wallace believes that not all practical or value judgments are perspectival in this way, he sets out to investigate the ones that are, and to understand what the affirmation of our contingent lives and attachments commits us to.

He differs significantly from Williams. Notably, Wallace doesn't believe in retroactive justification of a choice in light of how things turned out later. If someone breaks his promise to drive you to the airport, causing you to miss your flight, then even if the flight crashes with no survivors, your friend is not excused: he shouldn't have broken his promise. The retrospective effects of later outcomes have to do not with justification but with affirmation or regret, which are independent of justification or its absence. Just as you can't regret your friend's failure to keep his promise, so the present affirmation of their lives and projects—by the young girl's child, the disabled Paralympic athlete, or Gauguin—spreads backwards to encompass their historically essential conditions and blocks regret.

Wallace calls this the "affirmation dynamic," but it holds, he observes, only for unconditional affirmations, the kind typified by our attachment to a particular person whom we love, or to the projects that give our lives meaning. It does not apply to conditional affirmations: "Thus I might celebrate without reservation the heroism of the firefighter who rescued my kids from the flames, while regretting deeply the negligence on my own part that caused the fire, and which was therefore a necessary condition for the thing that I affirm." The conditional character of the affirmation is shown in this case by the fact that you would much prefer that neither the fire nor the rescue had occurred. (But what about the firefighter? If there were never any fires, his professional life would have no meaning, so perhaps he cannot feel unqualified regret.)

Wallace's general analysis, which applies to a wide range of cases, depends on the insight that different reasons can legitimately govern our attitudes to the same action, event, or circumstance when we view it from different temporal perspectives. This has practical implications. Here is what Wallace says about disabilities:

> Agents whose disabilities condition the projects that most importantly imbue their lives with meaning might well find that their affirmative attitude toward the lives they have led commits them to affirming their disabilities as well. They cannot wish on balance that they hadn't suffered from the conditions that disable them, since that would entail the absence from their lives of the very things that enable them to affirm those lives in the first place.
>
> From the fact that such agents have good reason to affirm their own disabilities, however, it doesn't follow that the condition that they affirm is generally a valuable one, something that in other contexts we have reason to promote or to encourage or to choose for people when there are alternatives available for them.

He draws the conclusion that deaf parents who are reluctant to authorize cochlear implants for their deaf children are making a mistake:

> There is no inconsistency whatsoever involved in being glad that one has suffered a given disability oneself, when one looks back on the life one has led, even while one chooses that one's children should not experience the same condition in the life that they are just embarking on.

The point applies more widely. Wallace does not discuss abortion, but anyone who is glad to be alive must be grateful they were not aborted. This has led some victims of congenital disabilities that are prenatally detectable to oppose prenatal screening, which results in decisions to abort, on the ground that this implies their lives are not worth living. But the affirmation of the value of their birth from the later perspective of the existing person does not by itself determine the reasons that should govern a decision from the earlier perspective of a pregnant woman. There is a painful clash of perspectives here, but no inconsistency. The pregnant woman can acknowledge that if she had the disabled child she would come to love it and would not be able to regret its birth, but that is not a reason for her now to carry it to term.

Wallace's discussion deals not only with such fraught cases. He offers a general account of how it makes sense to look back on one's life—on the good and bad things in it and the various contingencies that determine its meaning. To begin with, there is the question for each of us whether we can affirm our lives unconditionally. This is not a familiar, everyday concept, and perhaps most people have never asked themselves the question. But Wallace proposes to identify it with the question whether you prefer on balance that the series of events that constitutes your life had occurred, as against the alternative that you had not lived at all. As he notes, this "sets a very low standard for application of the notion of the affirmation of a life." But he believes interesting consequences can be drawn from it.

What kinds of regret are compatible with affirmation of one's life in this sense? Wallace believes the answer depends on the values that enable a person to look back favorably on his life in the way that he does. It depends on what in his actual life—what projects and attachments and achievements—give it its meaning. He cannot have what Wallace calls "all-in regret" for the things in his life that were essential conditions for those central elements of meaning, even if they included foolish or irrational or immoral choices, or misfortunes. That was Williams's point about Gauguin. If he had not abandoned his family, his life would still have been worth living, but it would have been a different life, and the way Gauguin values his actual life and work is incompatible with his wishing it had not included that desertion. As Wallace puts it, "His decision was a necessary historical condition for the values that shape his later point of view and ground his affirmative attitude toward the life he has actually led." The implied contrast is with other errors, failings, and misfortunes that one can simply regret, without qualification, because they did not play a role in grounding one's affirmation of one's life.

Wallace's view is more complicated than this, however, because it also has a place for what he calls "deep ambivalence." Sometimes we cannot avoid both affirming and regretting something that was objectionable but that has played too important a role in shaping our lives to be simply rejected. To take an example of a kind Wallace does not discuss, suppose someone fails to marry his true love—she marries someone else, or dies. He then marries someone with whom he is not in love, has children, and builds his life and commitments around these attachments. Though they are intimately involved in the way he values his actual life, he may always wish he had married the other woman, and regret that he didn't. Yet according to Wallace the affirmation of his actual life spreads backwards to encompass his not having done so, which is its necessary condition. If

Wallace is right about this, then deep ambivalence is inevitable in such a case: there is a real conflict between valuing one's actual life and regretting that it wasn't different.

The same might be said about other contingencies with which most lives are littered—accidents that determine one's occupation, for example. One's life can be formed around the pursuit of a particular profession, which contributes largely to what one finds valuable, but at the same time one may wish one had done something else, which would have given one's life a completely different kind of value—that one had become a cartoonist rather than an accountant, an anthropologist rather than a chef. One can't feel nothing but regret for having taken a path that grounds the value of one's actual life, but one may be constrained to ambivalence.

This in fact is what Wallace (disagreeing with Williams) thinks Gauguin should feel. He is not entitled simply to affirm his choice to abandon his family, without regret, in light of its consequences for his life. As Wallace explains, this is because the claims of his family remain alive, and are not affected by his success as an artist. They are not merely claims from the perspective of his past self: they come from other people whom he wronged in the past and who still exist. In this respect the case of Gauguin is different from that of the young mother. Her attachment to her child, and the child's attachment to life, make it impossible for either of them to regret the child's birth, and this leaves no one to be the source of a claim on the other side, a claim that would require deep ambivalence on the part of the mother:

> The main objections are of a moral nature, and I have suggested that they can be traced to the daughter's claim to an adequate level of attention and care from the mother who brought her into existence. But the bearer of that claim, the daughter, is also someone who is now deeply attached to the life she has led, and who by hypothesis strongly prefers that life to the alternative scenario that she should not have lived at all. This deprives the deliberative

objection of continuing force as a basis either for her or for her mother to prefer, retrospectively, that the decision to conceive should not have been made by the mother.

Having polished his concepts on these rather special cases, Wallace proceeds in the final chapters of his book to apply them in a radically extended way, arguing that he and all of his readers, and perhaps even all human beings, are in Gauguin's position, condemned to regard their lives with deep ambivalence and not with unconditional affirmation. He begins by trying to make the case to his readers, people who like him have comfortable lives, supported by rich institutions that enable them to pursue rewarding projects under conditions of freedom and at least moderate luxury. He says such lives, in the actual world, depend on a global system of extreme social and economic inequality, and are available only to those lucky enough to find themselves and those with whom they associate at the upper reaches of the distribution. Wallace believes these background conditions are so objectionable that they must be condemned even if they underpin the value and meaning of our lives. He calls this the "bourgeois predicament":

> Our ground projects are the basis of our affirmative attitude toward the lives that we lead. But their bourgeois character means that those projects implicate us in social and economic disparities that we cannot possibly endorse (not at any rate if we are reasonable and thoughtful).

One condition for this general invitation to hand-wringing is that the impersonal conditions that shape our lives, and not only our own choices and actions, come within the scope of the "affirmation dynamic." Another is the belief that our advantages depend on avoidable global injustice and that a just world would not include lives like ours. Thinking of his own case, Wallace says: "It is doubtful that contemporary research universities as we know them would survive if we made a serious effort to address these issues on a global scale." Wallace teaches at Berkeley, a public institution that makes enormous contributions to knowledge, both theoretical and practical, which benefit not only its members but the society of which it is a part and the world as a whole. To doubt that such institutions would exist in a just world seems to me pathologically pessimistic. Perhaps slavery was an indispensable condition for the cultural and intellectual flowering of ancient Athens, but we are not in a comparable position.

However, Wallace's argument does apply to the economic inequality that is such a conspicuous feature of our world, and that has been with us since the beginning of civilization. It seems fairly clear that a system that gave everyone at least a decent standard of living would depend on some method of financing that substantially reduced the disposable resources of the most affluent, and therefore changed what they could do with their lives. How bad should the recognition of this notionally possible alternative history ("notionally" because it has never been a real possibility in our past, whatever the future may hold) make us feel about our actual bourgeois lives? Wallace, embracing what he calls a "modest nihilism," thinks it condemns us to deep ambivalence: "There are genuine values that can be realized in our lives, and . . . these provide a real basis for affirmation, but . . . these grounds for affirmation are historically and socially connected to comparably weighty grounds for regret."

If you are skeptical about this, as I am, you may feel that a line needs to be drawn somewhere that limits our implication in the evils of the past that have played a role in creating us and the values that give meaning to our lives. This feeling is powerfully reinforced by Wallace's final extension of his affirmation dynamic to encompass anything in the past that was a necessary condition of our existence, or the existence of someone we love.

We can . . . readily imagine that somewhere along the line, the actual ancestors of those we love would not even have encountered each other if not for historical events that were momentously disastrous: a catastrophic and pointless war, for instance, that forced a distant progenitor into the refugee camp where she met her future husband, or a natural calamity of some kind that had a similar effect. Under these conditions, our unconditional affirmation of the person we love will commit us to affirming the objectionable historical conditions that were necessary for the individual person's existence.

Is someone who wouldn't have been conceived if Hitler had not come to power in Germany committed by his attachment to his own life to "affirming" the Second World War and the Holocaust? Wallace thinks we may have to affirm the entirety of world history, and suggests that this is the grain of truth in Nietzsche's doctrine of the eternal recurrence: "Only if we are prepared to will the totality of world history can we honestly adopt an attitude of unconditional affirmation toward our lives and the other things to which we are attached. Because for all we know, that attitude already commits us to affirming as well the most catastrophic and egregious aspects of the larger histories in which our lives are caught up."

In response to this extravagance it does not seem too defensive to suggest that our affirmation of anything—our own existence included—is bounded by a statute of limitations on its reach into the past. We can take much about the world that we have not created, good and bad, as simply given, and limit our affirmations and regrets to what is downstream from that. This would leave most of us with plenty to feel guilty or ambivalent about, and those feelings would not be diluted in the ocean of our universal implication in the horrors of history.

11

FOUR WOMEN

The appearance within a few months of each other of two books about the same four women is a bit startling, but on reflection the topic is so natural and interesting that one might even wonder why it hasn't been treated before. Elizabeth Anscombe, Philippa Foot (née Bosanquet), Mary Midgley (née Scrutton), and Iris Murdoch, four brilliant young women born in 1919 or 1920, all matriculated at Oxford in the late 1930s. When most of the men went off to war, they found themselves, as women philosophy students, in a very unusual situation—not in the minority and on the periphery, but central and predominant. (The rule in normal times had been that no more than one fifth of the undergraduates at Oxford could be women.) Midgley wrote later that the enhanced attention and absence of the usual competitive male atmosphere made it possible for her to find her voice as a philosopher. Distinctive and talented though each of them was, it still seems no accident that such a stellar group emerged from this atypical moment.[1]

Both books—Benjamin Lipscomb's *The Women Are Up to Something* and Clare Mac Cumhaill and Rachael Wiseman's *Metaphysical Animals*—explain how these women were formed, what they were like, their deep connections with one another, and the impact they had on the philosophy of their time. But they differ

This was a review of Benjamin J. B. Lipscomb, *The Women Are Up to Something: How Elizabeth Anscombe, Philippa Foot, Mary Midgley, and Iris Murdoch Revolutionized Ethics* (Oxford University Press, 2022) and Clare Mac Cumhaill and Rachael Wiseman, *Metaphysical Animals: How Four Women Brought Philosophy Back to Life* (Chatto and Windus, 2022).

[1] Did anything comparable happen in other male-dominated fields?

in scope and emphasis, so it is well worthwhile to read them both. Lipscomb is American; Mac Cumhaill and Wiseman are British. His book covers a longer time span, and goes more deeply into the philosophical controversies in which the four were engaged, particularly the transformation in moral philosophy that began with a revolt against analytic orthodoxy in the late 1950s and changed the field completely over the next twenty years. He has produced a superior work of personal and intellectual history, sensitive and finely written. Mac Cumhaill and Wiseman offer more biographical detail and information about secondary characters, but their detailed narrative stops in 1956, before the upheaval that is Lipscomb's focus. Co-directors of a project called Women in Parenthesis, which promotes the study of the four to demonstrate the importance of women in philosophy, they are broadly concerned with the way these women resisted the style and methods of the analytic mainstream:

> For all four friends, what mattered most was to bring philosophy back to life. Back to the content of the messy, everyday reality of human life lived with others. Back to the deep connection that ancient philosophers saw between Human Life, Goodness and Form. Back to the fact that we are living creatures, animals, whose nature shapes our ways of going on.

Murdoch became world famous as a novelist, and is the subject of a fine biography by Peter Conradi, but the lives of the others are not so well known. Anscombe, Murdoch, and Midgley all came from middle-class families in suburban London. Their abilities were evident early, and they were encouraged to go to university. Not so Foot. Philippa Bosanquet was born into a distinguished family, and was the granddaughter, on her mother's side, of the American president Grover Cleveland. Her parents were married in Westminster Abbey and she grew up in Kirkleatham Old Hall near Middlesbrough, a house with sixteen bedrooms. In her social class, girls were simply not educated; Foot spent a lot of time riding, and was taught chiefly at home by governesses who, she said, "didn't know anything." But she determined to escape from this world, and learned of a woman in Oxford who coached for the University entrance exams. She pulled it off and got into Somerville, the brainiest women's college, where Scrutton and Murdoch had started the year before.

Anscombe's path was unusual in a different way. Her parents had little interest in religion, and they were appalled when in adolescence she was drawn to Catholicism. After she was admitted to Oxford (she went to St. Hugh's) Elizabeth's father told her that they would cut off their support if she joined the Church. But in the spring of her first year she did just that. They backed down, and Catholicism would be central to her thought and action until the end of her life.

The four finished their undergraduate degrees in the middle of the war, each of them getting a first—Foot in Philosophy, Politics, and Economics and the other three in Greats, the classics degree that included philosophy and history. Foot, Midgley, and Murdoch then joined the war effort by entering the civil service. Murdoch had become a Communist at Oxford and was sure the civil service wouldn't want her, not "with a record like mine." But she was taken on at the Treasury, and duly copied documents which she hid in a tree in Kensington Gardens for transmission to the Soviets. She was also writing fiction and leading an adventurous personal life in the turbulent society of wartime London. Murdoch united incredible energy and productive discipline with emotional intensity. She fell in love as suddenly and violently as the characters in her novels, and sometimes found even ordinary relationships emotionally unmanageable: the wife of her Oxford philosophy tutor Donald MacKinnon made him stop seeing her; a crisis in her feelings for Anscombe caused her to destroy seven pages of her journals.

Foot and Murdoch shared a flat in London and became very close, but drama followed. Foot had been having an affair with the economist Thomas Balogh, who dropped her for Murdoch, who was involved with Michael Foot, an intelligence officer (the military historian M. R. D. Foot, not the politician). At Balogh's insistence, Murdoch broke up with Michael, who found comfort with Philippa; they were married after the war, from which Michael barely escaped with his life. Philippa seems not to have been fazed by the swap, but Michael was bitter toward Murdoch, and she felt guilty and estranged from both of them for some time—she described her own behavior as "nauseating," though we don't know exactly why.

Midgley didn't stay in the civil service but worked as a teacher for most of the war. Anscombe never left the academy. After completing her degree she married Peter Geach, another Catholic convert, who was her philosophical equal. He was also a conscientious objector and spent the war as a logger. They began immediately to have children (there would be seven in all). In 1942 Anscombe took up a research position at Cambridge, where she would encounter Wittgenstein—a turning point in her life. Over the next few years she went back and forth between Cambridge and Oxford; Geach stayed in Cambridge with the children, having found no steady employment after the war.

Anscombe had always been susceptible to classic problems of epistemology and metaphysics; she couldn't stop thinking about them and had a sense of their intractability. This made her naturally receptive to Wittgenstein's project of going behind the questions by which those problems were posed to reveal that they depended on misunderstandings of the way the relevant language works. And her uncompromising philosophical seriousness rivalled his. She taught herself German in order to read his current writings, and he selected her to translate his late work. She was a superb writer, and, as Mac Cumhaill and Wiseman say, "It is thanks to her translation that Wittgenstein's *Philosophical Investigations* is recognized as a literary, as well as a philosophical, masterpiece."

All four women continued in philosophy as graduate students after the war. Midgley got a lectureship at Reading, but left to raise a family in Newcastle, where her husband, Geoffrey (also a philosopher), taught, and to work as a free-lance writer and reviewer. It would be twenty years before she returned fully to the subject. Anscombe, Foot, and Murdoch found positions at Oxford that eventually became secure, but everything changed for them with the return of the men. Again in a minority, they were now in the midst of the rise to dominance of a new philosophical movement that did not engage their sympathies. Their resistance to this movement is the main philosophical theme of both books.

The revolution had been launched before the war. A. J. Ayer, encouraged by his teacher Gilbert Ryle, had gone to Austria to learn about the ideas of the Vienna Circle, a group of philosophers, scientists, and logicians who were developing the position known as logical positivism. Ayer returned to England and in 1936 published *Language, Truth and Logic,* a vivid, popular, and dogmatic statement of the theory. According to Ayer, only two kinds of statement are meaningful: (1) statements about the world that can be confirmed or disconfirmed by experience, and (2) analytic statements that are true simply in virtue of the logic of our language. This excludes all theological and metaphysical statements, and also, importantly, all moral judgments. The statement that stealing is wrong can be neither confirmed nor disconfirmed by experience, nor is it true by definition. It is neither true nor false, and can only be understood as an expression of emotion—in this case, antagonism to stealing. There is in consequence no such subject as ethics, if that means the search for true moral principles.

The book was a hit, providing a scalpel that could be easily wielded to cut out large chunks of discourse and label them nonsense. It also appealed to a sense that reality was the world of facts described by the natural sciences, and that there was no place for value in such a world. This left little for philosophy to do except clean up after itself. Many of its traditional questions and theories would have to be abandoned, and its positive role would be limited to conceptual and logical analysis of those uses of language that are not meaningless.

The Vienna Circle was especially interested in the logic of science and mathematics, but when its doctrines reached Oxford, the result was a concentration on natural or ordinary language—Oxford philosophers were nearly all trained as classicists, and lacked the scientific background of the Viennese. They engaged in linguistic analysis both to uncover the confusions behind traditional philosophical problems and for its own interest. Gilbert Ryle's *The Concept of Mind* (1949) was an early paradigm of the genre, and from his position after the war as Waynflete Professor of Metaphysical Philosophy at Oxford and editor of the leading philosophy journal *Mind,* he campaigned successfully to sweep the academy with analytic philosophy and philosophers of this stripe. J. L. Austin became the dominant figure of the movement in Oxford, with a distinctive style of minute attention to subtle distinctions in ordinary language. He conducted an informal discussion group on Saturday mornings to which the male teachers of philosophy in the University were invited, but no women.

All four women were resistant to this movement from the start, but only Anscombe, Foot, and Murdoch, who were teaching at Oxford, pursued this resistance at the time in public controversy and writing. Anscombe's hostility was virulent and personal. She loathed what seemed to her the clever superficiality and lack of seriousness about philosophical problems that typified ordinary language philosophers, in spite of the fact that they had taken from Wittgenstein, her idol, the idea that those problems could be dissolved by attention to language. But Wittgenstein's style was very different: he always insisted on the depth and grip of the problems, and agonized about them. "To think that Wittgenstein fathered that bastard," she said to Mary Wilson, a younger colleague, after attending one of Austin's classes. And she tried (unsuccessfully) to persuade Wilson not to marry Geoffrey Warnock ("that shit Geoffrey"), one of Austin's followers—just as she had tried earlier (also without success) to dissuade her undergraduate friend Jean Coutts from marrying Austin himself.

The most important conflicts were about ethics. The analytic orthodoxy was that there was an unbridgeable logical gap between facts and values, that statements of value or morality were neither true nor false, merely expressing the subjective attitudes or feelings of the speaker, and that there was no place in philosophy for an attempt to answer moral questions. There was a place, however, for a more precise account of the expressive function of moral language, and this project was taken up and carried out with exceptional skill by Richard Hare, a contemporary of the four who had returned to Oxford after a horrible wartime experience as a prisoner of the Japanese, working on the Burma-Thailand railway. (I once heard him say about the film *The Bridge on the River Kwai* that while the settings were disturbingly realistic, having been designed with the help of someone who had been a prisoner like himself, the plot was not: no British officer would have been so rational.)

Hare's book *The Language of Morals* (1952) held that moral statements were a special type of imperative, addressed not to one individual but to everyone, oneself included. So "stealing is wrong" means, roughly, "don't anyone steal, including me." Hare called his theory of the logic of moral language "universal prescriptivism." It conformed to the assumption that moral statements are neither true nor false, and it had the consequence that there are no restrictions on the content of morality: as a matter of logic, a universal prescription or imperative could be issued for or against anything—putting on your left sock before your right, for example—and it would count as a moral judgment. Someone who didn't care to issue universal imperatives would have no use for moral language. But if they did decide to use it, it was up to them which moral principles to endorse: each person formed their own moral commitments by choosing what universal prescriptions to make.

Murdoch had an unusual perspective on the proposal that we create morality by choosing. She was one of the first British philosophers to encounter French existentialism, having heard Sartre deliver a version of his manifesto, "Existentialism Is a Humanism," in Brussels in 1945. Having consumed the novels and philosophical writings of Sartre, de Beauvoir and others, she was one of very few persons at that time who could bridge the cross-Channel intellectual divide. Before the appearance of Hare's book, Murdoch noted the similarity between Sartre's view of value and that of Ayer, Hare's precursor: Both held that values are human projections onto a value-free reality. They cannot be right or wrong. As Lipscomb puts it, "We are condemned to be free, forced to invent values in a world where none can be found. This sounds grim, but it is also an invitation to heroism. . . . Making no excuses, but living authentically—in the root sense, as *authors* of ourselves—we acknowledge that we are whatever we summon the will to do." But Murdoch was scornful of this heroic self-image, writing that the gloom characteristic of existentialist writing "is superficial and conceals elation." She had no use for voluntarism about value in either its French or British form: value requires us to turn our attention away from ourselves, toward others and toward whatever demands recognition as good in itself. (She set out this view more fully in *The Sovereignty of Good*, published in 1970.)

Later, in *Moral Thinking: Its Levels, Method and Point* (1981), Hare would conclude that universal prescriptivism had much more restrictive consequences for the content of morality than he had first thought—he decided that correctly interpreted, it entailed utilitarianism—but Murdoch was hostile to a content-neutral theory of morality from the start. Though she always professed insecurity about her philosophical abilities, she had strong intuitive insight, and wasn't afraid to express it.

Foot, too, was unwilling to accept the elimination of truth from morality and its replacement by subjectivity. In 1945 she was shattered by seeing the newsreels of Buchenwald and Bergen-Belsen, with piles of corpses and skeletal survivors; a conception of morality that limited the response to such horror to a personal reaction could not be right. It took her some time to develop her philosophical response to Hare's British existentialism. When it finally appeared, in two essays published in 1958, it was squarely in the framework of analytic philosophy of language, and challenged the boundary between facts and values that was central to the positivist position. As Lipscomb explains, she began modestly:

> Foot asks, first, about the word "rude." "Rude," like "good" or "bad," "right" or "wrong," is plainly an evaluative word. Yet there are factual criteria governing its use. We do not have to—we do not *get* to—decide in anguished freedom what behaviors count as rude. Rather, to say that some behavior is rude means that it offends by showing disrespect. . . . If the factual criteria of rudeness are set aside, there is nothing left of the concept.

This blend of factual and evaluative meaning is characteristic of what are usually called "thick" concepts. But it is not just an arbitrary conjunction of a description and an attitude: the factual criteria of rudeness explain why it is objectionable, and this is reflected in our language.

> What about "good" and "bad," "right" and "wrong," as applied to human character and behavior? Are these judgments, too, "logically vulnerable to facts"? Or could any use of these words—so long as it's consistent—make sense? Consider, she asks: could we understand someone who says that someone is a good man "because he clasped and unclasped his hands" or refuses to "run round trees left handed, or look at hedgehogs in the light of the moon"? . . . *Just try* to talk about ethics while leaving behind considerations of what makes human lives go well or badly—the foundations on which Aristotle and Aquinas built their whole theories. It can't be done.

The content-neutral analysis of moral language fails at the linguistic level, but that is because the disconnect between fact and value on which it is based is false, and our language recognizes this. The names of the virtues and vices refer to qualities that contribute to a good or bad life, which is not a subjective matter, but a consequence of what humans need to live well—a consequence of human nature.

In my view, Foot's conception of objective moral truth, unlike Murdoch's, was limited by the Aristotelian assumption that it had to ground morality in the good of the moral agent. The doubt whether this could be done led her, later on, to a period of outright moral skepticism, expressed in "Morality as a System of Hypothetical Imperatives" (1972). But her challenge to the establishment had a lasting impact.

At around the same time, Anscombe had her brief but historic encounter with Oxford moral philosophy. It was characteristically polemical and denunciatory, in keeping with her temperament—so unlike either Foot or Murdoch. It began with her opposition, because of Hiroshima and Nagasaki, to Oxford's award of an honorary degree to Harry Truman in 1956. *The Women Are Up to Something*, the title of Lipscomb's book, is taken from *Mr. Truman's Degree*, a pamphlet Anscombe published afterwards, in which she set out with great clarity and force the prohibition in just war theory against targeting noncombatants. Before the Oxford meeting, she writes, "a fine House was whipped up to vote for the honour. The dons at St. John's were simply told 'The women are up to something in Convocation; we have to go and vote them down.'" Lipscomb reports that she got only three votes besides her own, but the position of righteous defiance suited her. At the end of the pamphlet she suggests not going to Encaenia, the ceremony at which Truman would receive his degree: "I, indeed, should fear to go, in case God's patience suddenly ends."

Much earlier, as an undergraduate, Anscombe, together with another student, had produced a pamphlet called *The Justice of the Present War Examined: A Criticism Based on Traditional Catholic*

Principles and on Natural Reason. The first part, "The War and the Moral Law," was written by Anscombe; she explains the prohibition against targeting civilians and predicts (this was in 1939) that it will not be respected. The Roman Catholic hierarchy forced Anscombe and her co-author, Norman Daniel, to withdraw the pamphlet shortly after publication, because they had used the word "Catholic" without getting an imprimatur. But while Catholicism was always central to Anscombe's moral outlook, the persuasiveness of her position did not depend on divine law, and it had a powerful influence on secular philosophical thinking about justice in war. More broadly, it clarified the nature of moral constraints on the means that may be used even in pursuit of good ends, and the difference in moral responsibility for harms that we intend and harms that are side-effects of our actions. Equally important in this area was Foot's 1967 essay, "The Problem of Abortion and the Doctrine of the Double Effect," which introduced the famous Trolley Problem. These writings challenged the positivist outlook by showing what it was like to reason philosophically about substantive moral questions, and not just about the logic of moral language.

Anscombe's attack on Truman's degree led to a more general broadside against recent moral philosophy. At the end of her pamphlet, she had written that all the prevailing theories "contain a repudiation of the idea that any class of actions, such as murder, may be absolutely excluded," and that this is entailed by the widely current view that moral principles merely express the attitudes of the speaker, freely adopted in a world without values. She suggested that this was not unrelated to the belief of nearly all of her Oxford colleagues "that a couple of massacres to a man's credit are not exactly a reason for not showing him honour."

Her comments caught the attention of someone at the BBC, and she was invited to give a talk on the Third Programme, which she entitled "Oxford Moral Philosophy: Does It 'Corrupt the Youth'?" Published in *The Listener,* it drew angry letters from Hare and others. She then pursued the subject in an article published in the journal *Philosophy* in 1958. As Lipscomb says, "that article, 'Modern Moral Philosophy,' would become one of the most cited philosophical publications of the twentieth century." Anscombe joins Foot in attacking the alleged gulf between facts and values, but also condemns the abandonment by modern philosophers of the absolute prohibition on certain actions that forms an essential part of the Hebrew-Christian ethic. Here is her most famous sentence:

> If someone really thinks, *in advance,* that it is open to question whether such an action as procuring the judicial execution of the innocent should be quite excluded from consideration—I do not want to argue with him; he shows a corrupt mind.

She claims, erroneously in my view, that all modern talk about moral principles and what we morally ought and ought not to do makes no sense without belief in a divine lawgiver who enacts those requirements—"the situation" is "the interesting one of the survival of a concept outside the framework of thought that made it a really intelligible one." Anscombe thought secular philosophers should return to the tradition of Aristotle and the virtues. "It would be a great improvement if, instead of 'morally wrong,' one always named a genus such as 'untruthful,' 'unchaste,' 'unjust.' We should no longer ask whether doing something was 'wrong,' passing directly from some description of an action to this notion; we should ask whether, e.g., it was unjust; and the answer would sometimes be clear at once." She and Foot were therefore responsible for the rise of what came to be called "virtue ethics," a significant part of moral philosophy ever since.

Midgley did not play a part in this revolt against the positivist consensus in the 1950s, because she had left philosophy, though she was an active and wide-ranging reviewer, essayist, and broadcaster. She returned to it later through an interest in biology and animal ethology, and the application of insights from those sciences to the study of human nature. With *Beast and Man: The Roots of*

Human Nature (1978), she became a leading exponent of a biological approach to the understanding of ethics and rationality. This had affinities with the Aristotelian revival, but brought in empirical results from modern evolutionary biology. Lipscomb rates her contribution highly:

> Midgley, writing from the margins of the discipline, was the first to present a positive proposal for the kind of moral philosophy recommended but never developed by Anscombe, Foot, and Murdoch: a *naturalistic* moral philosophy, grounded in the character and needs of the human animal. Indeed, she was the only one who could, the only one who knew both enough biology and enough moral philosophy to relate the two fields.

The result was what Lipscomb calls "an ethics of self-integration, of thinking through how to do justice to our whole selves." It begins from the instincts and motivational tendencies that are biologically given, goes on to awareness of the inner conflicts they generate, and leads to the capacity to resolve them creatively. Midgley's philosophical background ensured that her biologically informed understanding of humans did not fall into the kind of reductionism typified by E. O. Wilson's sociobiology. But whatever its merits as imaginative extrapolation from empirical science, Midgley's work seems less interesting philosophically than that of the other three. It does not grapple with the hardest conceptual problems about the content and structure of morality, and whether there is such a thing as moral truth. Her influence on academic philosophy has accordingly been less, though she had great success with a wider audience, and battled publicly with biologists like Richard Dawkins.

These books tell their stories in a way that does not require any knowledge of philosophy from the reader, and should interest many people outside the field. But for a philosopher they are irresistible. I found them highly evocative, since I knew two of the principals, Anscombe and Foot, extremely well (I met Murdoch only a few times, and didn't know Midgley). I was present for some of the developments to which Lipscomb assigns the greatest importance. As an undergraduate at Cornell I had been a student of Norman Malcolm—like Anscombe a student and close friend of Wittgenstein—and when I went to Oxford as a graduate student in 1958, it was with an introduction from him to Anscombe. I knew her as the translator of Wittgenstein's *Philosophical Investigations*, as the author of the pathbreaking monograph *Intention*, and as the unsuccessful opponent of Truman's degree. I spent many hours discussing philosophy in her chaotic house in St. John Street, full of children and smoke (at the time one could buy cigarettes in boxes of a hundred, and there was always such a box next to her). She had a beautiful, ethereal voice and a beautiful face with one lazy eye, and her body was hidden in shapeless steerage clothes.

Anscombe was intimidating not just because of her powerful intelligence, which was always at full throttle, but because of her strongly moralistic attitude to practically everything—a trait I associate with students of Wittgenstein. When this is part of the intellectual atmosphere, it generates useless anxiety, and I always suspected she must disapprove of me, though she was very generous. My adviser was J. L. Austin, and I spent enough time with members of the male philosophical establishment to pick up on their distaste for Anscombe; she returned it in full, defiant in her lack of gentility.

Foot was completely different—slim, handsome, unobtrusively well turned out, refined in speech and manner, effortlessly self-possessed. I attended the classes in which she presented her objections to Hare, and was invited with other students for discussion at her home. Her teaching made a strong impression on me, but in 1959 her husband left her, ostensibly because she couldn't have children, and she withdrew in misery from the public scene. She ended up teaching in the U.S., where I saw her often. She was witty. To an American friend who asked, "Philippa, how can one tell the difference between an upper-class and a lower-class British accent?" she replied, "My dear, *any* accent is lower-class." And in a backhanded tribute to Hare's intellectual agility, she said, "Of course he's up the wrong tree, but it's wonderful to watch him swinging from branch to branch."

Both books show the central role of their protagonists in overthrowing a consensus that had stifled philosophical thought about ethics since the rise of logical positivism. But Anscombe, Foot, Midgley, and Murdoch were not alone in their resistance. There was also an American branch to the revival of substantive moral theory, partly influenced by Anscombe and Foot in particular, but in some ways different. The seminal figure here was John Rawls, a contemporary of theirs. His work culminated in *A Theory of Justice,* published in 1971, but he had from the beginning of his career tried to develop ways of addressing real moral questions of right and wrong philosophically, in disregard of the metaethical arguments that this was impossible because there was no such thing as moral truth. His work encouraged the belief that convincing examples of substantive moral thought and moral argument could themselves show that there was a real subject here, even without a fully worked out theory of moral truth and moral language.

Rawls's subject was the justice of political and social institutions, but others, including Judith Jarvis Thomson, Robert Nozick, Ronald Dworkin, Michael Walzer, and T. M. Scanlon took up a range of topics, including the structure and content of individual rights, the problem of means and ends, and the moral content of law, as well as more specific issues like abortion and just war theory. Unlike Anscombe and Foot these philosophers did not assume that a secular account of objective moral truth had to be grounded in the good of the moral agent, like Aristotle's theory of the virtues. They were prepared to think about moral requirements, reasons, and principles as if they could be true in their own right, and investigated directly by moral judgment and moral argument. This is a crucial difference: it means that the investigation of interpersonal moral values like justice and rights can be based directly on the intrinsic value of other people's lives, and the reasons they provide. In a way this is closer to Murdoch's outlook, but more systematic.

I have left out a great deal, especially about the deep personal relations among the four. Both books bring to life an important episode in intellectual history, and have made me again grateful that I was for a time a contemporary of these unforgettable women.

12

LAW, MORALITY, AND TRUTH

Through his writings in *The New York Review of Books* on the law and politics of our time, Ronald Dworkin achieved a level of public recognition and influence that is rare for a legal academic. But much as he loved the public arena and the cultural limelight, he was fundamentally a theorist—originally a legal philosopher and then a moral and political philosopher whose interests expanded finally to include the theory of knowledge and the philosophy of religion. His theoretical development followed a personal path, and because he and I were friends and colleagues for many years, I saw much of it happen.

Dworkin and I were part of an unusually fortunate cohort of analytic philosophers and lawyers, formed in the 1960s, who were prepared to take moral questions seriously and who believed that both reasoning and intuition had a role in their resolution. Following the lead of John Rawls in the U.S. and H. L. A. Hart in England, a group of younger scholars began to write about substantive moral, legal, and political questions, and to talk to each other regularly about their work in progress. We were also exercised by political and legal developments like the Vietnam War, the civil rights movement, and controversies over abortion and sexual freedom.

Dworkin was a brilliant member of this group. He left Yale in 1969 to become Professor of Jurisprudence at Oxford, but he visited the U.S. regularly and in any case it was becoming a transatlantic

This was a review of Stephen Guest, *Ronald Dworkin* (Stanford University Press, 2013).

Analytic Philosophy and Human Life. Thomas Nagel, Oxford University Press.
© Oxford University Press 2023. DOI: 10.1093/oso/9780197681671.003.0012

conversation. A lot of important work in these fields appeared in the 1970s and 1980s, including two of Dworkin's most influential books, *Taking Rights Seriously* (1977) and *Law's Empire* (1986). By the time Ronnie began to split his time between Oxford and NYU Law School in 1987 and we began to teach together, he held a preeminent position as a philosopher of law. But his intellectual ambitions were much broader. As it turned out, he wanted to produce a modern version of Plato's *Republic*.

Ronnie presented his theoretical writings as they developed to the colloquium in law and philosophy that he and I conducted at NYU for twenty-five years. But mainly the colloquium was an occasion for intensive discussion with many of the people working in these fields, and for close critical attention to their work. We developed a format that almost always produced an illuminating discussion. A paper would be submitted in advance, to be read by all participants. On Thursday morning Ronnie and I would meet for an hour of preliminary dissection, and at noon the author would appear for two to three hours of questions and argument, continued over lunch.

We would then part to prepare for the public colloquium, which began at four with a presentation of the paper and initial questions by Ronnie or me, followed by responses from the author and further questions from the other of us. After that we opened it up to the audience, subject to an agenda of issues that we had identified. We ended at seven, but if the guest was not from NYU, this was followed by a dinner at which the discussion continued. The colloquium was a course that about fifteen law and philosophy students took for credit, but most of the audience were auditors, including many faculty from NYU and other universities in the area; so the students met separately with Ronnie in a seminar every Wednesday, to discuss the papers on their own.

Ronnie was always eager to present his own ideas as widely as possible, as shown by his Herculean schedule of global speaking engagements, but in the colloquium he focused happily, with admirable generosity and interpretive skill, on the work of others. He was usually critical and often combative, but the general reaction of those who were subjected to this nine-hour ordeal was gratitude. The advantage of all that work was that no one felt they hadn't been understood. I do remember one occasion, though, when we had Michael Walzer for a marathon engagement of two weeks in a row, and at the end we complimented him on his stamina and resourcefulness in responding again and again to all the questions, objections, and arguments we had thrown at him. "What was the alternative?" he replied sardonically.

When Ronnie or I presented a paper, the other took on the critical role alone, so I had a close view of the extension of his work into general moral and political theory, and the foundations of truth and objectivity in evaluative and other domains. He continued also to write about law, finding much to deplore as the Supreme Court moved to the right, but his search for the ultimate ground of his moral convictions led him gradually to quite another plane. He had never done graduate work in philosophy, but he succeeded, not without anxiety, in turning himself from a legal theorist into a general philosopher of large ambition and depth of view. It took courage, despite the air of effortlessness that was always his style.

Stephen Guest's comprehensive study *Ronald Dworkin*, now in its third edition, covers Dworkin's work from beginning to end, culminating in the big book *Justice for Hedgehogs* (2011), which brings everything together in a unified theory of value—personal, moral, political, and legal. The only thing missing is *Religion without God* (2013), but Guest discusses some of its themes in connection with an earlier book, *Life's Dominion* (1993), as well as *Hedgehogs*. Though Guest's book appears in a series called *Profiles in Legal Theory*, Dworkin's transformation has turned this final edition into something much broader: it is a valuable guide and reference to the full range of Dworkin's writings and the controversies to which they have given rise. It goes without saying that to appreciate Dworkin it is essential to go to the writings themselves, with their eloquence and argumentative density, especially *Law's Empire* and *Hedgehogs*.

Guest was a student of Dworkin's who remembers his supervisions as "brilliant occasions," and the spell has not faded; Guest writes as an uncompromising partisan, rebutting every criticism of Dworkin that he thinks significant enough to report, and showing little sympathy for the critics. This posture of defender of the faith is especially conspicuous in the first half of the book, where several chapters concentrate specifically on the philosophy of law, and the dispute between Dworkin and the legal positivists that first made him famous and that has been such a prominent feature of the literature of jurisprudence over the past forty-five years.

In the preface Guest observes with real insight that everything in Dworkin's philosophy follows from his acceptance of Hume's principle that you can't derive an "ought" from an "is." In other words, no matter how many descriptive facts you establish about a situation or an action, nothing follows about its rightness or wrongness, or about what ought or ought not to be done, without the addition of some further evaluative premise that can be applied to those facts. There is a big difference between Dworkin and Hume, however. Hume believed that value judgments were the expression of a special moral sentiment or feeling, and that they could not be true or false: the additional "premise" was not even a candidate for truth, so the resulting "ought" judgment couldn't be true either.

Dworkin, in contrast, believed that value judgments are not merely expressions of feeling or preference: they aim to say what is really good or bad, right or wrong, just or unjust, in virtue of the objective principles and reasons applicable to the choice before us. The right answer doesn't depend on one's belief, so value judgments, like statements of descriptive fact, may be either true or false. Most of Dworkin's work is a defense and exploration of this domain of objective value—an attempt to show that it makes sense to seek objectively right answers to difficult questions of law, of morality, and even of how to live. By "objectively right answers" he meant answers that depend not on our beliefs or attitudes, but solely on what is supported by the best reasons or the best arguments. And as Guest makes clear, Dworkin also held a radical view of the pervasiveness and inescapability in human understanding of this type of inquiry.

Dworkin believed that the domain of value—of norms determining what we should do—was one of those basic types of thought that could not be either justified or refuted from outside. Just as a mathematical proposition can be established or refuted only by a mathematical proof, and a scientific claim can be established or refuted only by scientific evidence, he thought a moral judgment can be supported or undermined only by moral argument. The fact that people engage in such arguments, and that they believe that others who disagree with them are mistaken, shows that most people take it for granted that value judgments can be objectively true or false. The contrary view that they are essentially subjective is a revisionist philosophical position that Dworkin says is incompatible with our everyday thoughts and practices.

But Dworkin also held definite and distinctive views about the content of this domain and the right method for discovering the truth about it, whether we are interested in justice, law, or the meaning of life. He argued, firstly, that the domain of value is a unity, and that its components must be consistent with one another: there cannot be irreconcilable conflicts among genuine values.

Secondly, the truth in this domain cannot be simply read off from our evaluative and moral concepts, because the content of those concepts is itself the object of evaluative disagreement: so the investigation of moral and evaluative truth must be a process of interpretation, and this interpretation must itself be an exercise of value judgment, trying to make the best unified sense of the whole system of our judgments of good and bad, right and wrong, by testing each of them in the light of the others. So if the values of liberty and equality seem to conflict, we must try to reinterpret them so that they do not.

Thirdly, the guiding value that succeeds in unifying our values is that of dignity, which in turn has two interdependent components: equality and individual responsibility. Dworkin believed that these complementary values enabled him to dissolve all the traditional tensions within moral and political theory—between morality and self-interest, between liberty and equality, between the right and the good.

This is a truly Platonic level of ambition. Plato argued for the convergence of justice and the good of the individual by identifying the virtue of justice with an ordered condition of the soul. Dworkin argues, as Guest puts it, that "the critically ideal life is the best life we could lead if we had at our disposal the material resources that the best theory of justice entitles us to have." So not only those who are unjustly impoverished are denied good lives, but also those who are unjustly enriched. If a more just system of taxation would leave a wealthy person with less disposable income and wealth than he actually has in a very unequal society, then according to Dworkin his life will be less of a success, whatever he does with it, than it could be if he lived under a more egalitarian system.

Likewise, there is no conflict between the values of liberty and equality, because the equality that morality requires of a political system is equality in the resources that people need to exercise their individual responsibility for their lives—equality in the conditions of liberty. That equality is a condition of the equal value of liberty for the different individuals in the society. By making people equal in their means, we leave them free to take responsibility for the choice and pursuit of their ends. A just society respects everyone's dignity in that sense—showing them equal concern, but also ensuring their personal responsibility for their lives.

This is undeniably a noble vision, opposed to the pluralism about values that implies that conflict among them is inevitable and that there is no social choice without loss. Isaiah Berlin was a prominent advocate of that pluralist position, and the title of *Justice for Hedgehogs* picks up the challenge of Berlin's distinction (in "The

Hedgehog and the Fox") between unifiers and multipliers to come down squarely on the side of unity. This also determines Dworkin's method of interpretation, which he believed applies in every domain where questions have to be answered that go beyond the purely descriptive or scientific facts.

Dworkin believed that whether we are asking about the meaning of a poem or the existence of a legal right in a difficult case, interpretation consists in making the object as good as it can be, relative to its purposes. In other words, given two readings that are consistent with the text, it is an argument for the truth of one of them that it would make the poem, or the law, a better poem or law than the other would. Thus truth in interpretation is dependent on value, and judgments in all domains requiring interpretation are necessarily value judgments of some kind or other—though they start out from the descriptive facts.

This general theory of interpretation is one of Dworkin's most controversial proposals. There seems clearly to be a difference between making the best sense of something and giving it a reading that makes it as good as possible. It is true that whenever we are faced with a normative system like law, whose point is to govern conduct, we cannot understand it simply as a pattern of behavior. We have to see it as an internalized set of standards and principles that the participants take to justify their behavior. But we need not share that point of view in order to understand it, even though we must rely on our own capacity for value judgments when we interpret how others see things as right that we believe to be wrong, and vice versa. We will not understand a bad system unless we see how its participants see it as good. But that seems different from showing it in its best light, as Dworkin proposed.

The evaluative basis of interpretation is central to Dworkin's conception of law, and its application to that case need not depend on its truth for artistic or historical interpretation. In *Justice for Hedgehogs* Dworkin finally declared that law is a part of morality—not just that moral reasoning plays a part in determining what the law is. Of course he meant that it is a very special part of morality, concerned with what, in light of general principles of political legitimacy and fairness, together with the pertinent legislation, institutions, and precedents, a society is morally justified in coercing people to do or not do.

By the same token, Dworkin believed that a legal right is a moral right—the right to be free from interference by the state or other individuals in its exercise. This doesn't mean there is no distinction between what the law is and what it ought to be. But it means that even an unjust law creates legal rights and obligations only in virtue of a moral justification for enforcing the decisions of a democratically elected legislature, for example. In hard cases where a result cannot be read off from the facts, statutes, and precedents, the answer has to be determined by the best moral interpretation of the principles that justify the legal system.

The positivist view to which Dworkin's is opposed—represented notably by H. L. A. Hart—is that law is a social institution and that what the law is depends on social facts about legislation, courts, etc., from which it can be empirically determined, without relying on value judgments or moral reasoning, what rules are actually in force. Sometimes there are hard cases to which no right answer can be deduced from the existing social materials. In those cases, positivists hold, judges who are required to make a decision will in effect make new law, which is then added to the social facts in the form of a precedent. They may very well engage in moral reasoning to arrive at their decision, asking for example what is the best interpretation of "equal protection of the laws" in respect to the federal government's treatment of same-sex marriage. But contrary to Dworkin, they would argue that this is not a way of discovering what the law is: rather it is a reason for deciding that this is what the law will be from now on—just as when a legislator votes for or against a law because he believes it would be right or wrong.

There is a much cruder form of positivism according to which value judgments have no place whatever in the process of adjudication. This has become the standard declared jurisprudential theory of nominees to the U.S. Supreme Court, but nobody believes it, least of all the nominees. When Chief Justice John Roberts said his role was like that of an umpire, calling balls and strikes, he was saying what everyone in earshot knew to be false, because this pious falsehood has become an obligatory part of the confirmation ritual.

In fact, judges have to make value judgments all the time, not only in major constitutional cases, but in cases of negligence, employment discrimination, defamation, copyright infringement, and so on. Moreover, the public, insofar as it takes an interest in legal developments, expects the justices of the Supreme Court to make their decisions on moral grounds. They know which justices are liberal and which are conservative, they can often predict how the vote will go on a controversial issue, and even if they disagree with the outcome most of them don't think there is anything wrong with the process, provided the justices are really deciding on the basis of principles they believe to be correct.

As for the dispute between Dworkin and the positivists over how to describe what is going on in such cases, my impression is that for the most part both the judiciary, whatever they may say in confirmation hearings or in their theoretical moments, and the public understand the process in Dworkin's way. Judges on multi-judge panels who disagree about the disposition of a contested case think and say that the other side is wrong about what the law is—that they are making a mistake of law, not merely—as a positivist would have to say—a mistake about the best way to decide this case, given that the law is indeterminate.

Of course this could be a collective illusion, perhaps one that serves to inflate the law's authority and majesty, by attributing to it both a moral aura and an unearned objectivity when it goes beyond its basis in clearly established social fact. Guest defends Dworkin's view that the only way to make sense of positivism is to see it as a morally based view of the law—an interpretation in something like

Dworkin's sense—whereby it is *morally* best to count as law only what can be derived from statutes and other social facts without moral reasoning, both because this makes the law clearer and more predictable, and because it usefully shrinks law's moral authority. Guest quotes H. L. A. Hart, arguing in favor of a clear separation of the identification of law from its moral assessment:

> What surely is most needed in order to make men clear sighted in confronting the official abuse of power, is that they should preserve the sense that the certification of something as legally valid is not conclusive of the question of obedience, and that, however great the aura of majesty or authority which the official system may have, its demands must in the end be submitted to a moral scrutiny.

If one thinks of the American legal system before the Civil War, with its constitutionally protected compromises over slavery, it seems strained to understand the truth about what the law was as part of morality—what was morally required and permitted in light of the morally best overall justification of the existing institutions, laws, and precedents. Looking at it from our external perspective, a positivist reading seems both more natural and morally preferable. But Dworkin's alternative is possible; indeed it may correspond to the understanding of many of the participants at the time, including Abraham Lincoln.[1] And it is certainly attractive as an aspiration for the kind of moral authority we should want to create in the legal systems under which we live.

---

[1] Dworkin's view about this example was complicated. He believed that the Fugitive Slave Law was not constitutionally valid, but that even if it had been, the rights it gave to slaveowners for restitution of their property would have been overridden by a much more powerful nonlegal moral right. In other words, though the law might have created a prima facie moral right, law is only part of morality, and extralegal moral reasons would make such a law, though valid, too unjust to enforce.

As Guest points out, resistance to Dworkin's theory often comes from the belief that there really isn't any objective truth about morality or other values—that there are just conflicting attitudes—so that a moral interpretation of law would destroy law's objectivity. Dworkin's conviction that law is part of morality and that the good of individuals, political justice, and legal rights can be unified in a mutually supporting system flows from his unshakable conviction that questions of value have answers, just as do questions of fact, and that there is a distinctive way to think about them—though just as in science, the quest for truth is open-ended. Fortunately he had time to set out this vision in full, in a body of work that will keep his memorable voice alive.

13

THE ILLUSION OF TAX FAIRNESS

By Liam Murphy and Thomas Nagel

Public debate about the Bush Administration's recently proposed tax cuts has largely revolved around their economic impact: How will they affect the deficit, public and private spending, investment, employment, and productivity? These are vital concerns. But there is another aspect of the debate—and an increasingly prominent part of tax politics in recent years—that is seriously confused. This is the issue of "tax fairness." The idea that there are standards of fairness that apply specifically to taxes is based on an illusion that threatens to distract attention from what really matters.

Fairness is a constant drumbeat in President Bush's rhetoric about taxes. He has condemned the estate tax as unfair because it taxes people's earnings twice. ("I just don't think it's fair to tax people's assets twice regardless of your status. It's a fairness issue. It's an issue of principle, not politics," he said about the estate tax during the 2000 campaign.) He argues against the taxation of dividends, which are generally paid by corporations out of after-tax income, for the same reason. ("It's fair to tax a company's profits. It's not fair to double tax by taxing the shareholder on the same profits," he said in January, 2003.) And Bush insists that if there is a tax cut it would

This was a precis of the central claim of our book *The Myth of Ownership: Taxes and Justice* (Oxford University Press, 2002). Though it appeared in the context of debate over tax cuts proposed by the George W. Bush Administration, the issues are perennial, and what we say applies to current debates.

be unfair not to share it out among everybody who pays taxes: "All people who pay taxes should get tax relief. This is a fair plan."

But it isn't only Republicans who appeal to tax fairness. Liberals typically insist that the rich should "pay their fair share," and identify this with progressive taxation—the rule that those who have more money should pay a progressively higher percentage of it in taxes than those who have less. Those who resist the President's proposals point out that under them the rich would get much larger tax reductions than middle and low earners. Reductions in income tax rates, elimination of the estate tax, and elimination of the tax on dividends will reduce the progressivity of the tax system, and that, they claim, is unfair.

There is something wrong with this entire debate. It proceeds, on both sides, as if the fairness of taxes could be evaluated just by looking at the distribution of tax burdens among taxpayers. The reasoning is that taxes are a way of sharing the cost of government among individuals, so the question to ask is this: How much is it fair for the government to take from each individual, as a proportion of what they have before taxes?

But there is no meaningful way to consider the fairness of taxes in isolation from the government's other economic policies and the functioning of the economy as a whole. Whether we are conservatives or liberals, it is what people end up with *after* taxes, as a result both of private efforts and of public policy, that should determine our assessment of any tax program. Progressivity and double taxation in themselves are neither fair nor unfair. They have to be judged by their larger economic effects, and by political and social values broader than the fairness of taxes alone.

The persistence of the idea that the distribution of tax burdens can be fair or unfair in itself stems from a very natural, but mistaken, picture of the relation between taxes and property rights: According to this picture, we own our pretax income, so in taxing us the government takes away some of our private property to pay for its activities. But in fact we don't own our pretax income, and what we do own is defined by a legal system of private property in which taxes play an indispensable role.

This claim may seem outrageous, but a little reflection shows that it must be so. Notice that we couldn't, as a matter of logic, have unrestricted property rights in the whole of our pretax income, because without taxes there would be no government, and consequently no legal system, no banks, no corporations, no commercial contracts, no markets in stock, capital, labor, or commodities—in other words no economy of the kind that makes all modern forms of income and wealth possible. There could be no private property rights in any of the things that a modern economy makes possible if those rights were not circumscribed by a built-in system of taxation.

Modern property rights are not part of nature; they are created and sustained by a legal, political, and economic system of which taxes are an essential part. This doesn't mean that everything really belongs to the government, except what it decides to give us. What it means is that property rights in a modern state, including the division between private and public property, depend for their existence on a legal system that does not and could not assign full property rights in pretax income. What we own depends on how we and others interact in the context of that system, and our private property is what we end up with after taxes, not before. Whether the result is fair depends on the legitimacy of the overall system, and we are collectively responsible, as a society, for the rules of that system.

Rights of private property are extremely important. In addition to playing a vital role in the working of the economy, they are as central to personal liberty as freedom of speech or religion. People need to be secure in the possession and use of what is theirs, protected both from theft and from arbitrary expropriation. But there remains the question of what forms modern property rights should take, or what legal rules and economic policies should determine their formation and transmission. John Locke, in the 17th century, argued that a man has natural rights to the fruits of one's labor on unowned land, even in the absence of government. But even if such primitive natural property rights exist, they hardly correspond with anyone's right to shares of a mutual fund. Modern property is not natural but conventional, and it has to be legally defined.

This definition will include taxes. The question, *How much of "our money" may the government take in taxes?* is logically incoherent, because the legal system, including the tax system, determines what "our money" is. The real moral issue is how the legal system that governs property rights should be designed, and with what goals. What kinds of markets will best promote investment and productivity? Which goods, at what level, should be provided by collective public decision and which goods by private individual choice? Should all citizens be guaranteed a minimum level of economic protection? To what extent should equal opportunity be publicly supported? Are large social and economic inequalities morally objectionable, and if they are, what may legitimately be done to discourage them?

These are questions of social justice and efficiency, not of tax fairness. They cannot be answered by a choice between flat and progressive taxes, or between income and expenditure taxes, or by principles making taxes dependent on people's ability to pay or on the benefit each taxpayer receives from government. The justice of a system of taxation depends on its overall effect on the creation, allocation, and use of public and private resources. How such a judgment is made will depend on one's political values, and here there are deep disagreements in American society—disagreements which have to be fought out in democratic politics.

At one end of the spectrum are hard-core conservatives, who believe that the legitimate role of government is limited to the provision of certain goods that are in each person's self-interest, but that cannot be provided except by collective action—goods such as police protection, national defense, public health and safety, a system of both criminal and civil law, competitive markets, and some level

of public education. At the other end of the not very broad U.S. political spectrum are egalitarian liberals, who believe that, in addition to providing public goods that benefit everyone, government
should use law and fiscal policy to promote equality of opportunity, to provide a decent standard of living even for those with low
earning capacity, and to inhibit the development of large hereditary
inequalities of wealth—partly as a way of inhibiting the political
inequalities that result.

In a genuine argument about the justice of tax policy, the main
issue is whether government should be concerned about social
and economic inequality. Surely those who believe it should not
can nevertheless agree that property rights are created by the legal
system, and that taxes don't take away money that is really yours to
begin with. The real disagreement—and it is a fundamental one—
is about how the legal rights of property should be designed, and
how they should determine what people end up owning and what
they can do with it. But the different answers depend on different
views about collective responsibility and the legitimate function of
government. Disputes about progressivity, estate taxes, negative income taxes, and so forth must be fought out against the backdrop of
these larger values.

By focusing on tax fairness instead of social justice the Bush
Administration is trying with some success to cut off public debate about these issues. Since the New Deal, most Americans
have believed that one of the functions of government, and its tax
system, is to ameliorate the extreme inequalities that result from
letting the chips fall where they may in a market economy. Strict
conservatives do not accept the goal of distributive justice in this
sense, but believe that government has the more limited function
of enabling the pursuit of individual and collective self-interest. By
depicting taxes as a form of expropriation and focusing on the percentage of one's pretax income taken in taxes, President Bush has
put a deceptive moral gloss on a radically conservative, and highly
controversial, political philosophy.

Opposition to the administration's tax policies on the ground that they promote inequality are met with the charge of class warfare. This, too, is revealing: It shows that even the President realizes that his policies can be sold to the public only if larger questions of social justice are ruled out of order.

MORAL PSYCHOLOGY

14

SCANLON ON THE REALITY
OF REASONS

1.

Philosophy has always been concerned with the largest questions of
what exists and what is the case. Not specific questions like "Is there
extraterrestrial life?" or "What is the speed of light in a vacuum?"
but maximally general questions about what kinds of things exist
and what kinds of facts there are—basic kinds that cannot be defined in terms of anything still more basic, and from which everything else is constituted. This is the subject matter of metaphysics.
A related question, how we can know about such things, is the subject matter of epistemology.

There is disagreement about how far a philosophical account of
existence, truth, and knowledge can depart from the assumptions
that underlie ordinary, commonsense thought and discourse about
what there is, what is the case, and what we know. Radical doubt is
not unusual: the basic reality of many things—matter, mind, space,
and time—has been called into question at one time or another; but
among the domains or areas of thought that are perennially thought
to pose problems, and that continue to be the focus of much discussion today, are morality and mathematics.

This was a review of T. M. Scanlon, *Being Realistic about Reasons* (Oxford University
Press, 2014).

Analytic Philosophy and Human Life. Thomas Nagel, Oxford University Press.
© Oxford University Press 2023. DOI: 10.1093/oso/9780197681671.003.0014

We frequently make moral judgments—that it was wrong of X to accuse Y of a theft of which X was in fact guilty, or that helping someone to commit suicide is not always wrong—but what, if anything, could make these judgments true, or false? They seem not to describe what exists or happens in the world but to say something further. What kind of fact could this be? We also have mathematical beliefs, for example, that $7 + 8 = 15$. Of course we use these beliefs in practical calculations about the material world, but we also think they are true in themselves—timelessly true. But what are they about, and what makes them true? The number 7 itself doesn't seem to be part of the world we see around us.

It is characteristic of our age that moral and mathematical truth are found philosophically puzzling because they seem so different from scientific truth about the natural world. Existence, truth, and knowledge in the natural sciences are regarded as relatively straightforward, though they depend on taking for granted the validity of the observational evidence and logical or mathematical reasoning used in the confirmation of scientific theories. Natural science is widely thought to provide a standard for robust reality that is difficult for the objects of moral judgment and pure mathematics to meet. That is why it is so easy to wonder whether numbers or wrongness really exist, outside of our thoughts.

Such doubts depend, however, on a crucial assumption. They assume that there is a universally applicable standard of existence and truth that determines the reality or unreality of any type of thing or fact. This means that the reality of what we are talking about when we talk about morality or mathematics must be established by appealing to a standard from outside those domains of thought—a standard that determines whether numbers and wrongness are really part of the fabric of the universe. Since the natural sciences are assumed to satisfy this supposedly universal standard, that leads to the search for things and facts analogous to but distinct from those described by natural science, which make the statements of morality and mathematics true. And that seems a fairly hopeless enterprise.[1]

2.

In his short, powerful book *Being Realistic about Reasons* T. M. Scanlon sets out, among other things, to refute this assumption and to present an alternative approach to the question of what, ultimately, is real—what kinds of things most basically exist and what kinds of facts are most basically true.[2] I have introduced the examples of morality and mathematics because they are important in Scanlon's discussion, but his main topic is that of normative reasons—reasons of the kind that specify what should or should not be thought or done. He is particularly concerned with reasons for action, of which morality and moral reasons form a special subpart. The comparison with mathematics is present here, as it has been in earlier writings of Scanlon, because of parallels between the philosophical problems posed by these two areas, and parallels between what he regards as the solutions to those problems.

The general category of the normative encompasses everything about what people should or shouldn't do or think, for reasons of any kind. These include reasons of self-interest, of sympathy, and of morality in the sphere of action, and reasons of empirical evidence and deductive logic in the sphere of belief. The life of a rational being is pervaded by normative thought about what to do and what

---

[1] A leading example of this type of skepticism is J. L. Mackie's *Ethics: Inventing Right and Wrong* (Penguin, 1977).

[2] Scanlon's general outlook has much in common with those of two other important recent works of moral theory, Ronald Dworkin's *Justice for Hedgehogs* (Harvard University Press, 2011) and Derek Parfit's *On What Matters* (Oxford University Press, 2011), and it is prefigured in his earlier major work, *What We Owe to Each Other* (Harvard University Press, 1998).

to think, in light of all the data and considerations bearing on the choices available. Normative thought is an essential part of our lives, and Scanlon holds that the irreducible core of such thought is found in the concept of a reason—a reason in favor of or against doing or thinking something.

Consider the following statement:

> For a person in control of a fast moving automobile, the fact that the car will injure and perhaps kill a pedestrian if the wheel is not turned is a reason to turn the wheel.

The normative character of this reason becomes clear if we contrast it with an explanatory reason. We can say that the reason why the driver turned the wheel was that he wanted to avoid hitting a pedestrian. That explains his action. But the normative reason—the reason to turn the wheel—is present whether he turns the wheel or not. It is a reason why he *should* turn the wheel. The normative reason enters into an explanation of action only if the driver recognizes it and is motivated by that recognition to act on it.

Scanlon calls his view Reasons Fundamentalism. He says the normative statement is obviously true (who could deny it?), and he contends that it is true in itself and is not equivalent to any other statement that does not itself make use of the concept of a reason. Scanlon holds that we all understand what it means for a reason of this kind to exist: the circumstances of the driver count in favor of turning the wheel. To ask what in the world makes this the case, demanding an answer that does not itself include a reference to reasons, is simply confused. Nothing else makes it the case, nothing that is not itself a normative truth—though often one can derive specific reasons from more general ones. Reasons are sui generis, and can be understood only from within the domain of normative thought. Much of the book is taken up with patient and trenchant refutations of the many ways philosophers have found of resisting this conclusion.

One such way is to interpret truths about normative reasons as truths about human motives—for example, it has been claimed that for someone to have a reason to do *a* is for *a* to be an action that would contribute to satisfying some desire that the person has—or perhaps a desire that he would have if he were fully informed about the facts. As Scanlon says, the trouble with this analysis is that it leaves out the specifically normative character of reasons—their "should" content. Reasons don't just say how people are or would be motivated: they say how we should be motivated, and that is simply a different kind of truth. If, on the other hand, the desire theory is interpreted as a genuinely normative claim, to the effect that what we have reason to do is what would satisfy our (factually informed) desires, then, first, it employs the concept of a reason and does not provide an analysis of reasons in purely psychological terms, and, second, it is not a credible normative claim, since a mere desire for something worthless does not give a reason to do what will satisfy it (unless satisfaction of the desire would produce a further effect, such as pleasure, which itself provides a reason).

The analysis of reasons in terms of desires is an attempt to show that normative statements are not basic by finding conditions for their truth in the sort of natural facts that a science like psychology can identify. A different strategy for analyzing the normative in naturalistic terms is to abandon the search for truth conditions altogether, and to interpret normative statements in such a way that they are neither true nor false because, despite appearances, they do not assert that anything is the case. This theory, which goes back to Hume, is called expressivism; it holds that normative statements—about what reasons there are, what we should and shouldn't do, think, or feel—are expressions of the speaker's attitudes, rather than claims that could be true or false. In other words, when you say that the driver has a reason to turn the wheel, or that it would be wrong not to turn the wheel, you are expressing your endorsement of his turning the wheel or your distress at the thought of his not doing so, or something of the kind—whether the driver is you or someone else.

Scanlon discusses sophisticated contemporary versions of expressivism such as that proposed by Allan Gibbard.[3] He argues that these views are incapable of accounting for the role of normative discourse in giving advice or justification to others, or for the process of trying to decide what reasons we ourselves have.

First, if someone objects to my having done *a*, and I reply by citing the fact that *p* as a good reason to do *a*, this will not serve as a justification if it merely expresses my personal feeling or attitude. For example, suppose I turn the wheel of a borrowed car to avoid hitting a cat, and as a result I hit a tree and crumple a fender. Then *p* is the fact that if I hadn't turned the wheel, I would have killed the cat, and my justification to the car's disgruntled owner is that that was in fact a good reason to turn the wheel. But this normative claim is a justification only if, in Scanlon's words, I am

> calling attention to what I claim to be a fact, independent of both of us, about what one has reason to do. . . . Whether the other person agrees with it or not, my claim that *p* was a reason for me to do *a* responds to his challenge, in a way that expressing my acceptance of a norm, or a plan, or an attitude of approval does not.

Second, whatever attitudes we ourselves may have (with regard to the value to be put on the lives of nonhuman animals, for example), we can always go on to ask whether we should have those attitudes, whether they are justified by good reasons. And that question is not answered just by noting that we have them (nor by finding that we have other attitudes that endorse them, since the same question can be asked about those higher-order attitudes). The search for justifying reasons, whether for ourselves or for others, has to be the search for something that is true independent of us and the attitudes we happen to have. The aim is to get it right—to bring

---

[3] In *Wise Choices, Apt Feelings: A Theory of Normative Judgment* (Harvard University Press, 1990) and *Thinking How to Live* (Harvard University Press, 2003).

our attitudes into conformity with the truth about what we should do and think, if we can discover it. That is the point of normative thought.

3.

But what kind of truth is this? Scanlon's positive conception of the normative is part of a larger pluralistic conception of reality, i.e., of existence, truth, and knowledge.

> Accepting science as the way of understanding the natural world entails rejecting claims about this world that are incompatible with science, such as claims about witches and spirits. But accepting a scientific view of the natural world does not mean accepting the view that the only meaningful statements with determinate truth values are statements about the natural world. . . .
>
> I believe that the way of thinking about these matters that makes the most sense is a view that does not privilege science but takes as basic a range of domains, including mathematics, science, and moral and practical reasoning. It holds that statements within all of these domains are capable of truth and falsity, and that the truth values of statements about one domain, insofar as they do not conflict with statements of some other domain, are properly settled by the standards of the domain that they are about. Mathematical questions, including questions about the existence of numbers and sets are settled by mathematical reasoning, scientific questions, including questions about the existence of bosons, by scientific reasoning, normative questions by normative reasoning, and so on.

The phrase "insofar as they do not conflict with statements of some other domain" is crucial. Scanlon holds that statements about the existence of reasons, numbers, and the collections called sets do not conflict with any true statements of natural science. It is not one of the claims of natural science that natural science contains all the truths there are, and statements about reasons and numbers, unlike statements about witches and ghosts, do not contradict anything that science tells us about the natural world and its causal order.

However, one might ask, if reasons and numbers, moral and mathematical truths are not part of the natural world in which we live, how can we know anything about them? If they are not in space and time, like stars and molecules, how can we make contact with them, how can they affect us? But this is just the old illusion raising its head again, the illusion that all existence, truth, and knowledge must conform to a single model: if these things have no spatial or temporal location they must exist "outside of space and time," and it becomes a mystery how we can have access to them. "But here," as Scanlon says, "the spatial metaphor has simply gotten out of hand." Instead of conjuring up a mysterious region to whose spooky occupants we could gain access only by a magical analogue of perception, what we need to understand is how we come to know certain familiar kinds of truth just by thinking about them in the right way.

Scanlon illustrates the systematic investigation of an autonomous domain with the examples of arithmetic and set theory. We employ precise concepts such as "successor" and "member" to formulate rules for the construction of numbers or sets, and axioms which seem clearly correct and whose further implications seem undeniable even after careful reflection. The concepts identify the kinds of truth involved, but most of the truths are not conceptual— i.e., they do not follow from the meaning of the terms in which they are stated.

Though the domain of reasons is entirely different in subject matter, and much less orderly, we also learn about it just by thinking about it in the right way—clarifying the relevant concepts, identifying statements that seem clearly true on reflection, formulating general principles that explain them and that seem true in themselves, and testing those principles against the fruitfulness and credibility, upon careful reflection, of their further consequences. Scanlon provides examples: in this book he offers a convincing account of the concept of a reason and the logical structure and boundaries of the normative domain, and in *What We Owe to Each Other* he presented a theory of the place of morality in the larger domain of reasons. But for reasons of space I will discuss only his general epistemological account of the method of thought involved, which applies to both mathematical and normative judgments.

4.

The method was given the name "reflective equilibrium" by John Rawls, who adopted it for his work in moral and political philosophy but noted that it has far wider application. It is a way of extending and rendering systematic one's understanding of a domain, by searching for an "equilibrium" in which convincing general principles account for the more specific judgments that one finds undeniable on reflection.

An example from moral thought is the complex process of reflection prompted by apparent counterexamples to the utilitarian principle that it is always right to do what will produce the best overall outcome. Would it be right, for example, to frame and execute one innocent man for an alleged interracial or interreligious crime if that is the only way to pacify an enraged mob that will otherwise attack an entire community, killing many innocent people? The considered judgment that this would be wrong even though it would result in fewer innocent deaths suggests several different hypotheses at the more general level:

(1) Perhaps every harmless individual has an inviolable right not to be killed merely as a means to some desirable end, and

perhaps the general principles of morality have to include universal rights of this kind, and not just requirements to minimize the number of deaths.

(2) Perhaps the execution of this one innocent man would corrupt the legal system and lead to further abuses, so that the balance of deaths now may not reflect its true cost; in that case the judgment that the act would be wrong may be supported by utilitarian principles after all.

(3) Perhaps our aversion to punishing the innocent man is an instinctive reaction that for biological or cultural reasons is found in human beings because of its general value in preventing violence; and perhaps if we recognize the general usefulness of the instinct, we should be content to act on it without trying to calculate in each case whether this will have the best consequences.

(4) Perhaps our instinctive reluctance to punish the innocent man, whatever its causes, is just wrong in this case, and should be overridden by utilitarian calculation, provided we can really be confident of the results.

There are also other possibilities, and this is only the beginning. Each general hypothesis must be evaluated for its intrinsic plausibility and the acceptability of its further consequences. How would a right not to be killed have to be modified to allow self-defense, or to allow causing one death as a side-effect of an action that saves many lives? Does the general usefulness of a disposition against killing, or of the institution of due process of law, justify our adhering to it case by case regardless of consequences? Can we come to regard our intuitive judgment of wrongness in this case not as an apprehension of the truth, but as a psychological quirk, akin to a phobia or an optical illusion? One tries to arrive at a stable conclusion by going back and forth between these judgments at different levels of generality, constructing alternative general hypotheses and comparing them in the light of their different implications.

The search involves repeated adjustments and revisions, at both general and specific levels, and each step is an exercise of judgment within the moral domain. The process is open-ended, and equilibrium is an ideal, rather than a static end point we can expect to reach. But someone who remains convinced of the wrongness of framing the innocent man will be led by this process to accept the general principle that seems to offer the most plausible justification of that judgment, on reflection. Sometimes, as in this case, people will disagree in their judgments of the correct result; but disagreement in judgments can be found in almost any area of inquiry, not just the normative.

The pursuit of scientific knowledge through the interaction between theory and observation has an analogous structure: we test theories against their observational consequences, but we also question or reinterpret our observations in light of theory. (The choice between geocentric and heliocentric theories at the time of the Copernican revolution is a vivid example.) The difference is that in mathematical or moral thought, instead of perceptual observations of events spatially distant from us, we start from considered judgments about specific statements within the domain (like a statement about the reason to turn the wheel, or not to frame the innocent man).

The method depends, as Scanlon says, on the assumption

that we have reason to believe the things that seem to us to be true about these subjects when we are thinking about them under the right conditions, and hence that it is appropriate for us to treat these beliefs as considered judgments in a process of seeking reflective equilibrium if we have no apparent reason to doubt them.

This seems like a platitude about how to pursue the truth, but it can be extraordinarily difficult to accept, or to understand. How can the mere fact that something seems to us to be true be a ground for believing that it is true? If seeming is all we have to go on, doesn't that mean that objective truth is unreachable or nonexistent, and all we can do is to explore the insides of our own minds?

But note that this form of skepticism is so general that it would destroy all thought, since the entitlement to believe what on careful reflection seems to be the case, where there is no reason to doubt it, is the necessary condition for being able to form any justified beliefs at all. Science would be impossible if we could not form warranted beliefs about the world around us on the basis of perception, which is just the way things seem when we use our senses. How things seem is the starting point for all knowledge, and its development through further correction, extension, and elaboration is inevitably the result of more seemings—considered judgments about the plausibility and consequences of different theoretical hypotheses. The only way to pursue the truth is to consider what seems true, after careful reflection of a kind appropriate to the subject matter, in light of all the relevant data, principles, and circumstances.

If someone objects that this shows that we are never talking about objective truth, but only about the realm of appearances, the reply is that that skeptical claim, too, is presented as something we should believe because it seems true on reflection. It relies on the very principle of belief that it denies, making an exception for itself from the general skepticism it proposes. Furthermore, it does not survive the test of seeming to be true on careful reflection, for when we reflect on the skeptical hypothesis it proves unbelievable: the things that seem to be the case—about the natural world, about morality, or about mathematics—continue to seem to be true in themselves and not just as descriptions of the inside of our minds.

5.

The internal pursuit of reflective equilibrium is the positive aspect of Scanlon's method for discovering the truth in a given domain. But there are also, importantly, two ways in which we may find that there is much less truth there than we had thought. This is important because it means that the standards for truth and knowledge are not too easily met.

The first possible ground for doubt is internal: it may turn out that the effort at systematic elaboration and explanation of our judgments within a domain fails repeatedly to arrive at stable conclusions—that nothing coherent emerges when we try, in discussion with others, to adjust general principles to particular judgments and vice versa. In that case we may be forced to conclude that we are not talking about an objective subject matter at all, but are merely giving voice to a set of subjective responses. (Something like this seems to have happened with the attempts in the nineteenth century, by figures as eminent as William James and Henry Sidgwick, to put communication with the dead on a scientific basis.)

This is not a problem for mathematics, given its extraordinary fruitfulness, order, and capacity to command unanimous conviction, but it must be taken seriously as a problem for morality, and for some aspects of practical reason in general. Scanlon's view is that we cannot hope for the kind of universal order and agreement in moral thought that we find in mathematics, and that the basis for confidence in determinate truth-values for statements about reasons will have to be piecemeal. He rejects any single all-encompassing moral principle like utilitarianism or Kant's categorical imperative. There are many claims we can be confident about, but we have no grounds for confidence that questions about what there is reason to do always have determinate answers. By contrast, we are confident that questions of arithmetic always have correct answers, even if we can't always discover them. (As Kurt Gödel proved, no consistent set of axioms can yield as theorems all the truths of arithmetic.)

The second challenge, alluded to earlier, is that claims that seem to be supported by judgments internal to one domain may conflict with the truths of another domain. Not all domains are self-contained in the way that mathematics is. Systems of religious belief, for example, may include claims about the natural world—e.g., about the creation of the universe—that are subject to refutation by the standards appropriate to that other domain.

Scanlon maintains that normative statements, including those of morality, do not entail or presuppose claims about the natural world that science gives us good reasons to reject. He says that the significance of the normative domain depends on there being rational agents—people who can act for reasons—but he believes "that rational agents are just a kind of natural organism, and that organisms of this kind do exist." Rational agents are capable of being motivated by their beliefs about normative facts, but this "does not involve causal interaction with these facts." Driving home the separation of the normative from the causal, Scanlon says:

> When a rational agent does something that he or she judges him or herself to have reason to do, this judgment makes sense of the action in normative terms and explains it, because the action is what one would expect of a rational agent who accepted that judgment. Presumably there is also a causal explanation of this connection, and of the more general uniformities . . . in virtue of which a being is a rational agent. But this causal explanation is another story, for neuroscientists to fill in.

I believe this carries the project of demystification too far. Normative rationality seems to require a kind of explanation of action and belief that consists neither of their merely "making sense" nor of their having certain neural causes. A rational being, unlike a calculating machine, responds to reasons because they exist and he recognizes them. How this explanation is to be understood is a deep question; but wherever the truth on this question may lie, Scanlon's defense of the reality of reasons is a great advance in our understanding of the subject.

15

KAHNEMAN'S THINKING

Humans are rational animals. In addition to the rich perceptual, cognitive, and motivational systems that they share with other creatures, they have a unique way of forming beliefs and preferences that is not instinctive but deliberate. They can form beliefs by logical inference, assessment of evidence, and statistical judgments of likelihood; and they can form preferences and make choices by the principled evaluation of alternative courses of action, on the basis of their rationally formed beliefs about the likely outcomes of those alternatives. The results of all these forms of reasoning can be preserved, recorded, and passed on to others, making possible the growth of knowledge and civilization. Reason has created our world.

However, reason depends on a constant supply of material from our prerational, animal nature—from perception, feeling, and natural desires. There is also an intermediate level of automatic judgment, some of it learned through experience, that operates more quickly than conscious reasoning and that is essential for navigating the world in real time. The relation among these faculties is complicated. Even when we think we are using reason to arrive at the right answer to some factual or practical question—taking the relevant data consciously into account—our reasoning may be influenced more directly, without our knowledge, by the instinctive forces with which it coexists.

This was a review of Daniel Kahneman, *Thinking, Fast and Slow* (Farrar, Straus and Giroux, 2011).

Analytic Philosophy and Human Life. Thomas Nagel, Oxford University Press.
© Oxford University Press 2023. DOI: 10.1093/oso/9780197681671.003.0015

Daniel Kahneman is one of the psychologists who has done the most to advance our understanding of how this complex set of mental factors works, and some of the problems that arise in the interaction among its components. His name will always be linked with that of Amos Tversky, whose early death in 1996 at the age of 59 brought their long intellectual collaboration to a close. Kahneman's book *Thinking, Fast and Slow* is dedicated to Tversky's memory, and it is a tribute to him and an admirable account of their work together. It is also a clear, comprehensive, and often witty introduction to an interesting area of research, written by a leading contributor with exceptional expository gifts.

Reason is traditionally divided into two types, theoretical and practical, which control the formation of beliefs and the determination of choices, respectively. It is a scarce resource in each of us; most of the time, in most respects, we have to operate on autopilot, because we can't spare the conscious attention to identify and weigh up the pros and cons for everything we do or think. Kahneman's aim in the book is not just theoretical but practical. He wants to provide us with a degree of self-understanding that will permit us to manage our thoughts and choices better, both individually and collectively. He says he cringes when his work with Tversky "is credited with demonstrating that human choices are irrational." This may seem an odd reaction, since they certainly showed that humans are systematically prone to make certain mistakes. But mistakes are not irrational until one has, and fails to use, the means to avoid them. Kahneman's aim is not to criticize human nature, but to identify features of the way human beings function that had not been recognized by influential theories of rational choice, and to suggest how we can guard against some of their untoward consequences.

The distinction in Kahneman's title, between thinking fast and slow, corresponds to a familiar distinction between two categories of mental functioning, which he follows common psychological usage in calling System 1 and System 2: "*System 1* operates automatically and quickly, with little or no effort and no sense of voluntary control. *System 2* allocates attention to the effortful mental activities that demand it, including complex computations. The operations of system 2 are often associated with the subjective experience of agency, choice, and concentration."

System 1 governs most of our perceptions, our use of language, our navigation through the world and our social interactions. We process so much constantly changing material from moment to moment that automatic responses are indispensable. Sometimes, however, these shortcuts give results that conscious reflection, calculation, or measurement carried out by System 2 would show to be wrong. We cannot in general displace System 1 responses by System 2 reflection—there just isn't time—but it pays to know when System 2 should be brought into action to correct for errors.

As Kahneman observes, System 2 is lazy. It is much easier to jump to conclusions than to weigh evidence and check the validity of arguments. Kahneman's strategy in overcoming this difficulty has two components: an empirically based account of how people actually think; and some recommendations for improvement through methods that correct for the most common errors produced by System 1. As I have said, the subject also divides between the formation of beliefs and the determination of choices—between fact and value—though some important mechanisms operate in both domains.

Consider for example the "anchoring effect," which has been demonstrated again and again in many contexts of both belief and choice. Where someone has to estimate a quantity, or make a quantitative choice, the mention in advance of a particular number, even if it comes from a completely irrelevant source, will have a strong influence on the answer. In one of their early experiments Kahneman and Tversky spun a wheel with 100 numbers, rigged to stop at 10 or 65, and asked people whether the percentage of African nations among UN members was greater or smaller than the number that came up. They then asked them for their best guess of the correct percentage. The average estimates of those who saw 10 and 65 were 25 percent and 45 percent, respectively. The "anchoring effect"— the ratio of the two differences—is 36 percent, which is typical. In another experiment, German judges read a description of a woman who had been caught shoplifting, and after rolling a pair of dice that were loaded to result in either a 3 or a 9, they were asked, first, whether they would sentence her to more or fewer months than that number, and then, what sentence they would give her. On average, those who had rolled a 9 said they would sentence her to 8 months; those who rolled a 3 said 5 months—an anchoring effect of 50 percent.

These influences are not conscious: everyone knows the numbers produced by the wheel or the dice are irrelevant. But in cases where an answer must be partly determined by guess or intuition, the suggestive prompting of such salient inputs is very powerful. Even if you try to resist it, you may fail, as was shown in an experiment with real estate agents, whose estimates of a reasonable buying price for a house they visited and examined carefully turned out to depend significantly on what they were told was the asking price, though they all took pride in their ability to ignore it. The anchoring effect was 41 percent.

Another important phenomenon is substitution: asked a question that would require some conscious reasoning to answer, one answers a different question that is easier. For example, when someone is given a description of someone's personality and asked about the relative likelihood of his being in a certain profession, the answer will usually depend entirely on how closely the description fits the stereotype of a typical member of the profession, ignoring the important factor of the different numbers of people in different professions. This is called base-rate neglect.

A similar error is involved in one of Kahneman and Tversky's most flagrant examples. Presented with a stereotypical description of a woman sympathetic to progressive social and political causes, most subjects thought the probability of her being a feminist bank teller was higher than the probability of her being a bank teller—a logical impossibility. It is like believing that a Norwegian is more likely to have blond hair than to have hair.

Kahneman describes the many ways in which intuitive judgments of likelihood tend to be unreliable—often with serious consequences for legal and policy choices. Salient examples that receive media coverage or make a strong emotional impression are given evidential weight independent of how typical they are. Small samples with unusual characteristics are taken as having causal significance, when they merely reflect random variation. The Gates Foundation spent $1.7 billion to encourage smaller schools, on the basis of findings that the most successful schools were small; but the least successful schools are also small. Both facts are a statistical consequence of the principle that the larger the sample from a population of individuals in which a characteristic like academic performance varies, the closer the sample's average level is likely to be to that of the population as a whole; whereas the smaller the sample, the more likely it is to diverge in one direction or another from that average. But people have a thirst for instructive causal explanations of what is good or bad, and tend to postulate them in many cases where an anomalous outcome is really due to chance. This is presumably at work in the current superstition that inoculations cause autism.

Kahneman is particularly hard on the stock market as a site of illusion. The lack of correlation in performance from year to year of almost all traders, advisers, and mutual funds shows that success or failure is essentially due to luck. Yet professional investors are rewarded on the basis of those results, which are not under their control. Kahneman explains that presentation of the statistical facts makes no impression on the participants because it cannot derail the subjective sense of informed judgment that accompanies these gambles. For similar statistical reasons Kahneman is skeptical about the contributions of CEOs' competence to the success or failure of their companies, which is due largely to factors beyond their control. "The CEO of a successful company is likely to be called flexible, methodical, and decisive. Imagine that a year has passed and things have gone sour. The same executive is now described as confused, rigid, and authoritarian." Where skill is decisive and much more important than chance, as in highly controlled accomplishments like orthodontia, golf, or musical performance, it will show up through the persistence over time of individual differences.

Kahneman's recommendation is that when making predictions or plans, one should try to identify a relevant class to which the case belongs, and take as a baseline the statistics of outcomes for that class, before factoring in any intuitive sense one may have about the particular case. And yet he also recognizes that unwarranted optimism in defiance of the statistical evidence may have its uses as an indispensable driving force in a competitive economy, and for that matter in scientific research, even though it usually results in failed restaurants, failed inventions, and failed experiments.

So far I have been talking mostly about errors due to System 1 in the formation of beliefs; but Kahneman's most influential contributions, for which he received the Nobel Prize in economics, have to do with the formation of preferences and choices. He and Tversky demonstrated that rational expectations theory, a model of choice widely used by economists, was seriously inaccurate as an account of how people actually behave, and they proposed an alternative that they called prospect theory.

Most choices, and all economic choices, involve some uncertainty about their outcomes, and rational expectations theory, also called expected utility theory, describes a uniform standard for determining the rationality of choices under uncertainty, where probabilities can be assigned to different possible outcomes. The standard seems self-evident: the value of a 50 percent probability of a given outcome is half the value the outcome would have if it actually occurred, and in general the value of any choice under uncertainty is dependent on the values of its possible outcomes, multiplied by their probabilities. Rationality in decision consists in making choices on the basis of "expected value," which means picking the alternative that maximizes the sum of the products of utility and probability for all the possible outcomes. So a 10 percent chance of $1,000 is better than a 50 percent chance of $150, an 80 percent chance of $100 plus a 20 percent chance of $10 is better than a 100 percent chance of $80, and so forth.

The principle of maximizing expected value was conceived both as a principle of what is rational and a way of predicting how cool-headed individuals will choose under conditions of uncertainty. But Kahneman and Tversky showed that people do not act in accordance with rational expectations theory—whatever may be the truth about the ideal standard of rationality. They do not care only about the value of outcomes, even discounted by probability. They care about whether the outcome is the result of a gain or a loss, and they assign greater importance to losses than to gains. Moreover, the weights they assign to outcomes are not uniformly proportional to probabilities; the relation is much more complicated.

In general, the negative trumps the positive: losses are more powerful than the corresponding gains. Most people won't accept a bet with a 50 percent chance of winning $125 and a 50 percent chance of losing $100. And for high probabilities, people are risk-averse with respect to gains and risk-seeking with respect to losses: they would choose $9,000 for sure over a 90 percent chance to win $10,000, but would prefer a 90 percent chance of losing $10,000 over losing $9,000 for sure. Yet when the probabilities are small, the preference is reversed. Most people prefer a 5 percent chance to win $10,000 over getting $500 for sure; and most people prefer a certain loss of $500 to a 5 percent chance of losing $10,000. For small probabilities the former, risk-seeking preference is why people buy lottery tickets; the latter, risk-averse preference is why people buy insurance. Kahneman brings in other factors as well, but these are particularly important, and he points out that they have an effect on the settlement of lawsuits, whose outcome is always uncertain: a big potential loser in a case with low probability of success will be more eager to settle than a big potential winner, so the plaintiff in a frivolous suit has a bargaining advantage over the defendant.

Another significant divergence from expected utility theory is found in the reaction to probabilities very close to zero. People tend either to ignore very small probabilities or overweight them: a cancer risk of .001% cannot be easily distinguished from a risk of .00001%. But if even a tiny cancer risk attracts attention, it is likely to be weighted out of proportion to its probability in the choice of actions or policies.

The phenomena of loss aversion, risk aversion, and risk seeking are sufficiently robust that prospect theory is now widely recognized as an improvement over expected utility theory as a predictor of individual choices. Behavioral economics is based on the systematic use of these findings. But Kahneman remains sympathetic to expected utility as a normative standard for rational choice, since it yields better results over the long term. He urges that we control the distorting emotional influence of our natural loss aversion by rehearsing "the mantra that will get you significantly closer to economic rationality: you win a few, you lose a few."

More recently, Kahneman has turned his attention to the measurement of happiness or well-being, and here again his claims take a dualistic form. He distinguishes between two selves, the experiencing self and the remembering self. In relation to an unpleasant experience such as a colonoscopy, for example, "The *experiencing self* is the one that answers the question: 'Does it hurt now?' The *remembering self* is the one that answers the question: 'How was it, on the whole?' Memories are all we get to keep from our experience of living, and the only perspective that we can adopt as we think about our lives is therefore that of the remembering self."

It turns out that the judgments of the remembering self bear a peculiar and indirect relation to those of the experiencing self. You might think that when asked to compare two unpleasant experiences after they are over, subjects would be influenced in their evaluation by the total amount of pain in each, which depends on both the duration and the average intensity. But this is not the case. Retrospective evaluation is determined by two other factors: the level of pain experienced at the worst moment of the experience and at its end. Duration seems to have no effect, and an unpleasant experience that differs from another only by having a period of less severe pain tacked on at the end will be remembered as less bad, even though it includes more total pain. Kahneman thinks there is clearly something wrong here:

> The remembering self is sometimes wrong, but it is the one that keeps score and governs what we learn from living, and it is the one that makes decisions. What we learn from the past is to maximize the qualities of our future memories, not necessarily of our future experience. This is the tyranny of the remembering self.

These misleading effects, which Kahneman calls the peak-end rule and duration neglect, apply to the evaluation of pleasant experiences as well. But surely there are other ways in which the overall evaluation of aspects of our lives, or of our lives as a whole, is not just a function of how experientially pleasant or unpleasant they are moment by moment. One of the most important influences on people's satisfaction with their lives is what their goals in life are, and whether they have achieved them. With unintentional comedy Kahneman reports that it required empirical research to bring him to the revelation that this should be regarded as an independent type of value, rather than some kind of mistake:

> In part because of these findings I have changed my mind about the definition of well-being. The goals that people set for themselves are so important to what they do and how they feel about it that an exclusive focus on experienced well-being is not

tenable. We cannot hold a concept of well-being that ignores what people want.

So he now holds a hybrid view. But the fact that it required psychological studies to convince him that what people want and what they achieve, and not just how they feel, is important for the evaluation of their lives, indicates that he started out with an unbelievably myopic conception of value. Kahneman continues to display the same blinkered hedonism when discussing the fact that those who suffer from major physical deficits, such as paraplegics and colostomy patients, don't have lower moment-to-moment experiential well-being than healthy people, though they give a much lower assessment to the quality of their lives. Kahneman regards this as an illusion:

> Experience sampling shows no difference in experienced happiness between these patients and a healthy population. Yet colostomy patients would be willing to trade away years of their life for a shorter life without a colostomy. Furthermore, patients whose colostomy has been reversed remember their time in this condition as awful, and they would give up even more of their remaining life not to have to return to it. Here it appears that the remembering self is subject to a massive focusing illusion about the life that the experiencing self endures quite comfortably.

Kahneman apparently regards the overwhelming desire of these patients not to spend their lives leaking excrement into a plastic bag as a "focusing illusion" because it produces experiential displeasure only when they think about it, which isn't most of the time. He can't imagine that the desire itself might be reasonable. Pleasure and the avoidance of pain are very important, but people care about a lot else. And to depart even farther from Kahneman's essentially utilitarian perspective: some of those things, including knowledge, freedom, and physical independence, are—dare I say it?—good in themselves, which is why people care about them.

Still, even if one takes a more sophisticated view of the sources of value, Kahneman's observations about how people make choices are highly relevant to public policy. This is not a work of moral or political theory, but it gives us important information about how to achieve our aims, whatever they may be, or at least how to improve the likelihood of success. If a society wants to encourage retirement savings, or organ donation at death, it can do so most effectively not by exhortation or coercion, but by setting a default position, so that people have to make a conscious choice to opt out of the pension plan, or to refuse to donate their organs. (This is known as libertarian paternalism, since it is not coercive, and it is elaborated in detail by Richard Thaler and Cass R. Sunstein in their book *Nudge*.) The anchoring effect of the status quo, or a neutral reference point, is enormous. But we must also be on guard against the malign influence of the status quo, which can lead us to throw good money after bad, because abandoning a failed project or investment for something more promising would require us to acknowledge the loss of what we have already wasted on it—the so-called fallacy of sunk costs.

Kahneman's findings should not surprise anyone who has had to make many decisions quickly on the basis of disparate information. My own academic experience of evaluating large numbers of candidates for appointment or for admission to graduate school does not inspire confidence in the accuracy of such judgments, or their insulation from unrecognized and irrelevant influences. Kahneman believes that the main practical lesson to take from his book is that one should cultivate the standpoint of the outside observer, or even the critical input of actual outside observers, to provide a warning when the gut responses of System 1 need to be reviewed by the more burdensome calculations and rule-governed procedures of System 2. But for any significant case, such methods have to be developed by insiders to the area of judgment.

These results leave open the question whether progress toward greater objectivity will come primarily from collective institutional practices or from the gradual internalization of critical standards by individuals. In some domains, such as science, law, and even morality, progress depends on reflection and the attempt to identify sources of error, carried out initially by a minority; then eventually institutions and cultural transmission lead to changes in many more people's habits of thought. Kahneman has provided a valuable service of consciousness-raising, but the design of remedies is an ongoing task.

16

THE CORTEX AND
THE TROLLEY PROBLEM

Joshua Greene is a leading contributor to the recently salient field
of empirical moral psychology, and *Moral Tribes* presents his
comprehensive view of the subject, and what we should make of
it. The grounds for the empirical hypotheses that he offers about
human morality are of three types: psychological experiments,
observations of brain activity, and evolutionary theory. The third,
in application to the psychological properties of human beings, is
necessarily speculative, but the first and second are backed up by
contemporary data, including many experiments that Greene and
his associates have carried out themselves.

But Greene does not limit himself to factual claims. He also asks
how our moral beliefs and attitudes should be affected by these psychological findings. Greene began his training and research as a
doctoral student in philosophy at Princeton, so he is familiar from
the inside with the enterprise of ethical theory conceived not as a
part of empirical psychology but as a direct first-order investigation of moral questions, and a quest for systematic answers to them.
His book is intended as a radical challenge to the assumptions of
that philosophical enterprise. It benefits from his familiarity with
the field, even if his grasp of the views that he discusses is not always
accurate.

This was a review of Joshua Greene, *Moral Tribes: Emotion, Reason, and the Gap between Us and Them* (Penguin, 2013).

Analytic Philosophy and Human Life. Thomas Nagel, Oxford University Press.
© Oxford University Press 2023. DOI: 10.1093/oso/9780197681671.003.0016

The book is framed as the search for a solution to a global problem that cannot be solved by the kinds of moral standards that command intuitive assent and work well within particular communities. Greene calls this problem the tragedy of commonsense morality. In a nutshell, it is the tragedy that moralities that help members of particular communities to cooperate peacefully do not foster a comparable harmony among members of different communities.

> Morality evolved to enable cooperation, but this conclusion comes with an important caveat. Biologically speaking, humans were designed for cooperation, *but only with some people.* Our moral brains evolved for cooperation *within groups,* and perhaps only within the context of personal relationships. Our moral brains did not evolve for cooperation *between groups* (at least not *all* groups). . . . As with the evolution of faster carnivores, competition is essential for the evolution of cooperation.

The tragedy of commonsense morality is conceived by analogy with the familiar tragedy of the commons, to which commonsense morality does provide a solution. In the tragedy of the commons, the pursuit of private self-interest leads a collection of individuals to a result that is contrary to the interest of all of them (like overgrazing the commons or overfishing the ocean). If they learn to limit their individual self-interest by agreeing to follow certain rules and sticking to them, the commons will not be destroyed and they will all do well. As Greene puts it, commonsense morality requires that we sometimes put Us ahead of Me; but the same disposition also leads us to put Us ahead of Them. We feel obligations to fellow members of our community but not to outsiders. So the solution to the tragedy of the commons has generated a new tragedy, which we can see wherever the values and the interests of different communities conflict, not only on an international scale but also more locally, within pluralistic societies that contain multiple moral communities.

To solve this problem Greene thinks we need what he calls a "metamorality," based on a common currency of value that all human beings can acknowledge, even if it conflicts with some of the promptings of the intuitive moralities of common sense. Like others who have based their doubts about commonsense morality on diagnoses of its evolutionary pedigree, Greene thinks that this higher-level moral outlook is to be found in utilitarianism, which he proposes to rename "deep pragmatism" (lots of luck). Utilitarianism, propounded by Bentham and Mill, is the principle that we should aim to maximize happiness impartially, and it conflicts with the instinctive commonsense morality of individual rights, and special heightened obligations to those to whom one is related by blood or community. Those intuitive values have their uses as rough guides to action in many ordinary circumstances, but they cannot, in Greene's view, provide the basis for universally valid standards of conduct.

Greene's argument against the objective authority of commonsense morality hinges on Daniel Kahneman's distinction between fast instinctive thought and slow deliberative thought. As Kahneman shows, these two modes appear in almost every aspect of human life, and we could not survive without both of them. Greene says that they are like the two ways a contemporary camera can operate: by automatic settings or by manual mode. Automatic settings enable you to point and shoot, without thinking about the distance or lighting conditions, whereas manual mode enables you to make adjustments to the focus, the aperture, and the shutter speed after conscious reflection on the specific conditions of the shot. The availability of both of these options makes for either efficiency or flexibility, depending on what is needed.

Our decision apparatus, according to Greene, is similar. When it comes to moral judgment—deciding whether an act would be right or wrong—we can be fast, automatic, and emotional, or slow, deliberate, and rational. Greene puts the distinction to work in his careful discussion of the trolley problem, a set of gruesome thought-experiments that has become a staple of recent moral philosophy, associated in particular with the writings of Philippa Foot, Judith Jarvis Thomson, and Frances Myrna Kamm. As Greene says, the problem boils down to the following question:

> When, and why, do the rights of the individual take precedence over the greater good? Every major moral issue—abortion, affirmative action, higher versus lower taxes, killing civilians in war, sending people to fight in war, rationing resources in healthcare, gun control, the death penalty—was in some way about the (real or alleged) rights of some individuals versus the (real or alleged) greater good. The Trolley Problem hit it right on the nose.

In the central case of the trolley problem, we are asked to compare two choices:

(1) The footbridge dilemma: A runaway trolley is headed for five railway workmen who will be killed if it proceeds on its present course. You are standing on a footbridge spanning the tracks, in between the oncoming trolley and the five people. Standing next to you is a 300-pound man. The only way to save the five people is to push him off the footbridge and onto the tracks below. The man will die as a result, but his body will stop the trolley. (You are only half his size and would not stop the trolley if you yourself jumped in front of it.)

(2) The switch dilemma: A runaway trolley is headed for five workmen who will be killed if nothing is done. You can save these five people by hitting a switch that will turn the trolley onto a sidetrack. Unfortunately there is a single workman on the side-track who will be killed if you hit the switch.

It turns out that most people the world over think that it would be wrong to push the fat man off the footbridge, but that it would be morally permissible to hit the switch—even though the outcomes of the two acts would be the same, one person killed and five saved. Other examples have been invented to refine the search for the determining characteristics that trigger a judgment of wrongness or permissibility, and various principles have been formulated to capture the results, but we need not go into those details here. The basic point for Greene's purposes is that we have strong moral reactions against certain actions that cause harm but serve the greater good on balance, but not to other actions that produce the same balance of good and harm.

There are two noteworthy differences between the two dilemmas. First, in "switch" there is nothing mysterious about the result; everyone gets the point of choosing the outcome with fewer deaths. As Greene observes, "No one's ever said, 'Try to save more lives? Why, that never occurred to me!'" But in "footbridge" the choice, however convincing, is mysterious; it seems to call for, but also to defy, explanation. What is it about pushing the fat man in front of the trolley that overrides the value of the five lives that would be saved? To say that it would violate his right to life, or that it would be murder, seems to repeat rather than to explain the judgment. Second, the response to "footbridge" has an emotional charge that is missing in the allegedly more rational response to "switch."

You can consult your own visceral reaction to the idea of pushing someone in front of a trolley, as opposed to your feeling about hitting the switch when you know that there is someone on the sidetrack. But Greene and his colleagues have added multiple studies, using brain imaging, to show that when people contemplate footbridge-type cases there is increased activity in the ventromedial prefrontal cortex, a part of the brain associated with emotion, whereas switch-type cases elicit increased activity in the dorsolateral prefrontal cortex, a part of the brain associated with calculation and reasoning. Moreover, people with damage to the ventromedial prefrontal cortex, who lack normal emotions, were five times as likely as others to approve of pushing the fat man off the bridge.

Greene offers much more experimental detail and some ingenious psychological proposals about why our gut reactions have the particular subtle contours that they do, but his overall conclusion, following Kahneman, is that we have a dual-process system of moral judgments: automatic settings charged with emotion and deliberative responses that depend on calculation. These two types of response will conflict in some cases, but he thinks both have their uses in the guidance of human behavior. As Greene says, "We wouldn't want to blindly condemn our moral intuitions with 'guilt by neural association.'" Still, the metaphor of camera settings and the appeal to evolutionary explanations for the automatic settings imply that Greene accords utilitarian values (minimizing the number of deaths) a different status from the kind of prohibition we find in "footbridge." He believes that although we cannot get rid of our visceral responses and in general should not want to, we can distance ourselves from them in a way that we should not distance ourselves from our utilitarian judgments. Utilitarianism, he believes, allows us to transcend our evolutionary heritage. The question then is whether he offers a coherent account of how and why we should give it this authority.

Greene wants to persuade us that moral psychology is more fundamental than moral philosophy. Most moral philosophies, he maintains, are misguided attempts to interpret our moral intuitions in particular cases as apprehensions of the truth about how we ought to live and what we ought to do, with the aim of discovering the underlying principles that determine that truth. In fact, Greene believes, all of our intuitions are just manifestations of the operation of our dual-process brains, functioning either instinctively or more reflectively. He endorses one moral position, utilitarianism, not as the truth (he professes to be agnostic on whether there is such a thing as moral truth) but rather as a method of evaluation that we can all understand, and that holds out hope of providing a common currency of value less divisive than the morality of individual rights and communal obligations. "None of us is truly impartial, but everyone feels the pull of impartiality as a moral ideal."

Utilitarianism, he contends, is not refuted by "footbridge"-type intuitions that conflict with it, because those intuitions are best understood not as perceptions of intrinsic wrongness, but as gut reactions that have evolved to serve social peace by preventing interpersonal violence. Similar debunking explanations can be given for other commonsense moral intuitions, such as the obligation to favor members of one's own group over strangers, or the stronger obligation one feels to rescue an identified individual who is drowning in front of you than to contribute to saving the lives of greater numbers of anonymous victims far away. According to Greene, it is understandable in light of evolutionary psychology that we have these intuitions, and for the most part it does no harm to let our conduct be guided by them, but they are not perceptions of moral truth, and they do not discredit the utilitarian response when it tells us to do something different.

While we cannot get rid of our automatic settings, Greene says we should try to transcend them—and if we do, we cannot expect the universal principles we adopt to "feel right." Utilitarianism has counterintuitive consequences, but we arrive at it by recognizing that happiness matters to everyone, and that objectively no one matters more than anyone else, even though subjectively we are each especially important to ourselves. This is an example of what he calls "kicking away the ladder," or forming moral values that are opposed to the evolutionary forces that originally gave rise to morality.

Yet Greene cannot seem to make up his mind as to whether utilitarianism trumps individual rights in some more objective sense. When he tries to describe the appropriate place of utilitarianism in our lives, this is what he says:

It's not reasonable to expect actual humans to put aside nearly everything they love for the sake of the greater good. Speaking for myself, I spend money on my children that would be better spent on distant starving children, and I have no intention of stopping. After all, I'm only human! But I'd rather be a human who knows that he's a hypocrite, and who tries to be less so, than one who mistakes his species-typical moral limitations for ideal values.

The word "hypocrite" is misused here. A hypocrite is someone who professes beliefs that he does not hold—but so far as I can tell Greene is accusing himself of failing to live in accordance with beliefs that he accepts, beliefs about ideal values.

This implies something that is clearly not a fact of empirical psychology: namely, that there are values by which we should "ideally" govern our lives, and that they are captured by the utilitarian aim of maximizing total happiness, counting everyone's happiness impartially as of equal value, with no preference for ourselves or our loved ones. Greene even offers an extravagantly philosophical argument in support of this ideal. He asks what you would do if you had the choice of creating a world full of people like us, or a world full of people whose natural motives were completely unselfish and impartial and who cared about everyone, not just their friends and families, as much as they care about themselves. He assumes you would choose to create the second species, and that this shows that there is something the matter with us and our species-typical moral responses.

Greene apparently believes that this bizarre creationist thought-experiment allows us to identify ideal values, because it calls forth a faculty of value judgment that is not tainted by our "species-typical moral limitations." He appears to think that the values that would animate this ideal species apply in some sense to us, even though we are very different. Yet he also believes it would be unreasonable to expect us to live up to them, and disastrous to insist that we do so:

If it seems absurd to ask real humans to abandon their families, friends, and other passions for the betterment of anonymous strangers, then that can't be what utilitarianism actually asks of real humans. Trying to do this would be a disaster, and disasters don't maximize happiness. Humans evolved to live lives defined by relationships with people and communities, and if our goal is to make the world as happy as possible, we must take this defining feature of human nature into account.

Greene is wrestling with an old problem, and his psychological approach does not enable him to solve it. When we want to arrive at standards to govern conduct, our own and that of others, we have to start somewhere, and that means starting from what seems right. When our intuitions are unequivocal, we can simply accept them; but sometimes they are not, and then we are faced with a choice. Should we distrust our intuitions about individual rights when they conflict with the intuition that it is always better to save more lives, or should we abandon utilitarianism because it allows intuitively unacceptable violations of individual rights? Greene says that the intuitive reaction in "footbridge" is analogous to an optical illusion like the Müller-Lyer, in which two equal lines appear to be of different lengths, because of a difference of context. The illusion doesn't go away even when we have measured the lines and found them to be equal. Yet the utilitarian calculation is not really like a physical measurement: it depends on a different form of evaluation, one which Greene describes as a human invention.

One of the hardest questions for moral theory is whether the values tied to the personal point of view, such as partiality toward oneself and one's family, and special responsibility for refraining from direct harm to others, should be part of the foundation of morality or should be admitted only to the extent that they can be justified from an impersonal standpoint such as that of impartial utilitarianism. To dismiss our counter-utilitarian attachments and intuitions, as Greene does, as "species-typical moral limitations," which must be seen as obstacles to the realization of the moral ideal, is to identify ideal morality as something more, or perhaps less, than human.

A more attractive alternative would be to combine some of the values that form a natural part of the personal point of view with universal and impartial values of the kind Greene believes we are also capable of. A project of this kind would require more subtlety about the different possible interpretations of impartiality than Greene displays: he identifies impartiality with happiness-maximization, and his brief discussions of Kant and Rawls show that he does not really understand their alternative conceptions—though I suspect that even if he did, he would still reject them in favor of utilitarianism.

Rawls's main objection to utilitarianism is that it fails to make the distinction between persons a fundamental factor in the construction of the moral point of view, so it settles conflicts between the interests of distinct persons by a method of cost-benefit balancing that is identical with the method that is appropriate when there are choices to be made between goods and evils within the life of one individual. Thus in utilitarianism a very severe cost to one person can be outweighed by the sum of small advantages to a sufficiently large number of other people. Rawls, in the tradition of Kant, tried to work out an alternative form of impartial equal consideration for the interpersonal case, based on priorities of urgency which limited such interpersonal tradeoffs. There is no space to discuss it here, but this is just one example of how the transcendence of our evolutionary heritage may be more complicated than Greene imagines.

The most difficult problem posed by Greene's proposals is whether we should give up trying to understand our natural moral intuitions as evidence of a coherent system of individual rights that limit what may be done even in pursuit of the greater good. Should we instead come to regard them as we regard optical illusions, recognizing them as evolutionary products but withholding our assent? Greene's debunking arguments add an empirical dimension to a venerable utilitarian tradition but they certainly don't settle the question. It is possible to defend a universal system of individual rights as the expression of a moral point of view that accords to each individual a sphere of autonomy in the conduct of life, free from interference by others, defined in such a way that the same sphere of autonomy can be accorded to everyone without inconsistency. This last condition means that sometimes the distinction between what does and does not count as a crossing of the boundary protected by rights may seem arbitrary—as in the distinction between "footbridge" and "switch," or between killing someone (strongly prohibited) and failing to save someone from death (permitted, unless it costs you very little). But the moral conception behind a system that embodies such distinctions cannot easily be dismissed as the equivalent of an optical illusion. Most people will regard a morality based entirely on such a system of equal liberty as unacceptable, but it can also be included, along with some requirements of impartial concern for the general welfare, as part of a more complicated morality that reflects the complexity of human nature.

Such disagreements are an inevitable part of the important enterprise of moral invention that Greene, along with many others, is engaged in. Humanity has, we may hope, a long road of moral development ahead of it.

17

MODULAR MORALITY

1.

Human beings want to understand themselves, and in our time such understanding is pursued on a wide front by the biological, psychological, and social sciences. One of the questions presented by these forms of self-understanding is how to connect them with the actual lives all of us continue to lead, using the faculties and engaging in the activities and relations that are described by scientific theories.

An important example is the universal human phenomenon of morality. Even if we come to accept descriptive theories of the different forms of morality, based on evolutionary biology, neuroscience, or developmental and social psychology, each of us also holds specific moral views, makes moral judgments, and governs his conduct and political choices partly on the basis of those attitudes. How do we combine the external descriptive view of ourselves provided by empirical science with the active internal engagement of real life?

This problem is posed and to some extent addressed by Jonathan Haidt's book *The Righteous Mind*, and part of the interest of the book lies in its failure to provide a fully coherent response. Haidt is a social psychologist, and he sets out his descriptive theory of the origins and nature of morality and of moral disagreement. But the

This was a review of Jonathan Haidt, *The Righteous Mind: Why Good People Are Divided by Politics and Religion* (Pantheon, 2012), and Michael Rosen, *Dignity: Its History and Meaning* (Harvard University Press, 2012).

book's overall point is partly normative, not just descriptive. Haidt makes definite recommendations of a clearly moral nature, and he seeks to support them with the help of his descriptive findings about morality. These two aspects of the project do not fit easily together.

Haidt's empirical theory, which he calls moral foundations theory, is an example of evolutionary psychology. It is the hypothesis that a set of innate "modules" of moral response were fixed in humans by natural selection, and that these responses, further shaped by cultural evolution in various more specific forms and combinations, underlie the widely divergent moralities that we observe not only across the globe but within pluralistic cultures like that of the United States. Specifically, Haidt argues that group selection—selection for genetic traits whose presence benefited social groups of early humans in competition with other groups, rather than individual selection for traits that enhanced the reproductive success of individuals in competition with other individuals—is responsible for the main moral dispositions. The existence of group selection is a contentious issue in evolutionary biology. Haidt defends it in this case on the ground that moral norms can include cheap enforcement mechanisms, such as forms of group pressure, that cancel the genetic advantage for any individual of trying to benefit from the group's success while not following the norms—free-riding, in other words.

Haidt distinguishes six basic types of moral response, which he likens to distinct taste receptors, so that different moralities are like different cuisines in the use they make of these responses. Each type manifests itself through intuitive emotional reactions, positive and negative, to a specific value or its violation, so he gives them double-barreled names: care/harm, liberty/oppression, fairness/cheating, loyalty/betrayal, authority/subversion, and sanctity/degradation. Haidt believes that all these responses developed in their basic innate form because they suppress or regulate self-interest and make cooperation possible among people who are not close relatives. Individual natural selection can explain psychological traits that benefit the individual and his close kin; but group selection, he argues, is needed to explain those traits that benefit individuals only by sustaining norms that preserve the cohesion of the group.

I will say more about these categories in a moment, but Haidt's general point is that functioning moralities must draw on these intuitive emotional responses to control behavior, and that reason plays a relatively minor role in morality—often merely as a source of rationalizations for what our gut feelings tell us is right or wrong. The main argument of the book is that the secular liberal moralities found in some parts of advanced Western societies assign too much importance to reason, and rely on only a subset of the basic responses he describes, whereas conservative moralities, in those societies or elsewhere, get their strength from invoking all of the moral categories equally. This explains what seems to liberals to be the irrational success of conservatism in American culture and politics. Haidt insists that it is wrong for liberals to regard the conservative outlook with contempt, and that they need to broaden the basis of their own moral appeal if they want to increase their influence.

Haidt describes his own research, based on interviews and questionnaires in the U.S. and abroad, about the distribution of different combinations of moral attitudes; he also offers evolutionary speculation, anthropological data, and evidence from brain research and studies of animal behavior. I will not attempt to discuss all this material. The contemporary phenomenon he describes is familiar to any socially conscious resident of the United States, even if the description is not fully accurate. Three of his categories—loyalty, authority, and sanctity (to shorten their double-barreled names)—are very important to conservatives but unimportant or even repellent to most liberals. Loyalty to a group excludes and devalues those outside it; authority suppresses the autonomy of the individual; sanctity (e.g., as a bar to stem cell research, euthanasia, pornography, and flag desecration) postulates values that do not depend on human interests. These norms clash with the concern for individual interests and aspiration to universality that are at the heart of liberalism.

According to Haidt, liberals appeal primarily to the care module, together with a version of liberty that makes it a bar to the oppression of the weak by the powerful. They have a lesser concern for fairness, interpreted by Haidt as a requirement of reward proportional to social contribution—not equality. In other words they ignore half of the possible emotional supports of morality, whereas conservatives care about all six of the basic values. Though liberals often fail to acknowledge it, conservatives don't care only about sexual morality, religion, and patriotism; but liberals, says Haidt, care only about poverty, civil rights, and civil liberties.

He credits Émile Durkheim with having understood that collective religious and patriotic emotions not only bind people together but give their lives meaning, and enable them to avoid the anomie—rootlessness and lack of norms—that results from an excessive preoccupation with individualistic aims. By contrast, he rejects John Stuart Mill's identification of morality with the universal advancement of individual interests and the prevention of harm done by one person to another.

2.

Haidt's evolutionary approach requires that an effectively motivated morality be grounded in dispositions that have been favored by natural selection. Universal, rather than group-centered, dispositions are not plausible candidates for such selection. This leads him to acknowledge only limited forms of the values of care and fairness. Care, he believes, is based on the need for human groups to protect the young during their lengthy period of helplessness; it cannot be naturally generalized to concern for the welfare of all humans, let alone all sentient beings. Fairness he identifies with the principle that participants in a cooperative enterprise should be rewarded in proportion to their contribution, and cheaters and free-riders should be punished. He denies that there is any moral interest in equality per se—only an aversion to excessive domination, a particular type of imposed inequality that goes beyond the legitimate hierarchy approved by the functional value of authority.

One of the things missing from this picture is a conception of fairness, important for American liberalism and the European left, that condemns as unfair those hereditary class inequalities that give some people much harder lives than others merely because of the accidents of birth. This is not an interest in equality per se, but an objection to certain social causes of inequality—and not just those causes like racial segregation that are infringements of liberty. There may not be a credible evolutionary explanation for this sense of unfairness, but it is real all the same, and it has motivated the left for some time. Yet such a response is probably too dependent on reasoning and requirements of moral consistency for Haidt to take seriously—just like the extension of concerns to provide care and avoid harm beyond one's own community.

> It would be nice to believe that we humans were designed to love everyone unconditionally. Nice, but rather unlikely from an evolutionary perspective. Parochial love—love within groups—amplified by similarity, a sense of shared fate, and the suppression of free riders, may be the most we can accomplish.

He urges liberals to respect the varying parochial moralities and religions that they are accustomed to deride as backward or intolerant, and to acknowledge their genuine moral character. However, Haidt insists that he is not a relativist. He has moral views of his own, and presumably this means that he believes that they are true, or at least more likely to be true than the alternatives. But what does it mean, in the light of Haidt's evolutionary perspective, to believe such a thing, and what grounds might he have for believing it?

What he says is that his descriptive theory of the six types of moral response and their group-preserving function works well "as an adjunct" to normative theories, "particularly those that have often had difficulty seeing groups and social facts." He himself favors what he calls a "Durkheimian utilitarianism," which

> would be open to the possibility that the binding foundations—
> Loyalty, Authority, and Sanctity—have a crucial role to play
> in a good society. . . . When we talk about making laws and
> implementing public policies in Western democracies that con-
> tain some degree of ethnic and moral diversity, then I think there
> is no compelling alternative to utilitarianism. I think Jeremy
> Bentham was right that laws and public policies should aim, as a
> first approximation, to produce the greatest total good. I just want
> Bentham to read Durkheim . . . before he tells any of us, or our
> legislators, how to go about maximizing that total good.

There are two problems about the relation of this view to the six modules theory. First, utilitarianism itself doesn't have a plausible foundation in any of them. The closest candidate is care/harm, but the utilitarian principle, which counts everyone's interests equally and requires that a society aim to maximize the total good, rather than merely protecting the helpless and suppressing intrasocietal aggression, is a huge expansion of the scope of care. It is the kind of principle that could only be based on reasoning of some kind, rather than instinct—even if it is applied only within the bounds of a single society.

Secondly, Haidt's Durkheimian utilitarianism reduces the values of loyalty, authority, and sanctity to a purely instrumental role. Religion, patriotism, and sexual taboos, for example, have no va-lidity or value in themselves, according to this view; they are merely useful in creating bonds that allow collective achievement of the greatest total good, which utilitarians identify with the satisfaction of individual interests. But can such values and practices serve this function if they are seen as purely instrumental? Can they even exist? The purely instrumental, utilitarian endorsement of these "binding" moral attitudes seems essentially that of an outsider, someone who does not share them in their authentic form.

When it comes to discovering factual truth Haidt is a great believer in reason, especially if it is exercised in the collective practice of mutual criticism characteristic of science. Reason is what allows us to go beyond instinct, intuition, and perception, as well as superstition and myth. But when it comes to normative truth Haidt is distrustful of reason, though he does not rule it out of bounds altogether. His conception of its place in moral thought is obscure (though at one point he suggests that a legislature might function as a site of collective reasoning about public policy). I have no idea what he thinks is going on in his argument for a Durkheimian form of utilitarianism. Is he expressing intuitions that he believes are present in him as the result of biological and cultural evolution? Or is he making a normative claim that takes those intuitions as data but rests on some further moral foundation? Or both?

We cannot ignore innate human instincts and cultural conditioning, but anyone who wants to think seriously about morality must be prepared to evaluate such motives from an independent point of view that is achieved by transcending them. For example, if one wishes to evaluate the various norms of sanctity and pollution, authority and hierarchy that still uphold the subordination of women to men in many societies, it is necessary first to ask whether the interests of men and women should be counted equally in assessing any such norms. If the answer is yes, that is essentially to deny that those norms carry their own intrinsic validity: if they devalue the interests of women, they should be rejected even if they are strongly resistant to being dislodged.

Reflection and argument of this kind have played a significant role in moral reform, but Haidt's picture of different moralities as composed, like different cuisines, from different blends of the six moral modules, suitably adapted to social circumstances, leaves little room for the pursuit of moral understanding and progress through rational reflection and the search for consistency. Yet this kind of thought is part of moral life, including Haidt's, and any theory of moral psychology should try to understand it. Social cohesion may be a necessary function of an acceptable morality, but it is not the only one.

3.

One of the main culprits of Haidt's book, for insisting that morality must be based on reason, not on feelings, is Immanuel Kant. Kant's influence has been very great, and Haidt believes it has sidetracked philosophers and others from the true path of understanding indicated by his predecessor David Hume, who maintained that reason was always subordinate to feeling or "sentiment" in the control of action, and therefore in morality. But it should be said that Hume's influence has been equally great, and that contemporary ethical theory continues to be dominated by the disagreement between these two giants.

Michael Rosen's stimulating and informative *Dignity: Its History and Meaning* is about a moral idea that is important in Kant's writings and influence, though Rosen also investigates the history of the concept of dignity before Kant and its place in other systems of thought, such as Catholic moral theology and German constitutional law. Rosen is not a social psychologist but a political theorist, and his investigations are historical, institutional, and textual rather than biological and psychological. Unlike Haidt, he does not propose a general theory of morality. Yet he is trying to understand a particular moral norm that in his reading functions rather like one of Haidt's moral modules.

Article I of the U.N.'s Universal Declaration of Human Rights begins: "All human beings are born free and equal in dignity and rights." Article I of the *Grundgesetz* (Basic Law) of the Federal Republic of Germany reads:

> Human dignity is inviolable. To respect it and protect it is the duty of all state power. The German people therefore acknowledge inviolable and inalienable human rights as the basis of every community, of peace and of justice in the world.

The prominence of dignity (*Würde*) in the German text reflects not only the influence of Kant but the need to exorcise the radically antiuniversal morality of Nazism. Both texts associate dignity with rights, a point Rosen will question.

In the aristocratic past, dignity was associated with high social status. Dignity demanded respect, but it was thought to be possessed not by all human beings, but only by an elevated few. Rosen points out that the reversal of this status hierarchy, so that "the last shall be first," is an important aspect of Christian social thought. But the conversion of dignity from an exclusive to a universal elevated human status was given its secular form by Kant, whose conception of the moral community is described by John Rawls as "the aristocracy of all."[1]

Kant famously held that the only thing that is good in itself and without qualification is a good will—a will that obeys universal laws of morality that it gives to itself. It is in virtue of their capacity for morality—as both the authors and the subjects of the moral law—that humans are ends in themselves and must always be treated as such. As Kant wrote:

---

[1] John Rawls, *Lectures on the History of Moral Philosophy*, edited by Barbara Herman (Cambridge: Harvard University Press, 2000) p. 211.

Morality is the condition under which alone a rational being can be an end in itself, since only through this is it possible to be a lawgiving member in the kingdom of ends. Hence morality, and humanity insofar as it is capable of morality, is that which alone has dignity.[2]

We give ourselves the moral law by applying the categorical imperative, whose first formulation (the formula of universal law) is: "Act only in accordance with that maxim through which you can at the same time will that it become a universal law." But Rosen is primarily concerned with the interpretation of the second formulation (the formula of humanity): "So act that you treat humanity, whether in your own person or in the person of any other, always at the same time as an end, never merely as a means."

What is it to treat humanity as an end in itself, and thus to respect the dignity of all human beings? Most interpreters of Kant take both the formula of universal law and the formula of humanity as injunctions to put yourself in other people's shoes. You are to ask not just, "What shall I do?" but, "What should anyone in my position do?" and the answer comes from subjecting your conduct to standards acceptable from everyone's point of view at once, or the points of view of all those affected—suitably idealized and combined.

Setting aside the difficult question whether such a method can yield definite moral requirements, and if so, what they are, this interpretation identifies the core of Kantian morality with some form of equal consideration for all persons, as a limit on the pursuit of one's own interests—not by maximizing aggregate welfare as utilitarianism requires, but by mandating certain forms of decent treatment of each person individually. But Rosen believes that this way of understanding Kant does not do justice to what he calls the extraordinary "austerity and radicalism" of the theory. Rosen believes

[2] Immanuel Kant, *Groundwork of the Metaphysics of Morals*, Ak. 4:435.

that its driving force is not concern for others, but something quite different.

4.

Admirers of Kant have always had difficulty with some of his views that seem impossible to account for on the humanistic conception I have described. One is his notorious insistence that it is not permissible to tell a lie even to save someone from being murdered. Another is the strict prohibition against suicide, even to escape unbearable suffering. Kant holds that this would violate the requirement to treat one's humanity as an end, and not merely as a means. But why wouldn't a person who ends his life to shorten the suffering of a terminal illness be treating himself not merely as a means—by ending his life—but also as an end—to shorten his suffering? If suicide for such a reason is a failure to treat oneself as an end, then Kant must be talking about a very different kind of value, one which cannot be understood as the satisfaction of human interests.

Rosen believes that a value of precisely this kind is expressed in the idea of dignity, and in the final section of the book, he explains his understanding of this value, and confirms its independence of human interests, by finding it manifest in yet another example (not taken from Kant), the requirement that the bodies of the dead be treated with respect, indeed with dignity. Some such requirement seems to be recognized by all cultures, and to have strong emotional support. It is not for reasons of public health that we would be appalled if someone ground up a dead relative for dog food. (We are clearly in Haidt's domain of sanctity/degradation.) Rosen believes this has nothing to do with the interests of the deceased or anyone else. It is just a requirement that we not do certain things to a person's body after they have died. It is a pure duty, corresponding to no one's right, and it doesn't benefit anyone.

Rosen holds that Kant's doctrine of dignity and of moral beings as ends in themselves is fundamentally a morality of duty—duty in essence to ourselves, to conduct ourselves in certain ways. Even if some of those ways concern the treatment of others, the point is not their benefit, but our conduct. This is an exaggeration, but Rosen makes a persuasive case that it is at least part of the truth. Our duty to treat morality and humanity's moral nature as an end in itself "consists not in trying to bring that timelessly valuable thing into existence or defending it from destruction (which is both impossible and unnecessary) but in acting in ways that are appropriate toward it." The distinction between a value that gives us a reason to produce more of what has it, like the value of human happiness, and a value that gives us a reason to treat what already has it with respect, like the value of human dignity, is an important one. The first might be called benefit-value, the second status-value.

Yet I believe Rosen finds too big a gulf between the two; both are important in Kant's theory. Rosen rejects the Kantian attempt to base human rights on human dignity, saying rights are better explained in terms of the benefit-value of the human interests that rights protect. But there is an element of pure status—a value that demands respect rather than increase—in the idea of basic rights. That is why a right may not be violated in order to minimize overall right-violations: one may not murder one innocent person even to save five others from being murdered. On the other hand, Rosen's "pure duty" reading ignores the fact that Kant's moral theory explicitly requires us to advance the interests of others as part of the requirement to treat them as ends in themselves: "For the ends of any person, who is an end in himself, must as far as possible also be my end, if that conception of an end in itself is to have its full effect on me."[3]

Rosen describes the role played by the concept of dignity in contemporary legal argument, often with questionable results. He

---

[3] Ak. 4:430

discusses the French case of Manuel Wackenheim, a dwarf who was prohibited from hiring himself out for dwarf-throwing contests on the ground that this was a violation of his dignity—a judgment upheld by the French Conseil d'Etat, the European Commission on Human Rights, and the Human Rights Committee of the United Nations. Rosen observes correctly that these judgments were based on a confusion between dignity as a moral status and dignity as "dignified" bearing:

> Doesn't being treated with dignity mean that we should have the right to make our own choices about whether to behave with dignity or not? Does the state's duty to protect "the dignity of the human person" entail that it has the right to prohibit people from choosing to behave in an undignified way?

Rosen is here appealing to a general principle of individual autonomy—something very different from respect for the bodies of the dead. Other violations of dignity may need to be explained by reference to fairness, the avoidance of humiliation, privacy, or bodily integrity. Without such interpretation the concept of dignity as requiring "appropriate" or "respectful" treatment is too vague to determine any definite standards. Rosen's attempt to redeem it as an independent basis for judgment is finally unconvincing. Here as elsewhere in moral thought, intuition may be an indispensable starting point, but justified confidence about right and wrong requires more.

18

FICTIONS AND IDEALS

1.

Kwame Anthony Appiah is a writer and thinker of remarkable range. He began his academic career as an analytic philosopher of language, but soon branched out to become one of the most prominent and respected philosophical voices addressing a wide public on topics of moral and political importance, such as race, cosmopolitanism, multiculturalism, codes of honor, and moral psychology. He even took on the "Ethicist" column in the *New York Times Sunday Magazine*, and it is easy to become addicted to his incisive answers to the extraordinary variety of real-life moral questions posed by readers.

As If: Idealization and Ideals is in part a return to Appiah's earlier, more abstract and technical interests. Its theme and its title pay tribute to the work of Hans Vaihinger (1852–1933), a currently neglected German philosopher whose masterwork, published in 1911, was called *The Philosophy of 'As if'*.[1] Vaihinger contended that much of our most fruitful thought about the world, particularly in the sciences, relies on idealizations, or what he called fictions— descriptions or laws or theories that are literally false but that provide an easier and more useful way to think about certain subjects than the truth in all its complexity would. We can often learn a great

This was a review of Kwame Anthony Appiah, *As If: Idealization and Ideals* (Harvard University Press, 2017).

[1] *The Philosophy of 'As if': A System of the Theoretical, Practical and Religious Fictions of Mankind*, English translation by C. K. Ogden (New York: Harcourt, Brace, and Co., 1924).

Analytic Philosophy and Human Life. Thomas Nagel, Oxford University Press.
© Oxford University Press 2023. DOI: 10.1093/oso/9780197681671.003.0018

deal by treating a subject *as if* it conformed to a certain theory, even though we know that this is a simplification. As Vaihinger says, such fictions "provide an *instrument for finding our way about more easily in the world.*"

One of the clearest examples Vaihinger offers is Adam Smith's assumption, for purposes of economic theory, that economic agents are motivated exclusively by self-interest—that they are egoists. Smith knew perfectly well that human motivation was much richer than that, as he demonstrated in his book *The Theory of Moral Sentiments*, a work less widely known than *The Wealth of Nations*. But as Vaihinger explains:

> For the construction of his system of political economy it was essential for Adam Smith to interpret human activity causally. With unerring instinct he realized that the main cause lay in egoism and he formulated his assumption in such a way that all human actions, and particularly those of a business or politico-economical nature, could be looked upon *as if* their driving force lay in one factor—egoism. Thus all the subsidiary causes and partially conditional factors, such as good will, habit, and so forth, are here neglected. With the aid of this abstract cause Adam Smith succeeded in bringing the whole of political economy into an ordered system.

Vaihinger explored the phenomenon in a wide range of cases, from mathematics, the natural sciences, ethics, law, religion, and philosophy. Appiah's range is equally wide, but his examples are different; he gives special attention to psychology, ethics, political theory, social thought, and literature. In general he defends the value of idealization, but he is also aware of its intellectual dangers. He emphasizes that it is essential to hold on to the contrasting concept of truth, and to keep in mind both the departures from truth that idealization involves and the specific purposes for which it is useful.

Appiah has packed into this short book an impressive amount of original reflection on a number of topics, so my discussion will have to be selective. He mentions some examples from the natural sciences, but in such abbreviated form that they cannot be understood by readers who are not already familiar with the theories in question.[2] I shall discuss some cases where Appiah's analyses of idealization are more accessible.

2.

The contemporary theory of what is standardly referred to as economic rationality is descended from Adam Smith's egoistic model of economic behavior; it is based on a much more sophisticated and quantitatively precise but still idealized model of the psychology of individual choice. The modern discipline of decision theory has permitted a great increase in the exactness of what we can say about this type of human motivation—by introducing quantitative measures of subjective degrees of belief and subjective degrees of preference.

If on a cloudy day you have to decide whether or not to take an umbrella when you go out, you face four possibilities: (1) rain and umbrella; (2) no rain and umbrella; (3) rain and no umbrella; (4) no rain and no umbrella. Obviously your decision will depend both on your estimate of the likelihood of rain and how much you mind getting wet, or alternatively how much you mind carrying an umbrella when it isn't raining; but decision theory makes this more precise. It says your choice is explained by the fact that you assign a probability p between zero and one to the prospect of rain, and (ignoring misty in-between states) a probability of one minus p to

<hr>

[2] At several points he references the philosopher of science Nancy Cartwright, who explored the phenomenon in her book *How the Laws of Physics Lie* (Oxford University Press, 1983).

the prospect of no rain, and that you assign a desirability, positive or negative, to each of the possibilities (1) to (4). By multiplying the probability and the desirability for each of these outcomes, one can calculate what is called the "expected value" of each of them, and therefore the expected value of taking an umbrella and of not taking an umbrella. The rational choice is to do what has the higher expected value.[3]

Decision theory applies this kind of calculus to choices among alternatives of any complexity, with any possible assignment of subjective probabilities and desirabilities. With the help of game theory it can be extended to multi-person interactions, as in a market economy. What interests Appiah is that the theory assigns these supposed quantifiable psychological states to individuals only on the basis of an idealization. They are not discovered by asking people to report their subjective probabilities and desirabilities: in general, people do not have introspective access to these numbers. Rather, precise psychological states of this type are assigned by the theory itself, on the basis of something to which people do have access, namely their preferences or rankings (better, worse, indifferent) among alternatives.

This by itself does not imply that the states are fictional: real but unobservable underlying causes can often be inferred from observable effects. The fiction comes from the way the inference proceeds in this case. Given a sufficiently extensive set of preferences (rankings of alternatives) by an individual, it is possible, employing relatively simple laws, to assign to that individual a set of subjective probabilities and desirabilities that would account for those preferences, *if the individual were rational in the sense of the theory*. But since rationality in the sense of the theory involves such

---

[3] For example, if your subjective probability of rain is 0.4 and your subjective desirabilities for the four possibilities are + 1, -1, -6, +2, then the expected values are + 0.4, -0.6, -2.4, +1.2. This makes the expected value for you of taking an umbrella -.2 and of not taking one -1.2, so it's rational to take one.

superhuman capacities as immunity to logical error, instantaneous calculation of logical consequences, and assigning equal probability and desirability to all possibilities that are logically equivalent, it is clear that no actual humans are rational in this sense. So if we use the theory of economic rationality to think about the behavior of real human beings, we are treating them *as if* they were superrational ("Cognitive Angels," in Appiah's phrase); we are employing a useful fiction, which allows us to bring human action under quantitative laws.

The fiction is useful only for certain purposes. If it is not to lead us astray, we have to recognize the ways in which it deviates from reality, and to correct for those deviations when they make a difference that matters. This is in fact the concern of the recently developed field of behavioral economics, which tries to identify the consequences of systematic deviations of actual human behavior from the standards of classical economic rationality. (For example, people often fail to count logically equivalent possibilities as equally desirable: an outcome framed as a loss will be counted as less desirable than the same outcome framed as the absence of a gain; an outcome described in terms of the probability of death will be evaluated differently from the same outcome described in terms of the probability of survival.) Appiah's point is more general: if we try to formulate laws of human psychology, we will inevitably have to ignore a great deal of the messy complexity of actual human life. This is sometimes legitimate, provided that we recognize the idealization, and are prepared to restore the complexity when necessary—when, for example, assuming the rationality of every free market would send us off an economic cliff.

3.

Consider next a completely nontechnical type of idealization that is omnipresent in contemporary thought and discourse: racial and

sexual categories such as "Negro" and "homosexual." The thought
that someone—oneself or another—is a Negro or a homosexual has
great personal, social, and political significance in our society. Yet
in light of the actual complexity and variety of people's biological
heredity and erotic dispositions these are very crude concepts; they
do not correspond to well-defined properties or categories in the
real world. Nevertheless, Appiah says, we may find it indispensable
to employ them:

> In earlier work of my own, for example, I have argued both
> that races, strictly speaking, don't exist, and that it is wrong to
> discriminate on the basis of a person's race. This can usually be
> parsed out in a way that is not strictly inconsistent: What is wrong
> is discrimination against someone because you believe her to be,
> say, a Negro even though there are, in fact, strictly speaking, no
> Negroes. But in responding to discrimination with affirmative
> action, we find ourselves assigning people to racial categories. We
> think it justified to treat people as if they had races even when we
> officially believe that they don't.

These cases do not start out as idealizations. "Negro" and "homosexual" became important social identities because it was widely
believed that they were essential properties possessed by some
people and not others, and that they had behavioral, social, and
moral consequences. Appiah maintains that when someone who
does not share these beliefs goes on using the terms, this is not just
the verbal acknowledgment of a misguided but tenacious social illusion; it is an example of fictional thinking. We do not truly distance ourselves from these categories and perhaps should not:

> Identities, conceived of as stable features of a social ontology
> grounded in natural facts, are often . . . assumed in our moral
> thinking, even though, in our theoretical hearts, we know them
> not to be real. They are one of our most potent idealizations.

This invites the question: When are these idealizations indispensable, and when on the contrary should we resist them, by appealing to the more complex truth? Appiah addresses this and related questions with great insight in an earlier book, *The Ethics of Identity*,[4] but not here.

Appiah considers another type of idealization that he calls "counter-normative": thinking or acting as if a moral principle is true although we know it isn't. He believes we do this when we treat certain prohibitions—against murder or torture, for example—as moral absolutes. His view is that strictly, there are exceptions to any such rule, but it may be better to treat it as exceptionless. In that way we will be sure to avoid unjustified violations, without countervailing risk, since "it is remarkably unlikely that I will ever be in one of those situations where it might be that murder was permissible (and even less likely that I will ever be in one where it is required)." Appiah adds that sometimes the advantage of the fiction will depend on its acceptance not by an individual but by a community. Perhaps the strict rule against making false promises would be an example, since even if it is not universally obeyed, the general belief that it is generally accepted encourages people to trust one another.

Which moral rules one regards as fictions or idealizations will depend on what one believes to be the basis of moral truth. Appiah does not take up this large topic, but his discussion seems most consistent with the view that the ultimate standard of right and wrong is what will produce the best overall outcomes. Counter-normative fictions then become useful if we will not achieve the best overall outcomes by aiming in each case at the best overall outcome: it is better to put murder and torture entirely off the table. This is an area of perennial controversy, but those who think the prohibitions of murder, torture, and false promises have a different source, dependent on the intrinsic character of those acts rather than overall

---

[4] Princeton University Press, 2005.

outcomes, may be less prone than Appiah to attribute their strictness to idealization.

4.

Appiah concludes with a topic of great philosophical interest, that of idealization in moral theory itself. There is some possibility of confusion here, because he is talking about idealization in a sense somewhat different from that discussed so far.

Every morality is an ideal; it enjoins us to conform to standards of conduct and character that we are often tempted to violate, and it is predictable that ordinary human beings will sometimes fail to conform, even if they accept the morality as correct. This by itself does not involve idealization in Appiah's sense. The moral principles need depend on no assumptions that are not strictly true. A morality describes not how people do behave but how they should behave; and it has to assume only that they could behave in that way, even if at the moment many of them do not.

The idealization that interests Appiah occurs when political thinkers or philosophers theorize about morality. In developing their accounts, they will often imagine situations or possibilities that differ from what is true in the actual world, as an aid to evaluating moral or political hypotheses. One type of idealization consists in evaluating a moral or political principle by considering what things would be like if everyone complied with it. But as Appiah points out, this is far from decisive:

> Consider a familiar kind of dispute. One philosopher—let us call her Dr. Welfare—proposes that we should act in a way that maximizes human well-being. What could be more evident than that *this* would make for the best world? Another—Prof. Partiality—proposes instead that we should avoid harm to others in general but focus our benevolence on those to whom we have

special ties. There is every reason to doubt that this will make a world in which everyone is as well off as could be. But a world in which everyone is succeeding in complying pretty well with Prof. Partiality's prescription might be better (by standards they share) than a world where most of us are failing pretty miserably to comply with Dr. Welfare's. And given what people are actually like, one might suppose that these are the likely outcomes.

An ideal that cannot be implemented is futile. The question is, how much of a drag on moral ideals should be exercised by the stubborn facts of human psychology? How far can moral ideals ask us to transcend our self-centered human dispositions without becoming unrealistically utopian? As Appiah says,

> Some aspects of human nature have to be taken as given in normative theorizing . . . , but to take us exactly as we are would involve giving up ideals altogether. So when should we ignore, and when insist on, human nature?

I would suggest that to idealize in this context is not to ignore human nature but to regard it, rightly or wrongly, as capable of change. Only if the change is impossible or undesirable is the idealization utopian.

Appiah illustrates a different kind of reason to avoid excessive idealization with the example of immigration policy. To even pose the problem that faces us we have to take the existence of national boundaries as given, as well as the fact that some states treat their own citizens with flagrant injustice or are beset by chaos and severe deprivation. In thinking about what obligations such a situation places on stable and prosperous states, it is no use imagining a unified world without state boundaries, or a world of uniformly just states in which people are free to move from one to another. Such ideal possibilities do not tell us what we should do now, as things are.

Appiah's response relies on the idea of fortunate nations each doing their fair share toward alleviating the plight of those seeking asylum, while acknowledging that many nations probably won't meet this standard. This too is an ideal, but it doesn't depend on imagining a world very different from the actual one.

Immigration is a special case, but Appiah deploys a more general form of the argument—unsuccessfully, in my view—to criticize the structure of John Rawls's theory of justice. Rawls presents his most general principles of justice by the device of what he called "ideal theory." That is, he tries to describe the structure and functioning of a fully just or "well-ordered" society, in which "everyone is presumed to act justly and to do his part in upholding just institutions." Rawls held that ideal theory was the natural first stage in formulating principles of justice, before proceeding to a systematic treatment of the various forms of injustice and the right ways to deal with them—such as the criminal law and principles of rectification. The latter enterprise he described as "nonideal theory," and he held that it depends on the results of ideal theory.

Appiah objects that the description of a fully just society is no help with the problem we actually face, which is how to make improvements in our actual, seriously unjust society. He adds:

> The history of our collective moral learning doesn't start with the growing acceptance of a picture of an ideal society. It starts with the rejection of some current actual practice or structure, which we come to see as wrong. You learn to be in favor of equality by noticing what is wrong with unequal treatment of blacks, or women, or working-class or lower-caste people. You learn to be in favor of freedom by seeing what is wrong in the life of the enslaved or of women in purdah.

But this is misguided as a response to Rawls, whose method in moral theory is to begin precisely with intuitively obvious examples of injustice like those Appiah cites. Rawls's philosophical project is to discover general principles that give a morally illuminating account of what is wrong in those cases by showing how they deviate from the standards that we should want to govern our society. Such general principles are needed to help us judge what would be right in less obvious cases. Both levels of inquiry are essential to the systematic pursuit and philosophical understanding of justice, and the whole aim of Rawls's theory is to unite them. It is highly implausible to claim that an understanding of the general principles that would govern a fully just society will not help us to decide what kinds of social or legal or economic changes to our actual society will make it more just.

There is much more in this rich and illuminating book, including a fine discussion of our emotional response to fiction and drama. Appiah's insight is that when we feel genuine sadness at the death of Ophelia, it is not because of what Coleridge called the "willing suspension of disbelief," but because of the suspension of "the normal affective response to disbelief." We react as if we believe an unhappy young woman has died, although we do not believe it; so this is another case of idealization.

The many examples that Appiah discusses are interesting in themselves, but he also thinks they offer a larger lesson:

> Once we come to see that many of our best theories are idealizations, we will also see why our best chance of understanding the world must be to have a plurality of ways of thinking about it. This book is about why we need a multitude of pictures of the world. It is a gentle jeremiad against theoretical monism.

It isn't just that we need different theories for different aspects of the world, but that our best understanding may come from theories or models that are not strictly true, and some of which may contradict each other. This is a liberating outlook, though care must be taken not to let it become too liberating. As Appiah insists, we should not allow the plurality of useful theories to undermine our belief in the existence of the truth, leaving us with nothing but a disparate collection of stories. It is conscious deviation from the truth that makes a theory an idealization, and keeping this in mind is a condition of its value.

REALITY

19

THE CORE OF
MIND AND COSMOS

The scientific revolution of the seventeenth century, which has given rise to such extraordinary progress in the understanding of nature, depended on a crucial limiting step at the start: It depended on subtracting from the physical world as an object of study everything mental—consciousness, meaning, intention, or purpose. The physical sciences as they have developed since then describe, with the aid of mathematics, the elements of which the material universe is composed, and the laws governing their behavior in space and time.

We ourselves, as physical organisms, are part of that universe, composed of the same basic elements as everything else, and recent advances in molecular biology have greatly increased our understanding of the physical and chemical basis of life. Since our mental lives evidently depend on our existence as physical organisms, especially on the functioning of our central nervous systems, it seems natural to think that the physical sciences can in principle provide the basis for an explanation of the mental aspects of reality as well—that physics can aspire finally to be a theory of everything.

However, I believe this possibility is ruled out by the conditions that have defined the physical sciences from the beginning. The

This is a brief statement, written for *The Stone*, of positions defended more fully in my book *Mind and Cosmos: Why the Materialist Neo-Darwinian Conception of Nature Is Almost Certainly False* (Oxford University Press, 2012). The book attracted a good deal of critical attention, which is not surprising, given the entrenchment of the world view that it attacks. It seemed useful to offer a short summary of the central argument.

physical sciences can describe organisms like ourselves as parts of the objective spatio-temporal order—our structure and behavior in space and time—but they cannot describe the subjective experiences of such organisms or how the world appears to their different particular points of view. There can be a purely physical description of the neurophysiological processes that give rise to an experience, and also of the physical behavior that is typically associated with it, but such a description, however complete, will leave out the subjective essence of the experience—how it is from the point of view of its subject—without which it would not be a conscious experience at all.

So the physical sciences, in spite of their extraordinary success in their own domain, necessarily leave an important aspect of nature unexplained. Further, since the mental arises through the development of animal organisms, the nature of those organisms cannot be fully understood through the physical sciences alone. Finally, since the long process of biological evolution is responsible for the existence of conscious organisms, and since a purely physical process cannot explain their existence, it follows that biological evolution must be more than just a physical process, and the theory of evolution, if it is to explain the existence of conscious life, must become more than just a physical theory.

This means that the scientific outlook, if it aspires to a more complete understanding of nature, must expand to include theories capable of explaining the appearance in the universe of mental phenomena and the subjective points of view in which they occur—theories of a different type from any we have seen so far.

There are two ways of resisting this conclusion, each of which has two versions. The first way is to deny that the mental is an irreducible aspect of reality, either (a) by holding that the mental can be identified with some aspect of the physical, such as patterns of behavior or patterns of neural activity, or (b) by denying that the mental is part of reality at all, being some kind of illusion (but then, illusion to whom?). The second way is to deny that the mental requires a scientific explanation through some new conception of the natural order, because either (c) we can regard it as a mere fluke or accident, an unexplained extra property of certain physical organisms—or else (d) we can believe that it has an explanation, but one that belongs not to science but to theology, in other words that mind has been added to the physical world in the course of evolution by divine intervention.

All four of these positions have their adherents. I believe the wide popularity among philosophers and scientists of (a), the outlook of psychophysical reductionism, is due not only to the great prestige of the physical sciences but to the feeling that this is the best defense against the dreaded (d), the theistic interventionist outlook. But someone who finds (a) and (b) self-evidently false and (c) completely implausible need not accept (d), because a scientific understanding of nature need not be limited to a physical theory of the objective spatio-temporal order. It makes sense to seek an expanded form of understanding that includes the mental but that is still scientific—i.e., still a theory of the immanent order of nature.

That seems to me the most likely solution. Even though the theistic outlook, in some versions, is consistent with the available scientific evidence, I don't believe it, and am drawn instead to a naturalistic, though non-materialist, alternative. Mind, I suspect, is not an inexplicable accident or a divine and anomalous gift but a basic aspect of nature that we will not understand until we transcend the built-in limits of contemporary scientific orthodoxy. (I would add that even some theists might find this acceptable; since they could maintain that God is ultimately responsible for such an expanded natural order, as he is for the laws of physics.)

20

PLANTINGA ON SCIENCE AND RELIGION

1.

The gulf in outlook between atheists and adherents of the mon-
otheistic religions is profound. We are fortunate to live under
a constitutional system and a code of manners that by and large
keep it from disturbing the social peace; usually the parties ignore
each other. But sometimes the conflict surfaces and heats up into a
public debate. The present is such a time.

One of the things atheists tend to believe is that modern science
is on their side, whereas theism is in conflict with science: that, for
example, belief in miracles is inconsistent with the scientific conception of natural law; faith as a basis of belief is inconsistent with
the scientific conception of knowledge; belief that God created man
in his own image is inconsistent with scientific explanations provided by the theory of evolution. In his absorbing book, *Where the
Conflict Really Lies*, Alvin Plantinga, a distinguished analytic philosopher known for his contributions to metaphysics and theory
of knowledge as well as to the philosophy of religion, turns this alleged opposition on its head. His overall claim is that "there is superficial conflict but deep concord between science and theistic
religion, but superficial concord and deep conflict between science

This was a review of Alvin Plantinga, *Where the Conflict Really Lies: Science, Religion,
and Naturalism* (Oxford University Press, 2011).

and naturalism." By naturalism he means the view that the world describable by the natural sciences is all that exists, and that there is no such person as God, or anything like God.

Plantinga's religion is the real thing, not just an intellectual deism that gives God nothing to do in the world. He himself is an evangelical Protestant, but he conducts his argument with respect to a version of Christianity that is the "rough intersection of the great Christian creeds"—ranging from the Apostle's Creed to the Anglican Thirty-Nine Articles—according to which God is a person who not only created and maintains the universe and its laws, but also intervenes specially in the world, with the miracles related in the Bible and in other ways. It is of great interest to be presented with a lucid and sophisticated account of how someone who holds these beliefs understands them to harmonize with and indeed to provide crucial support for the methods and results of the natural sciences.

Plantinga discusses many topics in the course of the book, but his most important claims are epistemological. He holds, first, that the theistic conception of the relation between God, the natural world, and ourselves makes it reasonable for us to regard our perceptual and rational faculties as reliable. It is therefore reasonable to believe that the scientific theories they allow us to create do describe reality. He holds, second, that the naturalistic conception of the world, and of ourselves as products of unguided Darwinian evolution, makes it unreasonable for us to believe that our cognitive faculties are reliable, and therefore unreasonable to believe any theories they may lead us to form, including the theory of evolution. In other words, belief in naturalism combined with belief in evolution is self-defeating. However, Plantinga thinks we can reasonably believe that we are the products of evolution provided we also believe, contrary to naturalism, that the process was in some way guided by God.

2.

I shall return to the claim about naturalism below, but let me first say more about the theistic conception. Plantinga contends, as others have, that it is no accident that the scientific revolution occurred in Christian Europe and nowhere else. Its great figures, such as Copernicus and Newton, believed that God had created a law-governed natural order and created humans in his image, with faculties that allowed them to discover that order by using perception and reason. That use of perception and reason is what defines the empirical sciences. But what about the theistic belief itself? It is obviously not a scientific result. How can it be congruent with a scientific understanding of nature?

Here we must turn to Plantinga's general theory of knowledge, which is crucial to understanding his position. Any theory of human knowledge must give an account of what he calls "warrant," i.e., the conditions that a true belief must meet in order to constitute knowledge. Sometimes we know something to be true on the basis of evidence provided by other beliefs, or because we see that it is entailed by our other beliefs. But not every belief can depend on other beliefs. The buck has to stop somewhere, and according to Plantinga this happens when we form beliefs in one of the ways that he calls "basic."

The basic belief-forming capacities include perception, memory, rational intuition (about logic and arithmetic), induction, and some more specialized faculties, such as the ability to detect the mental states of others. When you look in the refrigerator and see that it contains several bottles of beer, you form that belief immediately without inferring it from any other belief, e.g., a belief about the pattern of shapes and colors in your visual field. When someone asks you whether you have had lunch yet, you can answer immediately because you remember having had lunch, and the memory is a belief not based on any other belief, or on perception, or on logical reasoning.

Beliefs that are formed in the basic way are not infallible: they may have to be given up in the face of contrary evidence. But they do not have to be supported by other evidence in order to be warranted—otherwise knowledge could never get started. And the general reliability of each of these unmediated types of belief-formation cannot be shown by appealing to any of the others:

> Rational intuition enables us to know the truths of mathematics and logic, but it can't tell us whether or not perception is reliable. Nor can we show by rational intuition and perception that memory is reliable, nor (of course) by perception and memory that rational intuition is.

But what then is the warrant for beliefs formed in one of these basic ways? Plantinga holds that the main condition is that they must result from the proper functioning of a faculty that is in fact generally reliable. We cannot prove without circularity that the faculties of perception, memory, or reason are generally reliable, but *if* they are, then the true beliefs we form when they are functioning properly constitute knowledge unless they are put in doubt by counterevidence.[1] Human knowledge is therefore dependent on facts about our relation to the world that we cannot prove from scratch: we can't prove the existence of the physical world, or the reality of the past, or the existence of logical and mathematical truth; but if our faculties do in fact connect with these aspects of reality, then we can know about them, according to Plantinga's theory.

For example, if our perceptual beliefs are in general caused by the impact on our senses of objects and events in the environment corresponding to what is believed, and if memories are in general caused by traces in the brain laid down by events in the past

---

[1] The details are complicated, and are set out in Plantinga's three-volume magnum opus, *Warrant: The Current Debate* and *Warrant and Proper Function* (both, Oxford University Press, 1993) and *Warranted Christian Belief* (Oxford University Press, 2000).

212 ANALYTIC PHILOSOPHY AND HUMAN LIFE

corresponding to what those memories represent, then perception and memory are reliable faculties, which can give us knowledge even though we cannot prove they are reliable.

So far we are in the territory of traditional epistemology; but what about faith? Faith, according to Plantinga, is another basic way of forming beliefs, distinct from but not in competition with reason, perception, memory, and the others. However, it is

> a wholly different kettle of fish: according to the Christian tradition (including both Thomas Aquinas and John Calvin), faith is a special gift from God, not part of our ordinary epistemic equipment. Faith is a source of belief, a source that goes beyond the faculties included in reason.

God endows human beings with a *sensus divinitatis* that ordinarily leads them to believe in him. (In atheists the *sensus divinitatis* is either blocked or not functioning properly.)[2] In addition, God acts in the world more selectively, by "enabling Christians to see the truth of the central teachings of the gospel."

If all this is true, then by Plantinga's standard of reliability and proper function, faith is a kind of cause that provides a warrant for theistic belief, even though it is a gift, and not a universal human faculty. (Plantinga recognizes that rational arguments have also been offered for the existence of God, but he thinks it is not necessary to rely on these, any more than it is necessary to rely on rational proofs of the existence of the external world to know just by looking that there is beer in the refrigerator.)

It is illuminating to have the starkness of the opposition between Plantinga's theism and the secular outlook so clearly explained. My instinctively atheistic perspective implies that if I ever found myself flooded with the conviction that what the Nicene Creed says is true,

---

[2] This is often the result of sin, though not necessarily the sin of the unbeliever; see Plantinga, *Warranted Christian Belief*, p. 214.

the most likely explanation would be that I was losing my mind, not that I was being granted the gift of faith. From Plantinga's point of view, by contrast, I suffer from a kind of spiritual blindness from which I am unwilling to be cured. This is a huge epistemological gulf, and it cannot be overcome by the cooperative employment of the cognitive faculties that we share, as is the hope with scientific disagreements.

Faith adds beliefs to the theist's base of available evidence that are absent from the atheist's, and unavailable to him without God's special action. These differences make different beliefs reasonable given the same shared evidence. An atheist familiar with biology and medicine has no reason to believe the biblical story of the resurrection. But a Christian who believes it by faith should not, according to Plantinga, be dissuaded by general biological evidence. Plantinga compares the difference in justified beliefs to a case where you are accused of a crime on the basis of very convincing evidence, but you know that you didn't do it. For you, the immediate evidence of your memory is not defeated by the public evidence, even though your memory is not available to others. Likewise, the Christian's faith in the truth of the Gospels, though unavailable to the atheist, is not defeated by the secular evidence against the possibility of resurrection.

Of course sometimes contrary evidence may be strong enough to persuade you that your memory is deceiving you. Something analogous can occasionally happen with beliefs based on faith, but it will typically take the form, according to Plantinga, of a change in interpretation of what the Bible means. This tradition of interpreting scripture in light of scientific knowledge goes back to Augustine, who applied it to the "days" of creation. But Plantinga even suggests in a footnote that those whose faith includes, as his does not, the conviction that the biblical chronology of creation is to be taken literally can for that reason regard the evidence to the contrary as systematically misleading. One would think that this is a consequence of his epistemological views that he would hope to avoid.

3.

We all have to recognize that we have not created our own minds, and must rely on the way they work. Theists and naturalists differ radically over what justifies such reliance. Plantinga is certainly right that if one believes it, the theistic conception explains beautifully why science is possible: the fit between the natural order and our minds is produced intentionally by God. He is also right to maintain that naturalism has a much harder time accounting for that fit. Once the question is raised, atheists have to consider whether their view of how we got here makes it at all probable that our cognitive faculties should enable us to discover the laws of nature.

Plantinga argues that on the naturalist view of evolution, interpreted materialistically, there would be no reason to think that our beliefs have any relation to the truth. On that view beliefs are states of the brain, and natural selection favors brain mechanisms solely on the basis of their contribution, via behavior, to survival and reproduction. The content of our beliefs, and hence their truth or falsehood, is irrelevant to their survival value. "Natural selection is interested, not in truth, but in appropriate behavior."

Plantinga's version of this argument suffers from lack of attention to naturalist theories of mental content—i.e., theories about what makes a particular brain state the belief that it is, in virtue of which it can be true or false. Most naturalists would hold that there is an intimate connection between the content of a belief and its role in controlling an organism's behavioral interaction with the world. To oversimplify: they might hold, for example, that a state of someone's brain constitutes the belief that there is a dangerous animal in front of him if it is a state generally caused by encounters with bears, rattlesnakes, etc., and which generally causes flight or other defensive behavior. This is the basis for the widespread conviction that evolutionary naturalism makes it probable that our perceptual beliefs, and those formed by basic deductive and inductive inference, are in general reliable.

Still, when our faculties lead us to beliefs vastly removed from those our distant ancestors needed to survive—as in the recent production and assessment of evidence for the existence of the Higgs boson—Plantinga's skeptical argument remains powerful. Christians, says Plantinga, can "take modern science to be a magnificent display of the image of God in us human beings." Can naturalists say anything to match this, or must they regard it as an unexplained mystery?

Most of Plantinga's book is taken up with systematic discussion, deploying his epistemology, of more specific claims about how science conflicts with, or supports, religion. He addresses Richard Dawkins's claim that evolution reveals a world without design; Michael Behe's claim that on the contrary it reveals the working of intelligent design; the claim that the laws of physics are incompatible with miracles; the claim of evolutionary and social psychologists that the functional explanation of moral and religious beliefs shows that there are no objective moral or religious truths; the idea that historical biblical criticism makes it unreasonable to regard the Bible as the word of God; and the idea that the fine-tuning of the basic physical constants, whose precise values make life possible, is evidence of a creator. He touches on the problem of evil, and though he offers possible responses, he also remarks, "Suppose God does have a good reason for permitting sin and evil, pain and suffering: why think we would be the first to know what it is?"

About evolution, Plantinga argues persuasively that the most that can be shown (by Dawkins, for example) on the basis of the available evidence together with some highly speculative further assumptions is that we cannot rule out the possibility that the living world was produced by unguided evolution and hence without design. He believes the alternative hypothesis of guided evolution, with God causing appropriate mutations and fostering their survival, would make the actual result much more probable. On the other hand, though he believes Michael Behe offers a serious challenge to the prevailing naturalist picture of evolution, he does not think Behe's arguments for intelligent design are conclusive, and he notes that in any case they don't support Christian belief, and perhaps not even theism, because Behe intentionally says so little about the designer.

Plantinga holds that miracles are not incompatible with the laws of physics, because those laws determine only what happens in closed systems, without external intervention, and the proposition that the physical universe is a closed system is not itself a law of physics, but a naturalist assumption. Newton did not believe it: he even believed that God intervened to keep the planets in their orbits. Plantinga has a lengthy discussion of the relation of miracles to quantum theory: its probabilistic character, he believes, may allow not only miracles but human free will. And he considers the different interpretations that have been given to fine-tuning of the physical constants, concluding that the support it offers for theism is modest, because of the difficulty of assigning probabilities to the alternatives. All these discussions make a serious effort to engage with the data of current science. The arguments are often ingenious and, given Plantinga's premises, the overall view is thorough and consistent.

The interest of the book, especially for secular readers, is its presentation from the inside of the point of view of a philosophically subtle and scientifically informed theist—an outlook with which many of them will not be familiar. Plantinga writes clearly and accessibly, and sometimes acidly—in response to aggressive critics of religion like Dawkins and Daniel Dennett. His comprehensive stand is a valuable contribution to this debate.

I say this as someone who cannot imagine believing what he believes. But even those who cannot accept the theist alternative should admit that Plantinga's criticisms of naturalism are directed at the deepest problem with that view—how it can account for the appearance, through the operation of the laws of physics and chemistry, of conscious beings like ourselves, capable of discovering those laws and understanding the universe that they govern. Defenders of naturalism have not ignored this problem, but I believe that so far, even with the aid of evolutionary theory, they have not proposed a credible solution. Perhaps theism and materialist naturalism are not the only alternatives.

21

IS METAPHYSICS POSSIBLE?

The aim of metaphysics is to discover, in the most general terms, what the world is really like. A major part of the project is to determine what kinds of things exist or are the case independently of our responses and beliefs, and what kinds of things or facts have no existence apart from our responses. For example, a common metaphysical view is that physical facts are independent of human responses, but values are not. The "Mona Lisa" has a surface area of so many square centimeters. It is also very beautiful. The former is a truth about that object that does not depend on the response of human observers, but many people would say that the latter, if it is a truth at all, is a truth that depends on our aesthetic response to the painting.

Such a division between what is real independently of us and what is not seems natural, and the project of discovering which of the things we believe fall on either side of the line seems an entirely legitimate way to try to deepen our understanding of the world and our relation to it. But in his elegant, rigorous, and deeply original book *Engagement and Metaphysical Dissatisfaction* Barry Stroud argues that the project cannot be carried out, because we are too immersed in the system of concepts that we hope to subject to metaphysical assessment. This "prevents us from finding enough distance between our conception of the world and the world it is meant to be a conception of to allow for an appropriately impartial metaphysical verdict on the relation between the two."

This was a review of Barry Stroud, *Engagement and Metaphysical Dissatisfaction: Modality and Value* (Oxford University Press, 2011).

Stroud believes that we cannot succeed in reaching either a positive (often called "realist") or a negative ("antirealist") metaphysical verdict about a number of basic conceptions—that we cannot show either that they succeed in describing the way the world is independent of our responses, or that they fail to do so. He argues for this claim in detail with respect to three of the most fundamental and philosophically contested concepts: causality, necessity, and value. The argument has a general and powerful form. Stroud contends that the use of the very concepts being assessed, and judgments of the very kind being questioned, play an indispensable part in the metaphysical reasoning that is supposed to lead to our conclusions about those concepts and beliefs. If the conclusion is negative, our accepting it is inconsistent with the thoughts we have gone through in order to reach it. If the conclusion is positive, it is undermined by the antecedent unavoidability of our acceptance of the beliefs it endorses.

Stroud emphasizes that the inconsistency in the case of a negative verdict is of a special kind: although we cannot consistently arrive at such a verdict, it could nevertheless be true. In this respect it is like the inconsistency of saying, "I believe it is raining but it isn't." It is perfectly possible for someone to believe that it is raining when it isn't, but it is not possible for him to judge that that is so. This is known as Moore's paradox, after the philosopher G. E. Moore, who identified it. Stroud points out that if the impossibility of reaching a negative metaphysical verdict about our beliefs is of this kind, it does not support the alternative of a positive metaphysical verdict. All that has been shown is that we cannot consistently believe the negative verdict, and that doesn't mean it isn't true.

Most of the book is taken up with detailed application of this strategy to the major categories of causality, necessity, and value, but Stroud begins with a simpler example: the familiar adage about "beauty lying in the eye of the beholder." This is a negative metaphysical verdict because it says that the world does not really contain any objects that have a property of being beautiful or more beautiful than other objects. More precisely, it says that no objects have any such property independently of all "beholders'" responses to them.

But what would it mean to really believe this hackneyed thought? Would it mean giving up all judgments of beauty, and ceasing to believe, for example, that *The Marriage of Figaro* is more beautiful than "God Save the Queen"? Perhaps we could give up such judgments and replace them with expressions of personal aesthetic response that we acknowledged to be subjective. Or perhaps we could conclude that our judgments of beauty had really been nothing more than such expressions all along, so that they did not have to be revised or given up. (That would be the reductionist solution, which Stroud says probably distorts the understanding of our thoughts, in an effort to preserve their truth.)

A further question is how we could establish the negative metaphysical conclusion. It would require some conception of what the world is really like, independent of our responses, and the discovery that beauty is not to be found in that world. But it would not be enough simply to exclude beauty from the world at the outset. Instead, we would have to start out from everything we believe, and then arrive somehow at a more austere conception of reality that has the power to override our ordinary judgments of beauty and force us either to abandon or to revise them. Metaphysics, as Stroud says, has to be done "from within."

Stroud is uncertain whether such conclusions are possible even in the case of beauty. But he argues forcefully that they are not available for judgments of causality, necessity, and value. Those concepts, he contends, are irreducible, they cannot be abandoned, and they are indispensable for metaphysical thought.

Both causality and necessity are modal concepts: this means that they have to do not just with what actually happens in the world, but with what could happen or be the case, what must happen or be the case, and what would follow if things were different from the way they actually are. For example, "If I had let go of the plate, it would have dropped to the floor," is a counterfactual conditional that expresses a causal necessity, due to the law of gravity. It is because modal statements like this don't describe what actually happens that many philosophers have found them puzzling. What in the world could make such statements true, if not the concrete things and events of which the natural world consists? Possibilities, counterfactuals about what would have happened in other conditions, and the necessities from which those counterfactuals follow, all seem to have a much more ethereal and problematic reality.

That suggests an alternative, antirealist view, according to which such statements do not say what is true of the world outside of our minds, but reflect instead our responses or expectations. We impose or project causal and absolute necessities and possibilities onto the world rather than finding them there. Contemporary versions of this view are descended from Hume's claim that we never perceive anything causing anything else: All we see, for example, is one billiard ball hitting another followed by the second one moving: we do not see the first event *necessitating* the second. But the experience of seeing such sequences regularly sets up a pattern of expectation in our minds, which we project onto the external world as a judgment of causal necessity and natural law.

The idea that only what actually happens is real is remarkably seductive, but Stroud makes a convincing case that it collapses into incoherence if one tries to think it through. The belief in real causal dependence between things or states of affairs cannot be eliminated from our thoughts. We see it already in the statement of the antirealist view on causality itself. It is said that our perception of patterns of regularity in the external world produces a corresponding pattern of expectations in us, so that seeing the first billiard ball hit the second makes us expect the second to move. But there are two causal statements here: the regularity in the external world causes a corresponding regularity in the mind; and because of that regularity, a new perception causes the corresponding expectation. Furthermore, the idea of a world of independent, enduring objects with which we are in perceptual contact is itself saturated with causal beliefs.

One could avoid this problem if, like Hume, one held that all we really perceive are our fleeting sense impressions, and not external physical objects, which are also projections from our minds. But most latter-day followers of Hume on causation do not follow him in this: they are thorough-going realists about physical things and physical facts, whose existence independent of our minds is taken to be uncontroversial.

Another problem is how to apply the antirealist interpretation to our belief that there are many causal connections that neither we nor any other persons will ever be aware of. It is no good to say that these are instances of actual correlations that would lead people to form corresponding expectations if they observed them, because, as Stroud says, "this makes essential use of the very idea of counterfactual or law-like modality that was to have been explained."

One response to these problems with an antirealist view is to propose a reductionist analysis of causal statements, according to which their truth involves nothing beyond the actual regularities that occur in the world. But Stroud objects that this ignores the distinction between correlations that "just happen" to hold in the world and those that hold with a different or stronger modality. A pure regularity entails its instances but does not explain them. It is only if we take a regularity to be due to some kind of necessity that it supports belief about what would happen in other cases.

Seeing more and more objects passing relentlessly along a conveyor belt and finding all of them so far to be red (or to cost less than $50), we do not thereby get better and better reason to believe that all objects still to come along the belt will be red (or will cost less than \$50), or even that the next one will be, if we know or believe nothing involving any stronger or distinctive modality about what those objects are or where they come from or how they got there.

Stroud also examines and responds with care to the sophisticated neo-Humean projectivist view called quasi-realism, which is defended by Simon Blackburn. According to that view, we can continue to maintain all of our causal beliefs while acknowledging that they are projections of our attitudes onto a world that contains only actual successions of events, and no mind-independent causal necessity. Stroud argues that quasi-realism both fails to give a plausible reading of our ordinary causal beliefs and cannot avoid relying on mind-independent causal claims of the kind it professes to abjure:

> I think this . . . inconsistency cannot be avoided by any version of
> "projectivism"; the whole point of that theory is to give a causal
> explanation of our causal beliefs without holding that there is anything in the independent world answering to their contents.

In sum, we cannot consistently arrive at a negative metaphysical verdict about causal necessity or the individual causal and conditional statements that depend on it. We cannot dispense with or suspend that way of thinking, even in the course of metaphysical reflection about the relation of our causal beliefs to the reality outside our minds. But the impossibility of arriving at such a conclusion does not prove that it is false—only that we can't consistently believe it. So there is no satisfactory metaphysical conclusion to be had: we are stuck inside our way of thinking.

The basic elements of Stroud's discussion of causality—the unavoidability of the conception in question, both in ordinary life and in metaphysical reasoning itself, the failures of both projectivism and reductionism, and the impossibility of reaching either a negative or a positive metaphysical verdict—characterize the failure of the metaphysical project for all of the concepts Stroud takes up in this book. His next target is strict or absolute necessity, of the kind found in logic or mathematics. Perhaps it is logically possible that there could be a world in which a different law of gravitation held, so that causal necessities and counterfactuals regarding the behavior of bodies were different; but it is not in any way possible that there should be a world in which something that is red and round is not round, or in which $7 + 5$ is not equal to 12. Those are absolute necessities, which seem to hold independently not only of our beliefs and attitudes but of any other contingent truths.

Yet the philosophical temptation to deny that statements of logic really capture mind-independent truths about the world has been very powerful. The very fact of their necessity seems to create a problem: if nothing about the world could make it false that whatever is red and round is round, so that it is true whatever is the case, it doesn't seem to say anything at all. Nothing makes it true. Another problem is that necessary truths are typically known a *priori*—by pure thought rather than by observation. But how can finite creatures like us hope to find within ourselves the resources to establish truths that hold necessarily and universally in all possible worlds?

Questions like these have led repeatedly to attempts to place the source of apparent necessary truths in ourselves—explaining them in terms of the meanings of words, or other conventions of language, or in terms of our inability to avoid certain forms of thought, for example that any alternative to $7 + 5 = 12$ is inconceivable to us. Stroud's reply, in brief, is that all response-dependent interpretations of necessity fall into the incoherence of asserting that necessary truths depend on something that might not have been the case. This kind of "explanation" simply denies that they are necessarily true.

But the main problem is that we can't think at all without thinking that some things necessarily follow from or are inconsistent with other things. In particular, we can't even argue for the conclusion that nothing really holds with necessity in the independent world, without depending on such logical reasoning. The arguments needed to arrive at a negative metaphysical verdict about necessity are inconsistent with its conclusion.

Stroud's final topic is value, in which he includes not only moral judgments of right and wrong, but all judgments about reasons for and against doing or believing anything, so that value judgments are involved in thought as well as in action. As he says, the antirealist view is especially prevalent in this case.

> There is no question that we all have evaluative attitudes like this, and perhaps that we could not live without them. But there is a very widespread and firmly held metaphysical conviction that what those attitudes are concerned with—what is good or best for someone to do or what there is reason in favor of or against doing—depends always on the wants or desires or feelings or other attitudes of some or all of the people involved.

The classical source of this view was again Hume. One of his arguments was that value judgments are capable of motivating action, and mere beliefs, without the help of some desire, sentiment, or "passion," are incapable of motivating. Stroud replies that this is a misinterpretation of how reasons for action work. A competent practical reasoner just is someone with a settled general disposition to do things on the basis of what he takes to be reasons to do them, without the need for some further motive or desire prompting him to do what he believes he has a reason to do. In this respect practical reasoning is like the reasoning that leads to the formation of beliefs. If someone believes that p, and that if p then q, he draws the conclusion that q in virtue of his settled disposition to form beliefs in accordance with the law of logic called *modus ponens*, and not because he has a further motivation, or even belief, that gets him to do it.

Similarly, when someone helps a friend in distress, we can say that he wants to relieve the friend's distress, but it is the distress itself, and not his wanting to relieve it, that is the source of his reason for action. He wants to help because he recognizes distress as a reason to help and is the kind of person who is moved to act by the recognition of reasons.

Ordinary intentional action, and ordinary belief formed on the basis of evidence, cannot be understood apart from the recognition of reasons that do not depend on one's attitudes or desires. This is true even when the aim of the action is to satisfy a desire. When I buy a drink because I am thirsty, it is because I recognize that the fact that it will quench my thirst is a reason to buy a drink, and that judgment is not based on a further desire.

Stroud's general point is that the metaphysical project is doomed because it begins with an unsustainable separation between ourselves and our thoughts, on the one hand, and the world, on the other. Because we are parts of the world, in thinking about ourselves and our relation to the rest of the world we cannot avoid thinking the kinds of thoughts whose relation to reality we are putting into question.

We cannot even understand the existence of persons who have beliefs about causality, necessity, and value without engaging in judgments of causality, necessity, and value. We understand people's beliefs as *caused* in large part by their interaction with the world they perceive. We cannot make sense of the idea of a thinker who never believes that a certain thought he entertains could, or must, be true if a certain other thought is true. And accepting value judgments to the effect that something is a reason to do or believe something is completely indispensable both in thinking or acting ourselves and in understanding others as thinkers or agents.

That we cannot consistently arrive at a negative metaphysical verdict on these inescapable judgments does not prove that they are true. But it means that there is a kind of higher-order assessment of them that we cannot reach, however much we may yearn for it.

Has Stroud blocked all the exits? I believe there may be room for a partial escape in the domain of value, because it combines reasons for action with reasons for belief. Realism about reasons for belief seems unavoidable in any process of thought, including the thought that leads to metaphysical conclusions. But realism about reasons for action, while it is equally embedded in our lives, might be separated off as a kind of thought that is not directly involved in drawing the metaphysical conclusion that such reasons or values ultimately "depend on our attitudes." We might, then, be able to suspend or detach from such judgments for purposes of metaphysical inquiry (though of course they would be involved in the decision to undertake such an inquiry), just as we might be able to suspend judgments of beauty to ask whether beauty lies in the eye of the beholder. The issue is whether there is a sufficient core of purely "intellectual" norms to permit metaphysical criticism of the rest of the domain of value. If so, that would be compatible with either a positive or a negative metaphysical verdict.

But there is a deeper question about Stroud's general position. Why isn't the demonstrable impossibility of reaching a negative metaphysical verdict tantamount to a positive metaphysical verdict on the concept in question? Stroud says that the negative verdict could still be true though we couldn't consistently arrive at it. But these cases are not like the inconsistency of "I believe it is raining but it isn't." Even though I can't consistently believe that conjunction, I can perfectly well conceive of its being true. But if I accept Stroud's argument that I can't consistently arrive at the conclusion that logical necessity depends on my responses, I am left with all my logical convictions at full strength. I cannot conceive of the possibility that he thinks is left open: that although I cannot help believing that they are true independent of my responses, they are not. Perhaps realism about the things we can't help believing is the default position after antirealism has been excluded as an option.

These are speculative responses. Even if Stroud's proof of the impossibility of metaphysics is not complete, it is very unsettling.

22
CREATORS OF
THE MODERN MIND

1.

It is fascinating to learn about the concrete historical circumstances under which great philosophical works—works that have become timeless classics—were produced, and about the relation to their own times of the extraordinary individuals who produced them. For those with limited first-hand knowledge of the works this biographical approach can serve as an accessible introduction to the thought of some of the most important creators of our intellectual world. Anthony Gottlieb, a former executive editor of *The Economist* who is not a philosopher but a philosophical enthusiast, is writing just such a history of the entire course of Western philosophy. The first volume, *The Dream of Reason*, took the story from ancient Greece to the Renaissance. The second volume, *The Dream of Enlightenment*, ends in the eighteenth century; a third volume will take us from Kant to the present day.

Gottlieb concentrates most of his discussion in *The Dream of Enlightenment* on six philosophers of the seventeenth and eighteenth centuries whose stature and influence are especially great—Descartes, Hobbes, Spinoza, Locke, Leibniz, and Hume—along with shorter treatments of Bayle, Voltaire, and Rousseau, and brief comments on many other figures. Here is what he says at the outset:

This was a review of Anthony Gottlieb, *The Dream of Enlightenment: The Rise of Modern Philosophy* (Liveright, 2016).

Analytic Philosophy and Human Life. Thomas Nagel, Oxford University Press.
© Oxford University Press 2023. DOI: 10.1093/oso/9780197681671.003.0022

It is because they still have something to say to us that we can easily get these philosophers wrong. It is tempting to think that they speak our language and live in our world. But to understand them properly, we must step back into their shoes. That is what this book tries to do.

Gottlieb exaggerates the intellectual distance of these figures from us: it isn't that they speak our language, but that we speak *their* language, because our world has been significantly formed by them. And he does not always succeed in stepping back into their shoes, which in the case of a great philosopher means understanding his thoughts from the inside, as well as in relation to his historical milieu. Nevertheless Gottlieb's biographical narrative is vivid and often illuminating. Most important, he emphasizes throughout that these men lived in a historical period dominated by dramatic developments and conflicts in three areas—science, religion, and politics—and that their thoughts and writings were dominated by the need to respond to those developments, and to understand the relations among them.

First, there was the scientific revolution, which introduced a new way of understanding the physical world through universal laws, mathematically formulated, that govern everything that happens in space and time. Although knowledge of those laws is based on observation and experiment, the reality they describe is not directly available to human perception, but can be known only by theoretical inference. Two of Gottlieb's thinkers, Descartes and Leibniz, were major contributors to the mathematical sciences—Descartes through the creation of analytic geometry (hence the term "Cartesian coordinates") and Leibniz through the invention of the calculus (which was created independently by Newton). Descartes also produced theories of mechanics, optics, and physiology, Leibniz made significant contributions to dynamics, and Spinoza worked in optics and conducted experiments in hydrodynamics and metallurgy. But all six grappled with the question of how the austere physical reality revealed by the new science is related to the familiar world that we perceive—and to our minds, in which both perception and scientific reasoning take place.

Second, after the Reformation and the terrible wars of religion it had become clear that the plurality of religious beliefs in Christendom was not going to disappear. This posed questions both about the grounds for religious belief and about how governments should choose between imposing a single orthodoxy and tolerating diversity. In addition, each of these philosophers had to be concerned about the relation of his own work to the religious orthodoxy of his community, and about the dangers of ostracism, repression, or persecution. Descartes was deterred by the condemnation of Galileo from publishing his cosmological theories, and Spinoza was excommunicated by the Jewish community of Amsterdam.

Third, the basis of legitimate political authority was coming seriously into question, with skepticism about the divine right of kings and support for the right of subjects to overthrow a ruler who abused his power. This was not just theoretical: it took concrete form in the English Civil War that culminated with the execution of Charles I in 1649 and the Glorious Revolution that replaced James II with William of Orange in 1688. Hobbes, Spinoza, Locke, Hume, and Rousseau all produced theories of political authority starting from the subject's rather than the ruler's point of view.

2.

The metaphysical and epistemological problems that arose out of the scientific revolution are particularly difficult and abstract, and the responses of these thinkers are among the most formidable structures that philosophy has produced. They were concerned, as philosophers have always been, to understand the nature of reality in the broadest sense: what kinds of things and facts ultimately constitute everything there is. They were also concerned with whether we humans have the capacity to discover the answers to those questions, and if not, what limits to our knowledge are imposed by our finite human faculties. The advances of the scientific revolution gave these problems a new form.

Given how much he has to cover, Gottlieb does a pretty good job of summarizing the complex speculative responses of his philosophers. They are contributions to a collective intellectual inquiry that has continued ever since, and their value lies in working out some of the main alternative possibilities for making the most general sense of reality. Others can then explore, refine, and elaborate those proposals, and attempt to refute or defend them, or at least to evaluate their relative plausibility. I will confine myself— with apologies for the capsule presentation—to one metaphysical example, the mind-body problem, which grew directly out of the scientific revolution and is very much still with us.

The problem arose because the new mathematical conception of physical reality dehumanized it. Among other things, it left out all the rich qualitative aspects, such as color, smell, taste, and sound, with which the world appears to our senses. These so-called "secondary" qualities were interpreted as effects on our minds, as opposed to the geometrically describable so-called "primary" qualities like shape, size, and motion, which are features of the physical world as it is in itself, independent of our minds.

The question was: How complete an account of the nature of reality could the new physical science in principle provide? Do our minds necessarily escape its reach, even if our bodies are part of the physical world? Hobbes gave the most radically materialist answer to this question, holding not only that we, with all our thoughts and perceptions, are nothing but matter in motion, but that even God is a physical being. A scientifically updated version of this view— with mechanics replaced by quantum theory, molecular biology, and neuroscience, and God eliminated from the picture—is the dominant form of contemporary naturalism. It holds that physics can aspire to be the theory of everything.

But in different ways, the others took mind to be an aspect of reality not captured by physical theory. Descartes, famously, was a dualist, who believed there were two fundamental types of things: matter, which was extended in space, and mind, which was non-spatial and capable of thought and perception, but also in the case of human beings intimately linked during life to a material body. Spinoza, in contrast, believed that there was only one type of thing, but that it had different aspects. Gottlieb explains:

> For example, if we want to describe some piece of human be- havior, we may focus either on the psychological state of the person concerned—i.e., on what he thinks, feels and desires— or else on his physical state—i.e., on what is happening inside his brain and other parts of his body. According to Spinoza, these are merely alternative ways of describing the same chain of events; they are explanations of one thing from two different perspectives.

And while Descartes believed God, the divine mind, was separate from the physical world, Spinoza believed that God and Nature were not two distinct things but two aspects of one thing, and that this entity—God or Nature—was in fact the only independently existing reality, of which we and everything else were merely de- pendent features.

Leibniz, the polar opposite of Hobbes, believed that mind, not matter, was fundamental, and that reality consisted of an infinite number of beings he called monads—with different perceptual perspectives, each of which represents the entire universe with more or less clarity. Matter exists within these perspectives, but not independently of them. God, the supreme monad, created our world out of all the logically possible worlds by creating the

perspectives of a coordinated but noninteracting set of monads—
including ourselves—in whose perceptions the history of this
world is reflected.

The view that mind is the basis of all reality is known as idealism,
and though it was dominant in the nineteenth and early twentieth centuries, it is not now a common view among philosophers.
Materialism is for the moment in the ascendant. However, there is
some support for dualism, not in the form proposed by Descartes,
with a separable soul, but as the view that mental phenomena involve additional non-physical events associated with the neural
states of animal organisms—and also for dual aspect theories of
the type Spinoza favored, according to which the mental and the
physical are distinct but inseparable aspects of a single more basic
reality.

Commenting on Leibniz's belief that only monads have absolute reality, Gottlieb says, "Nowadays, philosophers do not have
much use for talk of what is absolutely real. Something either exists
or it doesn't, and there are no halfway houses." This is completely
wrong. The term "absolute" may not be in vogue, but a great deal
of philosophy nowadays is occupied with what is fundamental—
i.e., not analyzable in terms of anything else—and what by contrast
is dependent on and grounded in something more fundamental.
Whether mind has an independent reality that is irreducible to
the physical, and whether ethics, logic, probability, necessity, and
causality are real in themselves or are mind-dependent, as Leibniz
thought matter was, are central questions of contemporary philosophical debate.

3.

In contrast with these four bold metaphysicians Gottlieb finds
Locke refreshingly agnostic on the relation of mind and matter:

While Descartes, and indeed most other thinkers, maintained—
at least in public—that it was impossible for mere matter to think,
Locke could see no reason why God could not create purely physical beings who had the power of thought. We simply don't know
enough to decide whether or not such a thing is possible.

This brings out an important difference between Locke (and
Hume) on the one hand, and Descartes, Spinoza, and Leibniz on
the other: a difference in their views of the grounds of our knowledge of reality and how far that knowledge can penetrate into the
hidden nature of things.

It is a weakness of Gottlieb's account that he does not understand
and therefore dismisses the importance of this difference, now
standardly denoted as the opposition between rationalism and empiricism. "The distinction is a vague and confusing one, anyway,"
he says.

Several of the so-called rationalists of the seventeenth century
took a greater interest in the empirical sciences than their "empiricist" counterparts; Leibniz and Descartes knew far more about
these sciences than Locke or Hume ever did.

This is a surprisingly superficial remark. The difference between
rationalists and empiricists was not over the validity of empirical science, but over how much could be known on the basis of a
priori reasoning, rather than observation. Observations alone do
not create scientific theories: they have to be created by reasoners,
who construct possible laws of nature and calculate their observable consequences for the purpose of experimental confirmation or
disconfirmation.

Even where the empiricists admitted nonempirical certainties,
as in mathematics, they interpreted them as apprehensions of the
relations among our ideas, and that leaves it unclear how far such
knowledge reaches beyond our own minds. The logical positivist

view that necessary truths are tautologies that depend on the rules of our language is a direct descendent of this empiricist conception of a priori knowledge. The rationalists, by contrast, believed that reason could give us direct knowledge of necessary truths about a reality independent of our minds—logical, mathematical, and metaphysical truths—and this has important consequences for the interpretation of the empirical sciences.

Gottlieb shows his sympathy for empiricism in his attitude to Descartes, who he says "tried to work out too much in his head." Most philosophers would agree with Gottlieb that Descartes relied on flimsy arguments for the existence of a nondeceiving God to defend his trust in his own reasoning and perception. But there is no consensus that anyone else, however ingenious the attempts in the centuries since, has come up with a satisfactory answer to radical skepticism.

In spite of this, most of us, whether we are engaged in ordinary life or in the pursuit of science, rely on both experiential evidence and a *priori* reasoning to acquire what we regard as knowledge of a mind-independent reality. And in reasoning, we take ourselves to be justified by what seems plainly self-evident—what Descartes called the "natural light" of reason. If we do not take this as a method of learning about reality, whether in mathematics or in science, it is difficult to avoid retreating to an empiricism that makes most of human knowledge an exploration of the insides of our own minds, and of how things appear to us.

4.

Religion was a major concern of all these thinkers, and in some cases a source of trouble in their relation to society. The casual unbelief so common among today's intellectuals would have seemed very foreign to them. Both Hobbes and Spinoza were widely condemned as atheists, though Gottlieb argues persuasively that

Hobbes, in spite of his materialism, was not one; and of Spinoza he says charmingly:

> Spinoza's God is admittedly so different from anyone else's that a case can be made for saying that he was an atheist without realizing it; but it does appear that he believed that he believed in God.

Descartes, Locke, and Leibniz were sincere Christians, though Descartes' works were condemned by the Catholic Church as incompatible with orthodoxy. But Hume, though he veiled it in his publications, was clearly a religious skeptic, and produced a devastating argument against miracles, based on the maxim: "No testimony is sufficient to establish a miracle unless the testimony be of such a kind that its falsehood would be more miraculous than the fact which it endeavours to establish."

In the relation of God to the world there was one problem of particular difficulty: the so-called Problem of Evil. If God is omniscient, omnipotent, and infinitely good, why does he not prevent all the evils that we see in the world around us—all the suffering and wickedness? Spinoza's response was that our concepts of good and evil are relative to our parochial human interests, but, as Gottlieb puts it, "nothing is either good or bad from God's perspective, which is to say from the point of view of nature or the universe as a whole."

Leibniz, however, did not avoid the problem in this way, but embraced a solution that is probably his most famous claim, and the one that has made him a figure of popular ridicule ever since (unforgettably caricatured as Dr. Pangloss in Voltaire's *Candide*): namely that this is the best of all possible worlds, even though from our limited perspective that may not be obvious. Leibniz's hypothesis about how this could be so was that, of the infinity of possible universes that God could have created, this one achieves the best possible balance between simple laws and desirable effects. That requires assigning great value to the simplicity of the laws of nature.

It depends also on a fundamental tenet of Leibniz's thought: the Principle of Sufficient Reason, according to which nothing happens without a reason. God had to choose, from among all the logical possibilities, which world to make actual, and his reason could only be that it was better than the alternatives. Theists continue to explore solutions to the problem of evil, but secularists typically regard its insolubility as one of the strongest arguments for atheism, and for the view that there is no reason why this universe exists rather than another.

5.

There is a remarkable parallel between Hobbes's project in moral and political theory and Descartes' project in the theory of knowledge. Each of them attempted to dismantle and then reconstruct a complex edifice of thought and practice that is usually supported by tradition, custom, and authority on a new foundation that depended solely on what could be found in the point of view of a single individual. In this they were the creators of an individualistic method of justification that has marked the modern world ever since, even though it has also provoked resistance.

As Descartes attempted to ground all knowledge starting with nothing but the capacities of his own mind or that of any other person, Hobbes attempted to ground morality and political authority in the motives and reasoning of any person subject to them: the justification for abiding by the rules had to work for each individual separately, in virtue of the human nature we all share. Hobbes appealed in this justification to a minimal foundation, the rational motive of self-interest, and in particular the dominant motive of self-preservation, together with facts about the human condition that made morality and government the indispensable means to serve those interests. Objective requirements were constructed starting from the subjective point of view.

Gottlieb doesn't understand Hobbes, and it will take a bit of space to explain why. What was distinctive about Hobbes's theory, and what led to his being attacked as a moral nihilist, was his refusal to appeal to any concern for the good of others or the collective good as a basis for moral motivation. He demonstrated that the familiar rules of morality, which he called the laws of nature, are principles of conduct such that if everyone follows them, everyone will be better off. But the fact that everyone will be better off if everyone follows them gives no individual a reason to follow them himself. He can have a reason to follow them only if that will make him individually better off. And there is no natural guarantee that individual self-interest and the collective interest will coincide in this way.

Hobbes concluded that although we all have a reason to want to live in a community governed by the moral rules, we cannot achieve this unless we bring it about that it is in each person's individual interest to abide by those rules. And the method of doing that is to agree with one another to support a powerful sovereign with a monopoly on the use of force, who will use it to punish violators. Only then can each individual be confident that if he obeys the rules, he will not be laying himself open to assault and dispossession by others. Without the trust engendered by the knowledge that violators will be punished, civilization is impossible and individual self-interest—the same rational motive that supports morality—leads to perpetual conflict and constant insecurity. This is the famous Hobbesian state of nature, and Hobbes was most notorious for saying that in this condition, we are almost never obligated to obey the moral rules, because it is not safe to do so.

Gottlieb, failing to grasp the subtle and rigorous relation of self-interest, morality, and law in Hobbes's theory, says:

He wrote that "all men are permitted to have and to do all things in the state of nature," which was taken to mean that there was nothing really wrong with murder, theft, or anything else. In fact he was stating the tautology that nothing would be illegal if there were not yet any laws.

Whereas Hobbes was stating not a tautology but the substantive moral thesis that law is necessary to remove a condition of insecurity that would otherwise excuse us from the practical force of moral requirements:

> The laws of nature oblige *in foro interno*; that is to say, they bind to a desire they should take place: but *in foro externo*; that is, to putting them in act, not always. For he that should be modest, and tractable, and perform all he promises, in such a time, and place, where no man else should do so, should but make himself a prey to others, and procure his own certain ruin, contrary to the ground of all laws of nature, which tend to nature's preservation.[1]

Gottlieb is misled by Hobbes's statement that the laws of nature can be summed up in the Golden Rule. But for Hobbes, this is just a summary of the rules for peaceful coexistence that serve all our interests and that we are obligated to follow when it is safe to do so—not, as Gottlieb says, an "unselfish" principle that somehow supersedes their self-interested foundation.

Appalled by the disorders of the English Civil War, Hobbes did not believe in the possibility of limited government: he thought sovereign power had to be absolute and undivided, and that it extended to prescribing the forms of religious worship, since religious conflict was a major source of civil instability. Hobbes held that we were released from our obligation to obey the sovereign only when he lost the ability to protect us. Spinoza, though his political theory

---

[1] Thomas Hobbes, *Leviathan*, chap. 15.

followed Hobbes in being grounded in self-interest, defended more liberal and democratic institutions, with protections for freedom of speech and religion. But the most influential theorist of individual liberty and toleration as a condition of legitimate government was Locke.

For Locke the foundation of morality was not collective self-interest but the natural rights of each individual, given by God—rights to life, liberty, and property that men have reason to respect even in the absence of law. The state of nature, according to Locke, is therefore governed by morality in a way that it is not according to Hobbes:

> The *state of nature* has a law of nature to govern it, which obliges every one: and reason, which is that law, teaches all mankind, who will but consult it, that being all *equal and independent*, no one ought to harm another in his life, health, liberty, or possessions.[2]

Yet there is still a need to punish violators, and if this is left in the hands of individuals, the results are likely to be too unreliable and chaotic, so it is necessary to confer a monopoly of the enforcement power on a single authority, by a social contract that will ensure the protection of our natural rights.

Locke eventually concluded that this foundation for legitimate government entailed a right of resistance and even rebellion against a sovereign who grossly abused his power. Gottlieb explains the connection of Locke's theories with the efforts to prevent the accession of Charles II's Roman Catholic brother James to the English throne, and his eventual overthrow. But he adds that although Locke's name was invoked in support of the American Revolution, he would have been "aghast to discover that ideas from his book were later used against the British colonial regime, in which he himself played an enthusiastic part."

[2] John Locke, *Second Treatise of Government*, sec. 6.

6.

Hume did not believe in natural rights or in the social contract. He was a philosophical prodigy whose greatest work, *A Treatise of Human Nature*, written when he was in his twenties, offered an analysis of every form of thought, knowledge, and value through a comprehensive theory of the operations of the human mind. One of his most famous theses was that causal judgments express only habitual mental associations due to observed correlations, and do not identify necessary connections between events.

In ethics and political theory, also, his analysis took the form of a psychological account of our moral judgments—an account that explained both their nature and their content. Like Hobbes, he offered a secular account of morality and political obligation, but it was not grounded solely in self-interest. Hume held that there is a distinctive motive that he called the moral sentiment, which is based on the human affective capacity for sympathy with the happiness and unhappiness of others, together with the human intellectual capacity to take up a general and detached standpoint toward the world which abstracts from our own particular perspective and our own particular interests.

This standpoint, when infused with sympathy for everyone, enables us to judge acts or character traits or institutions or policies to be good or bad not for ourselves or for any other particular person, but impersonally. Such judgments are simply expressions of the moral sentiment, in which sympathy is mixed with detachment. They do not describe the world, either truly or falsely, but express a feeling or attitude, favorable or unfavorable; yet the feeling is of a kind that allows people to agree in their moral judgments, since it does not depend on their particular interests.

The details of Hume's moral theory are very sophisticated. It was an early form of utilitarianism, but it included a theory of property rights, contract, promises, and political obligation that explained them as the product of human conventions whose strict rules serve

242 ANALYTIC PHILOSOPHY AND HUMAN LIFE

the collective interest, even though in many individual cases they require actions that are contrary to the general welfare. (It is no defense against eviction that you need the rent money more than your landlord does.)

Hume, like all of Gottlieb's thinkers, was interested in practically everything, and I have barely sampled their creative achievements. Gottlieb offers a compact but fairly comprehensive survey, along with much historical detail. Except for Spinoza, these men did not live in an ivory tower; they were worldly, connected with royalty and the aristocracy, in some cases active as diplomats or in government service. Though it has shortcomings, Gottlieb's highly readable book is an engaging personal introduction to some of our most brilliant moral and intellectual ancestors. If it opens a path to the works themselves, so much the better.

23

DENNETT'S ILLUSIONS

For fifty years Daniel Dennett has been engaged in a grand project of disenchantment of the human world, using science to free us from what he deems illusions—illusions that are difficult to dislodge because they are so natural. In *From Bacteria to Bach and Back*, his eighteenth book (thirteenth as sole author), Dennett presents a valuable and typically lucid synthesis of his world view. Though it is supported by reams of scientific data, he acknowledges that much of what he says is conjectural rather than proven, either empirically or philosophically.

Dennett is always good company. He has a gargantuan appetite for scientific knowledge, and is one of the best people I know at transmitting it and explaining its significance, clearly and without superficiality. He writes with wit and elegance, and in this book especially, though it is frankly partisan, he tries hard to grasp and defuse the sources of resistance to his point of view. He recognizes that some of what he asks us to believe is strongly counterintuitive. I shall explain eventually why I think the overall project cannot succeed, but first let me set out the argument, which contains much that is true and insightful.

The book has a historical structure, taking us from the pre-biotic world to human minds and human civilization. It relies on different forms of evolution by natural selection, both biological and cultural, as its most important method of explanation. Dennett holds

---

This was a review of Daniel C. Dennett, *From Bacteria to Bach and Back: The Evolution of Minds* (Norton, 2017).

Analytic Philosophy and Human Life. Thomas Nagel, Oxford University Press.
© Oxford University Press 2023. DOI: 10.1093/oso/9780197681671.003.0023

fast to the assumption that we are just physical objects and that any appearance to the contrary must be accounted for in a way that is consistent with this truth. Bach's or Picasso's creative genius, and our conscious experience of hearing Bach's Fourth Brandenburg Concerto or seeing Picasso's *Girl Before a Mirror*, all arose by a sequence of physical events beginning with the chemical composition of the earth's surface before the appearance of unicellular organisms. Dennett identifies two unsolved problems along this path: the origin of life at its beginning, and the origin of human culture much more recently. But that is no reason not to speculate.

The task Dennett sets himself is framed by a famous distinction drawn by the philosopher Wilfrid Sellars between the "manifest image" and the "scientific image"—two ways of seeing the world we live in. According to the manifest image, Dennett writes, the world is

> full of other people, plants, and animals, furniture and houses and cars . . . and colors and rainbows and sunsets, and voices and haircuts, and home runs and dollars, and problems and opportunities and mistakes, among many other such things. These are the myriad "things" that are easy for us to recognize, point to, love or hate, and, in many cases, manipulate or even create. . . . It's the world according to *us*.

According to the scientific image, on the other hand, the world

> is populated with molecules, atoms, electrons, gravity, quarks, and who knows what else (dark energy, strings? branes?).

This, according to Dennett, is the world as it is in itself, not just for us, and the task is to explain scientifically how the world of molecules has come to include creatures like us, complex physical objects to whom everything, including they themselves, appears so different.

He greatly extends Sellars's point by observing that the concept of the manifest image can be generalized to apply not only to humans but to all other living beings, all the way down to bacteria. All organisms have biological sensors and physical reactions that allow them to detect and respond appropriately only to certain features of their environment—"affordances," Dennett calls them—that are nourishing, noxious, safe, dangerous, sources of energy or reproductive possibility, potential predators or prey.

For each type of organism, whether plant or animal, these are the things that define their world, that are salient and important for them; they can ignore the rest. Whatever the underlying physiological mechanisms, the content of the image manifests itself in what the organisms do and how they react to their environment; it need not imply that the organisms are consciously aware of their surroundings. But in its earliest forms, it is the first step on the route to awareness.

The lengthy process of evolution that generates these results is first biological and then, in our case, cultural, and only at the very end is it guided partly by intelligent design, made possible by the unique capacities of the human mind and human civilization. But as Dennett says, the biosphere is saturated with design from the beginning—everything from the genetic code embodied in DNA to the metabolism of unicellular organisms to the operation of the human visual system—design that is not the product of intention and that does not depend on understanding.

One of Dennett's most important claims is that most of what we and our fellow organisms do to stay alive, cope with the world and one another, and reproduce, is not understood by us. It is competence without comprehension. This is obviously true of organisms like bacteria and trees that have no comprehension at all, but it is equally true of creatures like us who comprehend a good deal. Most of what we do, and what our bodies do—digest a meal, move certain muscles to grasp a doorknob, or convert the impact of sound waves on our eardrums into meaningful sentences—is done for reasons that are not *our* reasons. Rather, they are what Dennett calls free-floating reasons, grounded in the pressures of natural selection that caused these behaviors and processes to become part of our repertoire. There are reasons why these patterns have emerged and survived, but we don't know those reasons, and we don't have to know them to display the competencies that allow us to function.

Nor do we have to understand the mechanisms that underlie those competencies. In an illuminating metaphor, Dennett asserts that the manifest image that depicts the world in which we live our everyday lives is composed of a set of user-illusions,

> like the ingenious user-illusion of click-and-drag icons, little tan folders into which files may be dropped, and the rest of the ever more familiar items on your computer's desktop. What is actually going on behind the desktop is mind-numbingly complicated, but users don't need to know about it, so intelligent interface designers have simplified the affordances, making them particularly salient for human eyes, and adding sound effects to help direct attention. Nothing compact and salient inside the computer corresponds to that little tan file-folder on the desktop screen.

He says that the manifest image of each species is "a user-illusion brilliantly designed by evolution to fit the needs of its users." In spite of the word "illusion" he doesn't wish simply to deny the reality of the things that compose the manifest image; the things we see and hear and interact with are "not *mere* fictions but different versions of what actually exists: real patterns." The underlying reality, however, what exists in itself and not just for us or for other creatures, is accurately represented only by the scientific image—ultimately in the language of physics, chemistry, molecular biology, and neurophysiology.

Our user-illusions were not, like the little icons on the desktop screen, created by an intelligent interface-designer. Nearly all of them, such as our images of people, their faces, voices, and actions, the perception of some things as delicious or comfortable and others as disgusting or dangerous, are the products of "bottom-up" design, understandable through the theory of evolution by natural selection, rather than "top-down" design by an intelligent being. Darwin, in what Dennett calls a "strange inversion of reasoning," showed us how to resist the intuitive tendency always to explain competence and design by intelligence, and to replace it with explanation by natural selection, a mindless process of accidental variation, replication, and differential survival.

As for the underlying mechanisms, we now have a general idea of how they might work because of another strange inversion of reasoning, due to Alan Turing, the creator of the computer, who saw how a mindless machine could do arithmetic perfectly without knowing what it was doing. This can be applied to all kinds of calculation and procedural control, in natural as well as in artificial systems, so that their competence does not depend on comprehension. Dennett's claim is that when we put these two insights together, we see that

> *all* the brilliance and comprehension in the world arises ultimately out of uncomprehending competences compounded over time into ever more competent—and *hence* comprehending—systems. This is indeed a strange inversion, overthrowing the pre-Darwinian mind-first vision of Creation with a mind-*last* vision of the eventual evolution of us, intelligent designers at long last.

And he adds:

> Turing himself is one of the twigs on the Tree of Life, and his artifacts, concrete and abstract, are indirectly products of the blind Darwinian processes in the same way spider webs and beaver dams are. . . .

An essential, culminating stage of this process is cultural evolution, much of which, Dennett believes, is as uncomprehending as biological evolution. He quotes Peter Godfrey-Smith's definition, from which it is clear that the concept of evolution can apply more widely:

> Evolution by natural selection is change in a population due to
> (i) variation in the characteristics of members of the population,
> (ii) which causes different rates of reproduction, and (iii) which
> is heritable.

In the biological case, variation is caused by mutations in DNA, and it is heritable through reproduction, sexual or otherwise. But the same pattern applies to variation in behavior that is not genetically caused, and that is heritable only in the sense that other members of the population can copy it, whether it be a game, a word, a superstition, or a mode of dress.

This is the territory of what Richard Dawkins memorably christened "memes," and Dennett shows that the concept is genuinely useful in describing the formation and evolution of culture. Dennett defines "memes" thus:

> They are a kind of *way of behaving* (roughly) that can be copied, transmitted, remembered, taught, shunned, denounced, brandished, ridiculed, parodied, censored, hallowed.

They include such things as the meme for wearing your baseball cap backward or for building an arch of a certain shape; but the best examples of memes are words. A word, like a virus, needs a host to reproduce, and it will survive only if it is eventually transmitted to other hosts, people who learn it by imitation:

> Like a virus, it is designed (by evolution, mainly) to provoke and enhance its own replication, and *every token it generates is one of*

its offspring. The set of tokens descended from an ancestor token form a *type*, which is thus like a *species.*

The distinction between type and token comes from the philosophy of language: the word "tomato" is a type, of which any individual utterance or inscription or thought is a token. The different tokens may be physically very different—you say "tomayto," I say "tomahto"—but what unites them is the perceptual capacity of different speakers to recognize them all as instances of the type. That is why people speaking the same language with different accents, or typing with different fonts, can understand each other.

A child picks up its native language without any comprehension of how it works. Dennett believes, plausibly, that language must have originated in an equally unplanned way, perhaps initially by the spontaneous attachment of sounds to prelinguistic thoughts. (And not only sounds but gestures: as Dennett observes, we find it very difficult to talk without moving our hands, an indication that the earliest language may have been partly nonvocal.) Eventually such memes coalesced to form languages as we know them, intricate structures with vast expressive capacity, shared by substantial populations.

Language permits us to transcend space and time by communicating about what is not present, to accumulate shared bodies of knowledge, and with writing to store them outside of individual minds, resulting in the vast body of collective knowledge and practice dispersed among many minds that constitutes civilization. Language also enables us to turn our attention to our own thoughts and develop them deliberately in the kind of top-down creativity characteristic of science, art, technology, and institutional design.

But such top-down research and development is possible only on a deep foundation of competence whose development was largely bottom-up, the result of cultural evolution by natural selection. Without denigrating the contributions of individual genius,

Dennett urges us not to forget its indispensable precondition, the arms race over millennia of competing memes—exemplified by the essentially unplanned evolution, survival, and extinction of languages.

Of course the biological evolution of the human brain made all of this possible, together with some coevolution of brain and culture over the past fifty thousand years, but at this point we can only speculate about what happened. Dennett cites recent research in support of the view that brain architecture is the product of bottom-up competition and coalition-formation among neurons—partly in response to the invasion of memes. But whatever the details, if Dennett is right that we are physical objects, it follows that all the capacities for understanding, all the values, perceptions, and thoughts that present us with the manifest image and allow us to form the scientific image, have their real existence as systems of representation in the central nervous system.

This brings us to the question of consciousness, on which Dennett holds a distinctive and openly paradoxical position. Our manifest image of the world and ourselves includes as a prominent part not only the physical body and central nervous system but our own consciousness with its elaborate features—sensory, emotional, and cognitive—as well as the consciousness of other humans and many nonhuman species. In keeping with his general view of the manifest image, Dennett holds that consciousness is not part of reality in the way the brain is. Rather, it is a particularly salient and convincing user-illusion, an illusion that is indispensable in our dealings with one another and in monitoring and managing ourselves, but an illusion nonetheless.

You may well ask how consciousness can be an illusion, since every illusion is itself a conscious experience—an appearance that doesn't correspond to reality. So it cannot appear to me that I am conscious though I am not: as Descartes famously observed, the reality of my own consciousness is the one thing I cannot be deluded about. The way Dennett avoids this apparent contradiction takes us to the heart of his position, which is to deny the authority of the first-person perspective with regard to consciousness and the mind generally.

The view is so unnatural that it is hard to convey, but it has something in common with the behaviorism that was prevalent in psychology at the middle of the last century. Dennett believes that our conception of conscious creatures with subjective inner lives—which are not describable merely in physical terms—is a useful fiction that allows us to predict how those creatures will behave and to interact with them. He has coined the term "heterophenomenology" to describe the (strictly false) attribution each of us makes to others of an inner mental theater—full of sensory experiences of colors, shapes, tastes, sounds, images of furniture, landscapes, and so forth, that contains their representation of the world.

According to Dennett, however, the reality is that the representations that underlie human behavior are found in neural structures of which we know very little. And the same is true of the similar conception we have of our own minds. That conception does not capture an inner reality, but has arisen as a consequence of our need to communicate to others in rough and graspable fashion our various competencies and dispositions (and also, sometimes, to conceal them):

> Curiously, then, our *first-person* point of view of our own minds is not so different from our *second-person* point of view of others' minds: we don't see, or hear, or feel, the complicated neural machinery churning away in our brains but have to settle for an interpreted, digested version, a user-illusion that is so familiar to us that we take it not just for reality but also for the most indubitable and intimately known reality of all.

The trouble is that Dennett concludes not only that there is much more behind our behavioral competencies than is revealed to the first-person point of view—which is certainly true—but that *nothing whatever* is revealed to the first-person point of view but a "version" of the neural machinery. In other words, when I look at the American flag, it may seem to me that there are red stripes in my subjective visual field, but that is an illusion: the only reality, of which this is "an interpreted, digested version," is that a physical process I can't describe is going on in my visual cortex.

I am reminded of the Marx Brothers line: "Who are you going to believe, me or your own eyes?" Dennett asks us to turn our backs on what is glaringly obvious—that in consciousness we are immediately aware of real subjective experiences of color, flavor, sound, touch, etc. that cannot be fully described in neural terms even though they have a neural cause (or perhaps have neural as well as experiential aspects). And he asks us to do this because the reality of such phenomena is incompatible with the scientific materialism that in his view sets the outer bounds of reality. He is, in Aristotle's words, "maintaining a thesis at all costs."

If I understand him, this requires us to interpret ourselves behavioristically: When it seems to me that I have a subjective conscious experience, that seeming is just a belief, manifested in what I am inclined to say. According to Dennett, the red stripes in my visual field are just the "intentional object" of such a belief, as Santa Claus is the intentional object of a child's belief in Santa Claus. Neither of them is real. Recall that even trees and bacteria have a manifest image, which is to be understood through their outward behavior. The same, it turns out, is true of us: the manifest image is not an image after all.

There is no reason to go through such mental contortions in the name of science. The spectacular progress of the physical sciences since the seventeenth century was made possible by the exclusion of the mental from their purview. To say that there is more to reality than physics can account for is not a piece of mysticism: it is an acknowledgment that we are nowhere near a theory of everything, and that science will have to expand to accommodate facts of a kind fundamentally different from those that physics is designed to explain. It should not disturb us that this may have radical consequences, especially for Dennett's favorite natural science, biology: the theory of evolution, which in its current form is a purely physical theory, may have to incorporate non-physical factors to account for consciousness, if consciousness is not, as he thinks, an illusion. Materialism remains a widespread view, but science does not progress by tailoring the data to fit a prevailing theory.

There is much in the book that I haven't discussed, about education, information theory, pre-biotic chemistry, the analysis of meaning, the psychological role of probability, the classification of types of minds, and artificial intelligence. Dennett's reflections on the history and prospects of artificial intelligence and how we should manage its development and our relation to it are informative and wise. He concludes:

> The real danger, I think, is not that machines more intelligent than we are will usurp our role as captains of our destinies, but that we will *over*-estimate the comprehension of our latest thinking tools, prematurely ceding authority to them far beyond their competence. . . .
>
> We should hope that new cognitive prostheses will continue to be designed to be parasitic, to be tools, not collaborators. Their only "innate" goal, set up by their creators, should be to respond, constructively and transparently, to the demands of the user.

About the true nature of the human mind, Dennett is on one side of an old argument that goes back to Descartes. He pays tribute to Descartes, citing the power of what he calls "Cartesian gravity," the pull of the first-person point of view, and calling the allegedly illusory realm of consciousness the "Cartesian Theater." The argument will no doubt go on for a long time, and the only way to advance understanding is for the participants to develop and defend their rival conceptions as fully as possible—as Dennett has done. Even those who find the overall view unbelievable will find much to interest them in this book.

TRIBUTES

24

BETSY DWORKIN 1933–2000

We all remember the first time we met Betsy; her impact was so immediate. In my case it was in New Haven, in 1968. I belonged to a small group that met regularly to discuss issues of legal, moral, and political philosophy—usually alternating between New York and Cambridge, but occasionally meeting in New Haven, because Ronnie was a member. At the time, he taught at Yale and was Master of Trumbull College, and we met in the Master's Residence. A bunch of us were sitting around wrestling with some knotty question about rights, or the relation between justice and equality, or war crimes, or affirmative action. I don't remember the topic; but I remember Betsy stepping into the room, just for a moment, to retrieve something she had left there, excusing her intrusion in that wonderful, low, rich, caramel voice, and with a somewhat inward smile. I remember exactly how she looked, what she wore, the perfection of finish even in this informal setting. The effect was startling. The sudden appearance of a beautiful woman in the middle of a philosophical argument may or may not reveal something about the cosmic order, but it certainly brings thought to a stop for a few seconds. We eventually took up the thread, whatever it was, but I remained impressed by the force of this incursion into an academic milieu of a very different kind of distinction, like a leopard visiting a company of elephants.

After that first encounter, as I came to know her, I developed an expanded sense of what made Betsy such a pleasure to be with. She was smart, funny, and beautiful, as we all remember. But she also had, in the highest degree, a quality of precise attention and an insistence on the nonapproximate rightness of things. It was this constant exercise of taste and judgment and exigent standards that made her such a strong presence, and that expressed itself in the extraordinary life she created for herself and Ronnie.

Her judgment was always at work. Aesthetically she was a perfectionist with strong responses to how everything looked and felt and functioned, and to the harmony of her surroundings. She knew how to create beauty and pleasure around her, whether she was cooking a delicious meal for a group of friends, or dressing for the evening, or designing and furnishing a house, or arranging a temporary home for a few weeks in some gorgeous part of the world. I remember visiting them in places in France and Italy where Betsy with her Midas touch had produced ideal surroundings and Ronnie sat happily clacking away at his computer and dealing with cascades of faxes from Bob Silvers, until lunch appeared magically on the terrace. Everyone who knew them benefited from this generous creativity of Betsy's; we were surrounded and pampered by the effects and discouraged from noticing the constant effort that lay behind them.

Betsy's perception, taste, and intelligence were also ceaselessly at work in her relations with other people. She had a profound interest in people and cared about their lives. Her friends felt this attention very strongly, and knew they could rely on it. But there was a still deeper quality that I think was her most distinctive virtue: Betsy had beautiful manners; and manners of the kind she displayed in all her contacts with the world, whether she was talking to a child or a statesman, are the expression of a sensitivity to others that is both precious and rare. Such manners cannot be learned as a set of rules. They come only from the constant exercise of a subtle awareness of the currents of feeling and social complexity that are present in any human encounter, and from a deep, instinctive considerateness that automatically arranges to shield others from awkwardness, embarrassment, or bruises to their vanity, and makes them feel good. In a world full of big egos, the constant exercise of this gift, unobtrusively and without flattery, and without any inhibition of her realism and wit, was a vital element of Betsy's aura.

Those beautiful manners reached their heroic height during her final illness. Her self-possession seemed designed to spare the rest of us the full awareness of what she must be going through. She was always her old self, with her wonderful voice and rich laugh, her big eyes focused warmly and attentively on us, whoever we were, and deflecting attention from herself. Now she can't pamper us anymore, and we are left to remember, with love and gratitude, the difference she made.

25

ROBERT NOZICK 1938–2002

I got to know Robert Nozick in the nineteen-sixties, when I was teaching at Princeton and he was at the Rockefeller University, and through a happy accident we lived in the same apartment building in Manhattan. We found ourselves on the same wavelength intellectually, particularly with regard to the inexhaustibility of philosophical problems and their resistance to programmatic elimination, either through linguistic analysis or through displacement by a scientific world view. Bob was truly brilliant in a way that is rare even among philosophers of great distinction—with a mind of incredible speed, power, and fertility, and an overwhelming excess of ideas and imagination that made it dazzling to be around him. He was also wonderfully playful and funny, and devoid of gravity.

In 1967 he and I founded a monthly discussion group called SELF (short for Society for Ethical and Legal Philosophy) whose members disagreed about practically everything except that the substantive moral and political questions we disagreed about were susceptible of rational thought and argument. This was a great break from the hands-off philosophical stance toward values that was one enduring legacy of the positivist tradition. Bob, with his strong views, exemplified confidence in the reality and independence of moral theory, and our discussions over the years, among a group whose work has transformed the subject, were the best I have ever known.

Bob could always combine wit and insight. In the early, environmentally primitive days of SELF I used to smoke during the meetings. On one occasion when I lit a cigar, Bob strode to the window and opened it wide. Knowing how much he admired

Analytic Philosophy and Human Life. Thomas Nagel, Oxford University Press.
© Oxford University Press 2023. DOI: 10.1093/oso/9780197681671.003.0025

market mechanisms, I proposed that we hold an auction for the air rights in the room. The high bidder would pay the loser his winning bid, and get his way with respect to my smoking. The bidding had got to five dollars, when Bob, after a moment's silence, said, "It's worth more than five dollars to me not to have you smoke, but it's worth much more than that not to have to pay you not to smoke!"

This is not the occasion to describe the substance of his philosophical contributions, but I would like to try to convey his distinctive philosophical character. Philosophy has always depended on the interaction and uneasy rivalry between the creative theoretical imagination, which tries to burst the boundaries of mental custom, and the disciplinary controls of logic and rational justification. These two forces of disorder and order have competed for dominance throughout the history of the subject. Both were present to the highest degree in Bob's temperament, and he tried to give them both maximum expression. He loved formal structures and logical argument, but his approach to philosophical problems was fundamentally intuitive. His logical speed, strength, and accuracy made him intellectually fearless, and he was prepared to follow his imagination and his instincts wherever they led.

In his youth he was known as the most lethal philosophical critic of his generation—someone who could come up with a counterargument or counterexample to any claim that even the most careful philosopher put forward. It must have occurred to Bob, as it occurred to others, that no philosophical theory that he might devise could possibly resist his own critical powers. But because he thought it was better to make something new than to avoid error by defensive caution, he adopted toward his own exuberant creative impulses a kind of disinhibiting acceptance, and he did not subject them to his full destructive capacities—something that was absolutely necessary to permit them to flourish. The fact that he could see and acknowledge in advance the objections that others might raise gave him the authority to take this freedom, and he used his dialectical skills to produce some of the most original and absorbing structures of thought in contemporary philosophy—complex theories of rationality, rights, value, knowledge, personal identity, explanation, consciousness, objectivity, and truth. The task led him far beyond the traditional bounds of philosophy, in a voracious attempt to grasp and make use of the major results of the social, physical, and biological sciences, and even Eastern mysticism. He was a philosopher of extraordinary range, and his deliberate recklessness together with the power and clarity of his mind gives his work an untamed but logically formidable character that sets it utterly apart.

Bob was unlike anyone else. There seemed to be no passivity in his nature. His force of will, clarity of outline, and personal and cerebral charm made him an unforgettable presence. Personally, politically, and intellectually he was outspoken, and would rather say something decisive with which others could strongly disagree than something qualified which might reduce conflict. He distrusted the impulse to round off the corners, because he knew that it was easy to lose definition and avoid difficult choices that way. It was a form of courage, really: he recognized that to be the complete author of his words, his actions, and his outlook took constant effort and the willingness to draw fire. He mellowed with time, but his fierce independence never diminished: his last book, *Invariances*, is at least as daring as any of those that came before.

Though he was an international celebrity, Bob was not at all worldly and never became a public figure, as he could so easily have done. He had the largest possible ambitions, but they were philosophical and spiritual, and he filled his life to its limits by using his extraordinary mental powers to transform his understanding of himself and the world and to express that understanding with a rare lucidity. In spite of its cruel curtailment it was a life of enormous size—adventurous, unprofessional, and full of joy.

26

JOHN RAWLS 1921–2002

I took my first course with John Rawls in the spring term of 1955, as a freshman at Cornell. At that time he had to contend with a serious stammer, which largely disappeared in later years. It must have made teaching difficult for him, though it also may have served to heighten attention by binding him and the students together in a common anxiety.

This was the only respect, however, in which he seemed vulnerable. Over the next forty-eight years, though I never ceased to be his student, I also became a friend. But I have to say that I have never had another friend so different from myself, toward whom the highest admiration and affection were mixed with the feeling that he existed on a completely different plane of humanity.

I am talking about his personal quality, not his achievements, though they are related. Everyone who knew Jack was impressed by his purity and his freedom from the distortions of ego, but this was something beyond virtue: I hope it will not be misunderstood if I say that my dominant sense of Jack was that he was a natural aristocrat.

He was of course profoundly egalitarian and democratic, lived very simply, even ascetically, was often threadbare, never spent a dime on himself. But he had a kind of deep self-assurance and inner remoteness that made him seem to hover above the rest of us, despite his true modesty and regular expressions of uncertainty. There was something self-sufficient about him that I can only describe as aristocratic. Though he shunned conflict and had exquisite tact, he didn't seem to need the approval of others. And his social and moral responses displayed a level of refinement that was out of the

Analytic Philosophy and Human Life. Thomas Nagel, Oxford University Press.

range of anything I was accustomed to. For example, I believe he never applied for federally funded research fellowships, because he didn't believe the state should support efforts such as his—though naturally he wrote recommendations for others.

All this made it difficult to go through the delicate transition by which a student and a teacher become friends. Such a process is never easy, but in this case it was complicated on my side by a sense of the huge personal gulf between the clumsy, inconsiderate, approval-seeking young person I was and the noble and self-sufficient figure whom I so much admired. I could not help seeing myself through his eyes as a ridiculous barbarian.

Over time I came to recognize that he didn't require others to be as free of vanity and related vices as he was, but I never got over the habit of seeing in his effortless unworldliness the standard by which I could measure my limitations, even if he did not.

I don't know if he affected other people in this way; I feel fairly certain that he didn't know the kind of unattainability he presented, because he assumed that such purity was within reach of everyone. It is significant that he describes Kant's moral vision as an "aristocracy of all."

To my mind, Jack's essence is best expressed by the beautiful closing sentences of *A Theory of Justice*, which will be familiar to many of you:

The perspective of eternity is not a perspective from a certain place beyond the world, nor the point of view of a transcendent being; rather it is a certain form of thought and feeling that rational persons can adopt within the world. And having done so, they can, whatever their generation, bring together into one scheme all individual perspectives and arrive together at regulative principles that can be affirmed by everyone as he lives by them, each from his own standpoint. Purity of heart, if one could attain it, would be to see clearly and to act with grace and self-command from this point of view.

27

BERNARD WILLIAMS 1929–2003

Bernard Williams was an improbable blend of rebellion and responsibility. On one hand he was institutionally apt, an exemplary citizen of the academic and public worlds who took on the most demanding official roles and carried them through with matchless effectiveness. On the other hand he had a deep skepticism about authority, including his own, and never became the august personage that in someone of a less subversive disposition would have formed naturally through the identification of the individual with such a position of public eminence.

Intellectually his rebelliousness led to an attack on morality as it has been widely conceived by philosophers, namely as a system of universal norms that appear when we view human life *sub specie aeternitatis*. That, Bernard insisted, was not a good perspective from which to view it. "The correct perspective on one's life," he said, "is *from now*," and his onslaught on what he took to be the excessive aspirations to objectivity and impersonality in moral theory made the field immeasurably more lively and less boring than it would otherwise have been, especially for those of us who disagreed with him. In his hands the treatment of moral questions completely lost its usual flavor of piety and acquired the vividness of imaginative literature, without ceasing to be analytically penetrating. I always suspected, though, that in mocking the impersonal voices of Sidgwick and Kant, Bernard was secretly reacting against a form of conscience that he knew from the inside, and that helped make him such a sterling character, though without the slightest whiff of rectitude.

Analytic Philosophy and Human Life. Thomas Nagel, Oxford University Press.
© Oxford University Press 2023. DOI: 10.1093/oso/9780197681671.003.0027

He had enormous facility, and he did not husband his resources but seemed to respond with spendthrift energy to almost every challenge or invitation for engagement that came his way. The prolific brilliance revealed early made him an object of admiration and high expectations for others, but he never took himself as seriously as they did; he was manifestly free of that brooding sense of duty to his own talents and their fulfillment that drives so many creative individuals.

Bernard retained throughout his life, without effort, the distinctive character of youth: he never accumulated a stock of customary, settled reactions and opinions but responded with fresh curiosity and original perception to everything he met. He was mischievous, irreverent, instinctively distrustful of orthodoxy, and a connoisseur of people's foibles and absurdities, something that must have made many of his friends wish they could enjoy the educational benefit of hearing what he said about them when they were out of earshot. Those of us who knew him will never forget the sparkling illumination of his consciousness in our lives.

28

DONALD DAVIDSON 1917–2003

I got to know Donald gradually over many years. As a graduate student at Oxford in the late fifties, before I had read anything he wrote—indeed before he had begun to publish the papers that would make him famous—I heard of him as a powerful and magnetic teacher at Stanford, and his appearance in the audience at J. L. Austin's class on excuses was publicly acknowledged by Austin in an uncharacteristic display of respect. When I began to teach at Berkeley several years later, I attended seminars at Stanford and a joint Berkeley-Stanford discussion group, and got to know him better. I then left for Princeton, and Donald joined that department not long after I did. After a few years he moved to the Rockefeller University, but since I lived in New York, I continued to see a good deal of him. Finally, when he was at Berkeley and married to Marcia, we began a series of trips to remote parts of the world—Patagonia, the Sahara, Botswana, Tanzania, the Turkish coast—that were for me and my wife among the richest experiences of our lives. One can't tell in advance how it will be to travel with others, but we found we were naturally attuned, and it was pure pleasure. Earlier Anne and I on our own had made some spectacular journeys on Donald's recommendation, first to climb Kilimanjaro, then two month-long treks in the Himalayas. Without his having told us these things were possible we would never have imagined it. In this way he had a huge effect on our lives; I'm only sorry he wasn't with us when we climbed over the Thorong La, the eighteen-thousand-foot pass that leads into the Kali-Gandaki Gorge, between the Annapurnas and the Daulaghiri Range—as Donald said, the deepest valley in the world, a place he longed to see but never did.

Analytic Philosophy and Human Life. Thomas Nagel, Oxford University Press.
© Oxford University Press 2023. DOI: 10.1093/oso/9780197681671.003.0028

Donald shared with his friend Quine a love of the surface of the earth, and I suppose many people would associate him philosophically with Quine, but I always thought they were poles apart. It's true that Davidson, like Quine, was formed in the logical empiricist branch of analytic philosophy that reached the United States directly from central Europe, rather than in the ordinary language branch that arrived from England. But Quine was by temperament a positivist and reductionist, and Donald was the reverse. In spite of his interest in formal systems and theoretical unification, he was wedded to a rich and generous sense of reality and truth, and this is what I found congenial in his philosophical outlook. He did not think of philosophy as an extension of science at its most reductive, and seemed to me never to lose sight of the unique character of philosophical questions.

He was absorbed not only by the natural order but by literature, music, history, and art, about all of which he was deeply knowledgeable. He had robust left-wing political convictions. (Perhaps that is why as chairman of the Princeton department he was democratic to a fault.) But his writings were always rather austere, and his breadth made itself felt in print only occasionally, in the stray literary reference.

Donald was a distinctly menacing character when I first got to know him—very competitive, rather guarded, always weighing his words with extreme care. There was a good deal of tension and not much forgiveness in his pursuit of a philosophical disagreement. I have seen him cause a graduate student in an oral examination to tremble and perspire visibly under his cold blue glare. He didn't mind scaring people. No doubt that contributed to his influence as a teacher, since the sense of danger makes it impossible to feel one is being ignored.

The competitiveness probably had something to do with his long reluctance to publish, but once the essays started pouring out, wide recognition came quickly; and as he began to take up and enjoy the prolific response to his work, he gradually mellowed—if one can mellow without exactly becoming mellow.

I found his taut, intense, and sometimes irascible temperament appealing, and it threw his warmth as a friend into relief—the warmth of someone who was not naturally easy-going, but who valued particular attachments to an exceptional degree.

I can't resist adding one other thing I found sympathetic: He was one of the most erotic members of our profession. No one is uninterested in sex, of course, but for some of us it is at the center of our experience of the world. This was true of Donald, as was evident to anyone who knew him well. I remember a small emblematic moment when we were walking in the country and came upon a large rhubarb plant bursting out of the ground with an extraordinary phallic thrust. Donald looked at it and said, "Father Nature."

He had a complex consciousness, and managed to realize its diverse aspects in an equally complex life. Few are so fortunate.

29

PETER STRAWSON 1919–2006

When I first came to Oxford in 1958 on a Fulbright scholarship, it was as a wide-eyed visitor to the center of the philosophical world from one of the outposts of empire. Because I had been an undergraduate at Cornell, and a student of Norman Malcolm, Max Black, and John Rawls, I had some familiarity with the new direction of analytic philosophy in England and the writings of its leading figures. To be in Oxford, the center of the movement at the high tide of its influence, was a heady and thrilling experience.

It's hard to remember now, but what made this movement seem so revolutionary at the time was that its most conspicuous public image, set by the diagnostic legacy of Wittgenstein and the verbal housecleaning program of ordinary language philosophy, was radically deflationary. Like logical positivism at an earlier stage, it presented itself as bringing the history of traditional philosophy to an end, and ushering in a post-philosophical, or at least post-metaphysical concluding movement that would free us of the confusions of the past. This was to be accomplished by uncovering the misunderstandings of the function of ordinary language that were at the root of philosophical problems.

Peter Strawson stood out in relief against this deflationary background because of his unapologetic attachment to the largest questions of traditional philosophy. He was enough a part of his philosophical age and influenced by the method of linguistic and conceptual investigation so that his ambitious philosophical project took a special form, which he called "descriptive metaphysics"— an exploration from within of the system of thought by which we humans make sense of the world and of ourselves. But while this

Analytic Philosophy and Human Life. Thomas Nagel, Oxford University Press.
© Oxford University Press 2023. DOI: 10.1093/oso/9780197681671.003.0029

project, with its human focus, carried a built-in resistance to the transcendent ambitions of much traditional metaphysics, there was nothing deflationary about it. The contrast between Strawson's writings and the bluff, commonsense, plain man style affected by his predecessor in the Waynflete professorship of metaphysics, Gilbert Ryle, could not have been greater. As a student I attended the lectures that would be published as *Individuals*, and the originality and ambition of this treatment of major metaphysical questions was startling, and very different from what anyone else was doing.

There is an even greater contrast between Strawson's work and the other main branch of analytic philosophy—the tradition of logical empiricism that originated with the Vienna Circle and migrated with its leading figures to the United States before World War II. That movement, which aspired to make philosophy into something as close as possible to science, and to give philosophical theories the technical power and precision of scientific theories, has in the long run had much more influence than the ordinary language movement. Sometimes it threatens to swallow up philosophy altogether as part of the general scientism that has come to pervade our culture. By contrast, Strawson's work provided a living example of what is distinctively philosophical in the central aims of human understanding—something more basic than natural science, and not merely its most general and abstract form.

For someone entering the field when the most salient conceptions of philosophy were the Wittgensteinian view that it was a kind of illness and the Quinian view that it was a kind of science, Strawson offered a liberating alternative ideal. He kept before our minds the inescapability and uniqueness of philosophical questions, and the continuity between our engagement with those questions and that of Descartes, Hume, Kant, and other great predecessors. Strawson represented what was deepest in philosophy, and his clear and beautiful writings, free of technical apparatus, provided an inspiring demonstration that rigorous philosophy could still be a form of literature.

In addition to his style and intellectual independence, something else set Peter apart from the field—his noncombativeness. Philosophy is, perhaps it has always been, a highly competitive subject, in which controversies and refutations play an important part in determining which writings and whose ideas are the focus of attention. Peter lacked the pugnacity that comes so naturally to most philosophers, and fuels the intellectual battles that give the philosophical scene its visible day-to-day shape. Peter's irenic disposition, his sheer reasonableness, and his extreme aversion to anything resembling self-assertion or self-promotion kept him out of the competitive spectator sport that is one of the less lovely aspects of academic philosophy.

In my personal memory, Peter is marked by two contrasting qualities: fastidiousness and generosity. On the one hand I always felt in his presence the operation of an acute sensitivity to any carelessness or infelicity of taste, of tact, of thought, or of language, and I always imagined, though it may have been a fantasy, that he must suffer far more aesthetic discomfort than most of us, just from the encounters of ordinary life. On the other hand, he responded with generous recognition to what was valuable wherever he found it, and was by preference receptive in expression—and gentle when he had to be critical.

He was very amusing, though not often on the page. One example is his unforgettable put-down of those who foresee the only true form of human self-understanding in a developed neuroscience, by contrast with (and I quote) "what is sometimes called, with apparently pejorative intent, 'folk psychology'; i.e., the ordinary explanatory terms employed by diarists, novelists, biographers, historians, journalists, and gossips, when they deliver their accounts of human behavior and human experience—the terms employed by such simple folk as Shakespeare, Tolstoy, Proust, and Henry James."

And I remember a philosophical discussion in which there was a question about the meaning of the word "actually." Peter produced the following illustrative dialogue:

"What was your regiment?"
"The Coldstream Guards, actually."

30

RONALD DWORKIN 2006

I first met Ronald Dworkin forty years ago in the bar of one of those faceless, interchangeable hotels where conventions of the American Philosophical Association always take place. Amid the general grunge that typically characterizes any gathering of philosophers, Ronnie with his beautifully tailored suit, gleaming cufflinks, and silk breastpocket handkerchief stood out as a visitor from another planet. He was in the company of my former teacher John Rawls, whose frayed cuffs, scuffed shoes, and otherworldly air made the contrast even more vivid.

The juxtaposition of Ronnie's worldly, elegant hedonism and Rawls's unworldly, tattered asceticism is an indelible dash of color in my image of the philosophical world. These two very different Americans were jointly responsible for an enormous change in our moral and intellectual environment during the latter part of the twentieth century—Rawls in political philosophy and Ronnie in legal philosophy. They brought the clarity and logic of analytic philosophy into normative fields from which they had been excluded by the earlier prejudices of logical positivism. Both of them deepened and gave articulate form to questions and arguments that arose from the most urgent political and legal issues of our time.

But Ronnie also did something else: he wrote for the public. Rawls, who did not have this gift, greatly admired Ronnie's capacity to explain difficult moral issues about law, politics, and society in lucid terms to a general, nonacademic audience—without in any

This was a contribution to the issue of the *New York University Survey of American Law* dedicated to Ronald Dworkin.

way watering them down or simplifying them. He said that in this respect Ronnie had made a contribution in our own day comparable to that of John Stuart Mill in the 19th century—a just and memorable tribute.

Ronnie's original point of entry, both as a theorist and as a public intellectual, has been law. This was possible because of the important philosophical dimension of constitutional law under our system, which he has done so much to explain. But his work has addressed larger issues of moral and political theory from the beginning, and he has done more than anyone to bring those fields into creative contact with one another.

That was the basis for the Colloquium in Law and Philosophy that he initiated at NYU in 1987, with the help of David Richards, Larry Sager, and myself, and that, to my occasional amazement, he and I are still conducting almost twenty years later. The mountains of theoretical material that we have subjected to critical analysis in those years includes some of the most interesting work on these topics, as well as some that is less interesting; but the constant element that always impresses me is Ronnie's tirelessness and his unforced enthusiasm. He is a superb intellectual host, always giving the impression that there is nothing he would rather be doing than talking with our guest of the week about his or her ideas. I have to admit that sometimes, when he and I meet for a preliminary discussion of a thinner-than-average paper for that week's colloquium, he will look at me ruefully and say, "We're going to have to do a lot of work." But as soon as the author walks through the door, Ronnie is the picture of eager engagement and interest, and an unstoppable discussion is launched.

One thing that makes this possible is that Ronnie cares more keenly about the answers to questions of moral, political, and legal theory, and about converting others to the right view, than almost anyone I know. This quality of temperament is more unusual among philosophers than you might think. I'm going to steal one of Ronnie's stories here. He once overheard a woman comforting

276 ANALYTIC PHILOSOPHY AND HUMAN LIFE

a friend who was evidently in great distress, by saying, "Be philosophical; don't think about it." Most of us don't go quite that far, but I believe the norm, after a certain number of rounds in the dialectical ring, is to feel that we can let fundamental disagreements continue unresolved, and that we aren't obliged to keep trying to convince our opponents.

Ronnie, by contrast, is always good for another round. So long as anyone on the other side is left standing and unconverted, he will keep the battle going, and will leave no objection or reply unanswered. This can create problems of graceful termination, particularly when Ronnie encounters an equally tireless adversary. Fortunately this is not a problem in the Letters column of *The New York Review of Books*, where Ronnie always has the last word.

Even though I have known Ronnie for forty years, I learned only recently, from an article in the *N. Y. U. Law School Magazine*, that after his appeals court clerkship with Learned Hand he had the opportunity to become a Supreme Court clerk for Felix Frankfurter; but he decided he'd had enough of schooling and apprenticeship and went to work for the firm of Sullivan and Cromwell instead. I wonder what would have happened if he had taken that clerkship. He might have followed it with work in government and perhaps real politics (the Kennedy administration was about to begin). Even if he had eventually entered the legal academy by this other route, I suspect that his concerns and his writings would have been different. He would probably not have concentrated on the largest philosophical questions to the same extent. So in closing, I would like to offer my thanks to Sullivan and Cromwell for enriching our philosophical lives, and for giving me a friend and colleague whom it has been such a joy to work with.

31

JOHN SEARLE 2009

I met John Searle the year before he came to Berkeley. When I arrived in Oxford as a Fulbright scholar in the fall of 1958, fresh off the boat (and it was a boat in those days—the *Queen Elizabeth* in my case), my first encounter with Oxford philosophy was a talk given at one of the university's discussion groups by Alison Knox, a graduate student in philosophy at the time. The talk was a response to John's article, "Proper Names," recently published in *Mind*, and John was the commentator. I don't remember the content of the discussion, only that the room was packed, the atmosphere intense, and that it gave me the sense that I was at the center of the philosophical universe, which was probably true at the time.

John was then a Lecturer in philosophy at Christ Church, the vast, beautiful, and imposing college attached to the cathedral of Oxford. He had arrived at the University in 1952 as a Rhodes scholar, somehow without bothering to complete his undergraduate degree at Wisconsin—I have never known how he managed that. He stayed on as a graduate student after getting his B.A. at Oxford, and when I met him he was completing the doctorate and was in his third year as a Lecturer. I was never a student of John's, but Oxford was teeming with philosophical activity, and I got to know him through encounters at talks and seminars. He was, as he has always been, superbly accessible and outgoing, and he immediately treated me for no good reason as an equal. He even invited me to dine at High Table in Christ Church, along with the canons of the

This was my contribution to a symposium celebrating John Searle's fifty years of teaching at Berkeley.

278 ANALYTIC PHILOSOPHY AND HUMAN LIFE

Cathedral and assorted dons in various stages of decay. John wore a three-piece suit, and for the only time in my life I took snuff when it was passed around in the senior common room after dinner.

John seemed perfectly at home in this venerable establishment, defiantly unanglicized, with his pure Western twang and blunt style—unassimilated but unselfconscious. I have always thought of his failure to pick up the slightest trace of a British accent during his lengthy stay in Oxford as a phonetic expression of his strong individual character. He also seemed at home in Europe. His passport had had to be expanded with a large, accordionlike insert to accommodate all the customs stamps from his frequent trips to France. He even had a French car, one of those gorgeous old low-slung Citroens of prewar design, with big, swooping fenders and a running board—a car I suspect most of you have never seen, unless you are a fan of old Jean Gabin movies. Automobiles have always been profoundly important to John, and this gave him in advance a natural affinity for California.

John and Dagmar were already an item at that time. She was still Dagmar Carboch, and held a research position in Politics at Nuffield College, having reached Oxford from Czechoslovakia by way of Australia. They were a vivid and irresistible cosmopolitan couple, and were wonderfully hospitable and kind to me. Their capacity for friendship and generosity is an enduring quality, of which I have been the beneficiary for more than fifty years.

John was very attached to Oxford, which had formed him and which was then at its peak of philosophical strength and excitement. While I was there I was able to study with J. L. Austin, Paul Grice, Peter Strawson, Elizabeth Anscombe, Philippa Foot, Isaiah Berlin, H. L. A. Hart, G. E. L. Owen, David Pears, James Thomson, Gilbert Ryle, and Bernard Williams. Austin was a commanding presence, dry, sarcastic, and devastating in public but remarkably kind to students one-on-one, in my experience. Austin was visiting the Berkeley philosophy department during the fall of 1958, so I encountered him only when he returned in January 1959. John told me that Austin had been seriously tempted by an offer to move to Berkeley—"You could build an empire there," John reported him as having said—but just at that point Austin became ill, and was diagnosed with cancer. He died in the spring of 1960, at the age of forty-eight.

In addition to being, along with Strawson, the most important early philosophical influence on John's work, I assume that Austin had a hand in his going to Berkeley. Austin must have seen the natural fit and recommended John to the University, and the University to John. Initially one might think it impossible to imagine two people less alike—Austin the austere, schoolmasterly Englishman and John the hedonistic American extrovert—but I think there was a natural sympathy between them. They shared a sense of comedy, and both were combative and competitive, but at the same time highly social, and committed to the advancement of the life of the mind through supportive institutions and collective effort.

They both thought of philosophy as a team sport (with winners and losers, I might add). And they were both attracted to philosophical topics that emphasized the embeddedness of the individual in a structure of social interactions, rather than the relation of the solitary individual to the universe. The theory of speech acts, so important in the work of both Austin and Searle, is a prime example of this interest. John never took up the method of linguistic connoisseurship that was Austin's trademark—for example the distinctions among shooting a donkey inadvertently, unintentionally, by accident, or by mistake. But John has always been drawn to empirical facts as a starting point for philosophical understanding, and the refusal to respect the boundary between the empirical and the a priori was also an important disposition of Austin's. Going through the Times Law Reports with Austin in his seminar on Excuses was a delicious treat. Austin was my thesis adviser at Oxford, and I assume that he had an even more memorable effect on John, who knew him better, than he had on me. The importance of Oxford in

John's formation cannot be exaggerated. He spent seven years there, and formed his philosophical style and some of his main interests during that period.

After John and Dagmar went off to Berkeley in 1959, I stayed in Oxford to finish the B.Phil., and then went to Harvard for the Ph.D. Barry Stroud and I overlapped as graduate students at Harvard in 1960–61, and then he too took a job at Berkeley. When I finished the degree in 1963, the job market was unbelievable. The postwar baby boom had reached college age, and state universities all over the country were expanding at warp speed. I went to Berkeley partly because John and Barry, two good friends, were there, and I suppose they had something to do with my being hired.

Berkeley was wonderful, in all the ways you are familiar with. John and Dagmar were thriving, and raising a family, and John was one of the most popular teachers in the university. When the student government course evaluations came out, I remember Tom Clarke saying that John's evaluations read as though they had been written by his mother. This was the period when the Berkeley philosophy department moved decisively into the mainstream of analytic philosophy, and John's presence was crucial. For some time Berkeley had had a stellar program in mathematical logic, but now the department began to reach out in other fields. This was part of a general tendency in the academic world away from institutional insularity and toward the creation of a dynamic international community.

And then there were all those students. In his book about the troubles of the sixties, *The Campus War*, John cites "sheer numbers" as one of the causes of campus unrest and the breakdown of authority. He is there referring to the huge enrollments at individual campuses. But I think the really important number was the size of the entire age cohort of students at that time, in this country and in other countries, which was quite out of proportion to the population of its elders. The baby boom generation, born in the years immediately after World War II, formed a society of its own, large enough and secure enough to set its own standards and not to feel that their lives depended on transforming themselves into grownups on the model of those who had left youth behind. The traditional source of adult authority—the desire of the young minority to be assimilated to the culture and norms of an adult world, was weakened by the sheer weight of numbers. That is why the baby boom generation has transformed American society so radically as it has passed like a huge lump through the national digestive tract.

Like John, I was here at the heady beginning of it all, in 1964, when the Free Speech Movement clashed with an administration that was under pressure from conservatives in state government and on the board of trustees. John, then still an assistant professor, was one of the first faculty members to side with the students. I remember him addressing a rally in Sproul Plaza, and noting that the faculty group invited by the administration to help solve the problem was limited to tenured faculty. "I like that touch," said John. He eventually took an administrative post himself, and the conflict in Berkeley became more and more absorbing and destructive in succeeding years. By the time he published *The Campus War* in 1971 his mood was grim.

I had decamped in 1966, to Princeton. Partly it was the pull of New York, which I had always loved, but partly it was the sense that the sources of conflict at Berkeley were deep, and would make it a battleground indefinitely. I was spending too much time thinking about the latest disaster, or the next. But John stayed, and with his combative nature, he seems to have managed to stay sane while embroiled in these battles, on one side or the other. We were now friends at long distance, linked in the larger philosophical world through conferences and conventions, and even, more recently, by a common love for Paris, where we often find ourselves together in June, and where it is always a pleasure to take up again our extended pursuit of the higher gossip.

The creative work of an intellectual discipline like philosophy is done in private, by solitary individuals or small groups interacting at a high level. John has been a major internal contributor to the field in this way, and I won't try to summarize his large theoretical achievements. But the place of the discipline in the wider world depends also on its having a public face, and the field of philosophy, and in particular analytic philosophy, is singularly fortunate that John Searle has been one of its most important representatives to the world at large in our time. This is due partly to his superb lucidity and force as a writer, comparable to that of Bertrand Russell in an earlier day. But it is due also to his powerful urge to engage with the significant intellectual forces, good and bad, in the civilization around him, to try to understand them, and to influence them by making available as widely as possible what can be learned from the insights and methods of contemporary philosophy.

There is a missionary element in John's makeup, as there was in Russell's. He is much more willing than most philosophers to expose himself to public conflict by attacking what he sees as the forces of darkness. While this is an expression of his essential nature, it is not without cost. Unlike some prominent polemicists, he goes into battle again and again without the benefit of a thick skin. Even though he has a fundamentally sanguine temperament, John takes things hard, harder than most people I know, and I am all the more grateful to him for so often leading the charge against sophistry and illusion.

But John is much more than a dragon-slayer. His extensive writings, both academic and popular, have given countless people throughout the world their primary understanding of the central questions in philosophy of language and philosophy of mind. He is one of the most famous and effective teachers of the subject in our time, and Berkeley is very lucky to be the place where for fifty years one has been able to encounter the man himself—an inimitable and unforgettable presence.

32

RONALD DWORKIN 1931–2013

Ronald Dworkin and I were friends for many years, starting in the 1960s, when we belonged to a monthly discussion group that included many of the leading contributors to moral, political, and legal philosophy of the succeeding decades. After he began to spend half of every year at NYU in 1987, I had the immense pleasure of his brilliant companionship every week as we conducted the colloquium in law and philosophy, which gave scope to his talent for logically complex and morally imaginative argument over the next twenty-five years. Knowing and working with him has been not only an intellectual treat but a party that seemed never to end and never to run out of steam. His presence in any conversation turned it into a delicious entertainment.

I won't talk about the substance of his intellectual contributions here, but will say something about his style and his attitude to life.

Ronnie was a consummate performer, whatever he was doing, whether animating a dinner party as host or guest, giving a public lecture, teaching, or writing. He always wrote and spoke beautifully, with enviable command and clarity of organization. Above all he carried it off with an air of complete effortlessness—made possible, of course, only by ferociously hard work and a terrific memory. This inspired the wonderful entry for Ronnie in the *Philosophical Lexicon*, a creation of Daniel Dennett, in which definitions are given for the names of philosophers. For example, "Heidegger" is defined as "a ponderous device for boring through thick layers of substance," as in, "It's buried so deep we'll have to go after it with a Heidegger."

Here is Ronnie's entry:

Analytic Philosophy and Human Life. Thomas Nagel, Oxford University Press.
© Oxford University Press 2023. DOI: 10.1093/oso/9780197681671.003.0032

Dwork (verb): (perhaps a contraction of *hard work*?) To drawl through a well-prepared talk, making it appear effortless and extemporaneous. As in the old American folk song, "I bin dworkin on de lecture circuit."

There was one aspect of Ronnie's style that was important, though he was not altogether pleased to be reminded of it. In addition to being a creative philosophical thinker, Ronnie never ceased to be a lawyer. His intellectual style was marked by the determination to make a case for his client—the truth as he saw it—if possible an overwhelming case, with concomitant demonstration that his opponent had no case. This take-no-prisoners style of intellectual combat is not unknown in philosophy, but I believe that in Ronnie's case it drew strength from his immersion in legal argument. It also fitted well with his conviction that there is always a right answer to any difficult moral, political, or legal question.

But what made Ronnie unlike anyone else I have ever known, and gave him his distinctive charm, was his omnivorous appetite for life. There is a famous poem by William Butler Yeats that begins:

> The intellect of man is forced to choose
> Perfection of the life, or of the work.
> And if it take the second must refuse
> A heavenly mansion, raging in the dark.

That is a choice that Ronnie emphatically refused to make. You would never catch Ronnie "raging in the dark." And a heavenly mansion, or a reasonable facsimile thereof—in New York or London or Martha's Vineyard or Tuscany—always seemed the natural setting for his relentless pursuit of perfection in the work he undertook.

This was a manifestation in the way he lived his life of the conviction, so fully expressed in his big book *Justice for Hedgehogs*, that there are no deep conflicts between values, and that what is good forms a coherent unity. Ronnie managed to combine creative intellectual achievement at the highest level, motivated by powerful moral and political convictions, with a life filled with pleasure, brilliant society, and aesthetic style, and he seemed to be able to give equal attention to them all. In a sense he never aged, but brought the same youthful enthusiasm to every new experience or new opportunity. He couldn't visit a beautiful part of the world without engaging in fantasies about acquiring some of the local real estate. He loved good food and drink, amusing company, interesting architecture, and he dressed beautifully, in a defiantly nonacademic style. In addition to teaching on both sides of the Atlantic, Ronnie maintained a Herculean schedule of international speaking engagements, and seemed to fill every minute with activity and experience. Once we were talking about how much in advance of a flight one should arrive at the airport, and he said, "If you haven't missed a few planes, you've led a wasted life."

In his existence there was absolutely no opposition, but rather a complete congruence between the life of the mind, often at its most abstract, and life in the world at its most concrete and delectable. This joie de vivre was brutally interrupted by Betsy's illness and death, but he found it again with Reni, for the final years of his life, which were also among his most creative.

The brilliant life is now over, and the brilliant work remains. Fortunately for all of us, Yeats stands refuted.

33
BARRY STROUD 1935–2019

Barry and I got to know each other in 1960–61, his last year in the philosophy graduate program at Harvard, and my first. He then took a job at Berkeley, and I followed him in 1963. I moved back east to Princeton in 1966, but for three years we were colleagues in that unique condition of subordinate equality which brings people so close together. We were present at the beginning of a transformation of the Berkeley philosophy department. Most of its tenure members, as I recall, were Berkeley Ph.D.s, far removed from current developments in analytic philosophy. Barry and I found an inexhaustible supply of things to deplore about how the department was being run, in our almost daily conspiratorial lunches. It should have been obvious that we and our ilk were destined to take over, but at the time we felt like the oppressed proletariat, and no doubt enjoyed it hugely.

Leaving Barry was for me one of the saddest things about leaving Berkeley, but as it turned out, our friendship was an enduring part of my life. We didn't correspond regularly, but although we saw each other only at unpredictable intervals, our connection when we met was immediate and always the same: we were infallibly on the same wavelength.

We shared a view of philosophy that was a minority position even when we were young, and that has become more unfashionable over the years since then—a view influenced by Wittgenstein, though less radical than the conception found in his later work, so far as I understand it. It is the view that the center of philosophy, its deepest and most interesting part, consists of certain philosophical problems that are different in kind from those in any other

Analytic Philosophy and Human Life. Thomas Nagel, Oxford University Press.
© Oxford University Press 2023. DOI: 10.1093/oso/9780197681671.003.0033

domain of thought. These problems are probably not soluble, but they are irresistible, and the attempt to solve them has yielded over the history of the subject, and continues to yield, brilliant and fascinating philosophical responses and theories, all of which have something wrong with them. The attempt to escape the labyrinth by diagnosing them as pseudo-problems is also a failure. Philosophy is inescapable, and it should have at its core the study of these problems themselves: a study of their sources—what in our concepts and practices and beliefs generates these questions—and of both the positive virtues or appeal and the inadequacies of different and mutually opposed responses to them. And finally, the view is that by exploring these impossible problems and their sources we can learn something about ourselves and our essentially problematic situation in the world, even as we fail to solve them. In this way the process serves the function of philosophy as the most extreme form of self-consciousness.

The problems that Barry devoted himself to in this way were multiple: epistemological skepticism, the a priori, realism versus subjectivism about value, secondary qualities, and modality, as well as problems about causality and perception. My own interests overlapped with his to some extent, but included other topics as well, such as free will, the mind-body problem, and the absurd. One has not really come to philosophical grips with these questions unless one finds them completely baffling. A rather small group of philosophers seemed to us to engage with the subject in the same, problem-centered way. Both of us found in our colleague Tom Clarke an especially powerful example of this outlook, and it had an influence on us.

Barry's writing was exceptionally pure, explicit, and unrhetorical. He had an exceptional gift for bringing out and making clear the logical structure of complex arguments and counterarguments and for detecting unspoken assumptions behind philosophical positions. He was patient, charitable, and cogent in criticism. The care, thoroughness, and trenchancy of his work seems to me to be an expression of his personality more generally. In life as in philosophy, he was intent on getting it right, on doing it as it should be done, and to a high standard. To put it negatively, he avoided any trace of sloppiness in his physical, personal, and mental life. All this was compatible with his being a hedonist, but one whose pleasures were richly informed by conscious attention.

He knew how to enjoy life, and he was a wonderful friend, but there was a grim side to his outlook that was also part of his appeal, at least to me. He did not have high expectations of his fellow human beings, and was rarely surprised by manifestations of vanity, dishonesty, or selfishness—and he detected human failings of these kinds with merciless accuracy. He wasn't moralistic, but he was distinctly lacking in illusions, and the consistent encounter with his realism was always instructive.

For all of us, there are a few people we feel particularly fortunate to have shared the world with. For me, Barry was one of these.

Index

For the benefit of digital users, indexed terms that span two pages (e.g., 52–53) may, on occasion, appear on only one of those pages

Note: Footnote references are indicated by an italic *n* following the page number